GAME PLAN

GAME PLAN

*A Geostrategic Framework
for the Conduct of the
U.S.–Soviet Contest*

by ZBIGNIEW BRZEZINSKI

The Atlantic Monthly Press

BOSTON / NEW YORK

FIRST EDITION

LIBRARY OF CONGRESS CATALOGING-IN-PUBLICATION DATA

Brzezinski, Zbigniew K., 1928–
  Game plan.

  Includes index.
    1. United States—Foreign relations—Soviet Union.
  2. Soviet Union—Foreign relations—United States.
  3. Geopolitics—United States. 4. Geopolitics—
  Soviet Union. 5. Soviet Union—Strategic aspects.
  I. Title.
  E183.8.S65B795 1986   327.73047   86-70889
  ISBN 0-87113-084-X

MV

Published simultaneously in Canada

PRINTED IN THE UNITED STATES OF AMERICA

For Muška

Contents

List of Maps	xi
Preface	xii
I. The Imperial Collision	3
The Map in Moscow	4
A Historical Contest	8
An Imperial Contest	16
A Global Contest	26
II. The Struggle for Eurasia	30
Russia and Eurasia	30
Three Central Strategic Fronts	41
Geopolitical Linchpin States	52
Soviet Geostrategy	65
III. Peripheral Zones of Special Vulnerability	76
Unstable Imperial Domains	77
Historical Enmity and Geopolitical Necessity	85
Stakes and Policies	92
IV. The One-Dimensional Rival: A Threat Assessment	99
Soviet Military Capabilities	100
Socioeconomic Liabilities	122
A World Power of a New Type	130
Domination and Disruption	135
U.S.–Soviet Scenarios: The Next Ten Years	141

V. U.S. Strategic Imperatives   145

    Strategic Impotence: The Threat of Arms Control   148
    Mutual Strategic Security   159
    Global Conventional Flexibility   168
    The Centrality of Technological Superiority   184
    An Integrated Strategic Framework   191

VI. U.S. Geopolitical Priorities   194

    A More Self-Reliant Europe   196
    The Pacific Triangle   210
    The Soft Underbelly   220
    Imperial Retraction   230

VII. Prevailing Historically   239

    Executive Summary   251
    Appendix: Where Major U.S. Defense Forces
      Stand   269
    Acknowledgments   275
    Index   277

Maps

The Global View from Moscow   4

The Global View from Washington   5

Geostrategic Distribution of Great Russians in the   18
    Soviet Union

The Centrality of Eurasia   32

Soviet Interest in the Persian Gulf   37

Railroad Imperialism in Central Asia before 19.6   38

Soviet Geopolitical Demands on the   40
    Diplomatic Record

The Three Central Strategic Fronts   42

Japanese Maritime Lifeline   48

Moscow's Strategic Perspective on the First Front   54
    Linchpin States

Moscow's Strategic Perspective on the Second Front   57
    Linchpin States

Moscow's Strategic Perspective on the Third Front   62
    Linchpin States

Target Coverage of Soviet SS-20 and NATO   74
    Pershing II and Ground-Launched Cruise Missiles

American Expansion at Mexico's Expense   86

Russian Expansion at Poland's Expense   87

Deployment of Soviet Missiles.   163

Forward Defense: Evolution of a Strategic Concept   178–179

European Political Divisions Today   200

Possible Future European Political Constellation   201

Preface

THIS book is based on a central proposition: the American-Soviet contest is not some temporary aberration but a historical rivalry that will long endure. This rivalry is global in scope but it has clear geopolitical priorities, and to prevail the United States must wage it on the basis of a consistent and broad strategic perspective. This book therefore is not an argument about the evils of the Soviet system compared with the merits of American democracy, but a practical guide to action.

Each of the chapters is designed to leave the reader with a clear message. The first defines the historical dimensions of the U.S.–Soviet conflict. The second identifies its geopolitical focus and central areas of contention. The third deals with special regional vulnerabilities of both powers. The fourth follows up with a comprehensive threat assessment, focusing on both Soviet strengths and weaknesses. The fifth and sixth chapters then systematically develop the required program of long-term U.S. strategic and geopolitical responses. Since the focus here is on the interaction between geopolitics and strategy in the U.S.–Soviet contest, such otherwise important bilateral issues as economic relations or human rights are not covered. The final chapter defines, in the context of the nuclear age, the historical meaning of prevailing. The argument of *Game Plan* takes as its point of departure the geopolitical struggle for the domination of Eurasia, but it also examines its peripheral and diversionary aspects as well as the rivalry on the oceans and in outer space that is an extension of the struggle for earth control, so as to provide an integrated geostrategic framework for the conduct of the historical American-Soviet contest.

The advent of highly destructive nuclear weapons has made it likely that the U.S.–Soviet rivalry will not be terminally resolved by war — unless a war occurs either through miscalculation or because one side achieves such overwhelming nuclear superiority that it is tempted to strike at the other. This means that the U.S.–Soviet conflict has been transformed into an endless ''game.'' Each side plays according to its own rules and keeps its own score; each side is restrained only by the fear of retaliation for the use of excessively provocative tactics. This unusual game, with no victory of the traditional type in sight, and with no formally defined rules, is being partially codified by experience and by limited understandings, such as arms control. But it still remains predominantly a mobile contest of maneuver, pressure, and even occasionally of force. Not to lose is the first objective; to score points according to one's own scoring system (or values) is the second; to prevail is the ultimate but remote goal. To stay in this historical game requires not only political will but also a long-term design. This volume seeks to outline the necessary trade-offs, given unavoidable budgetary constraints, and to provide the needed U.S. geostrategic game plan.*

---

*Note on terminology: the words *geopolitical, strategic,* and *geostrategic* are used to convey the following meanings: *geopolitical* reflects the combination of geographic and political factors determining the condition of a state or region, and emphasizing the impact of geography on politics; *strategic* refers to the comprehensive and planned application of measures to achieve a central goal or to vital assets of military significance; and *geostrategic* merges strategic considerations with geopolitical ones.

GAME PLAN

I

The Imperial Collision

E ARLY in 1985 a NATO foreign minister was being hosted in Moscow by his venerable Soviet counterpart, Andrei Gromyko. In a display of professional camaraderie, or perhaps as a courtesy induced by a touch of nostalgia over anticipated retirement, the Soviet host suddenly confided to his visitor that several times a week he made it a special point to retire from his busy office to a small and private study where he could meditate in solitude. Inviting his somewhat startled but also flattered Western guest to follow him, Gromyko with evident pride opened the doors to a small room, where a comfortable armchair faced a large wall map of the world. "For an hour or so," Gromyko said, "I do nothing but sit here, looking at that map and reflecting . . ."

Simple, yet impressive! How many Western foreign ministers, who are frequently unversed in foreign policy and typically hold their posts for three or so years at most, take the time to reflect systematically on the implications of geopolitics and strategy for their foreign policies? Indeed, one wonders whether many American secretaries of state (and there were nine of them during Andrei Gromyko's tenure of office) have spent much time in deep thought on the historical and geopo-

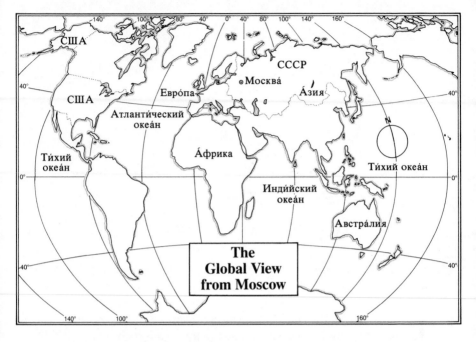

litical imperatives that shape a nation's relationship with the
world.

The Map in Moscow

One can only speculate on what might have passed through
Gromyko's mind as the veteran foreign minister of the Communist Great Russian empire — in this historical epoch rela-
beled as the Union of Soviet Socialist Republics — contemplated the flat rendition of our globe. By far the largest land
area on that map — in fact, its relative size was exaggerated
by the flat projection — was marked with the Cyrillic letters
"CCCP." It dominated with its bulk a huge single Eurasian
continent, with only the extremities not governed from Moscow, and with Africa to the south appearing almost as an ap-
pendage. Across a blue space of water was the visibly smaller
Western Hemisphere, dominated by the archrival state situated
in North America.

Looking at the world spread out flat in this manner, Gromyko must have found it unnatural, indeed perhaps even gall-

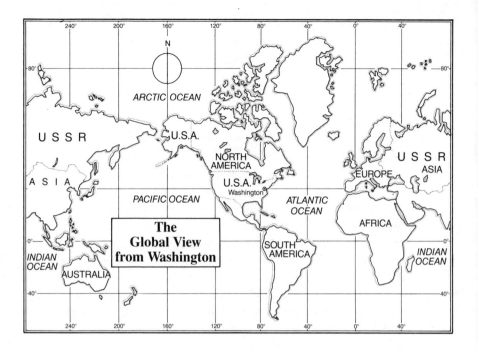

The Global View from Washington

ing, for the distant North American state to be so deeply involved in the political and economic matters of that central Eurasian landmass stretching from Kamchatka to Gibraltar. In the eyes of the meditating Russian statesman, only an aggressive design could explain the determination of that distant state to keep the peripheries — Western Europe, the Far East, and south Asia — out of Moscow's sphere of influence, a design obviously calculated to harm the legitimate continental interests of the USSR. Surely, he must have mused, the map clearly revealed certain evident "iron laws" of global politics: water should separate the North American intruder from these deviant peripheries of the central landmass, thereby providing for a "natural" geopolitical division of the world.

Admittedly, the foreign minister was not only a geopolitician but a statesman with an ideological bent. Such a "natural" division of global power, with Moscow holding sway over the central landmass and Washington confined to the Western Hemisphere, would tilt world power in favor of the forces of socialism, spelling the end of global preponderance by the hostile socioeconomic and political system led by the adversary in Washington.

But such global and rather apocalyptic ideological musings would not divert the experienced Russian foreign minister, nor his successors, from the more immediate policy tasks — and these are, indeed, geopolitically defined. The wall map helped to focus the mind, to refine and to reinforce priorities, to provide constancy, and to identify openings to be exploited as they appeared. The map was itself reinforced by an awareness of history, for Gromyko also confided that his favorite readings were the memoirs of his predecessors at the Foreign Ministry.

An enduring sense of direction thus gave geopolitical substance to Soviet foreign policy moves. In contrast, Gromyko's Western opponents all too often practiced foreign policy by reflex. They responded mainly to events, not to speak of the democratic temptation to place atmospherics above enduring historical propensities. As Gromyko once disdainfully remarked to an associate, his adversaries "mistake tactics for strategy. . . . The absence of a solid, coherent, and consistent policy is their big flaw."

Yet a map can mislead as well as enlighten. It can foster a false sense of the true distribution of power by distorting relative size and by creating a misleading sense of geographical centrality. Since a map must have an arbitrary center, it can be designed to put any country at the global midpoint; for a long time, for instance, Chinese world maps quite naturally confirmed the political significance of the term "the Middle Kingdom." It is not surprising, therefore, that the standard Soviet world map, including those in the official Soviet atlas, places the straight longitude line at 40 degrees, so that Moscow is the world's very center. The Western Hemisphere is way off, on the left. It faces across an ocean the huge and dominant landmass of Eurasia, with Africa attached to Eurasia's western half and Australia floating close to its southeast.

In effect, the visual impact carries a geopolitical message: a central continent, with a central capital, dominating the globe physically — and political realities should be in accord with these physical facts.

It hardly needs saying that this is not a fully accurate rendition of the world. A geopolitical appreciation of the globe rather than of a flat map yields other insights. For one thing, North America (which includes the United States and Canada) more closely matches the USSR in size than the Soviet map conveys. For another, oceans more effectively link than separate (as it seems on the map) the large floating islands called continents. The immense watery expanses serve as objects for the exercise of strategic control by dominant naval forces, as waterways for trade, and as avenues for cultural expansion. Such strategic control can therefore lead to the development of organic political, economic, and cultural ties between the peripheries of a continent and a distant transoceanic power.

Also, a map conveys neither a sense of the economic power nor an appreciation of the vitality and size of a population. The world looks vastly different when measured in these terms, and in a rendition of the world based on gross national product the United States emerges clearly as the preponderant power, dwarfing by a factor of two its nearest rival. Beyond these tangibles, one must also consider such intangible qualitative factors as social creativity and innovation in high technology, not to speak of cultural dynamism.

It would be most surprising if Gromyko and his heirs ignored these other considerations. Gromyko's experience certainly must have taught him to respect these factors, for they helped to frustrate the geopolitical determinism that would have yielded Moscow total control of the dominating central landmass. But other statesmen often make the opposite mistake: they too lightly discard the territorial view of foreign policy. Yet this perspective does focus attention on the intimate link between geography and political power, between territory and people, between historical drives and geopolitical priorities. Without it, foreign policy lacks the vital link between national power and global strategy.

A Historical Contest

The American-Soviet relationship is a classic historical conflict between two major powers. But it is more than merely a national conflict. It is also a struggle between two imperial systems. And it involves — for the first time in history — a two-nation contest for nothing less than global predominance. Of these three propositions, the American people are prepared instinctively to accept only the last. Most Americans realize that the American-Soviet rivalry is global in scope; they would be hard put not to, with almost every morning's newspaper and every evening's television news program providing graphic evidence of that fact. Americans today are "tuned in" to the world through mass communications, and hence their awareness of a pervasive, global competition comes to them relatively naturally.

Paradoxically, the other two propositions are less congenial. The notion of historical conflict — and the idea that the American-Soviet struggle is the latest in a long series of prolonged major national rivalries — is less digestible to a people who are short on historical memory and who tend to view peace as natural and war (or conflict) as an aberration. Even more alien is the notion that in a significant respect the American-Soviet contest is not only a struggle between a democratic and a totalitarian state but also the clash of two large imperial systems. Yet the fact is that the American-Soviet conflict has become a truly historical collision waged on a global scale between two dominant empires.

The United States and the Soviet Union have been in conflict for almost half a century, a period of time certainly of historical length. During these decades, each country has viewed the other as hostile and threatening to its vital interests and basic beliefs. During these decades, each has perceived the other as the main source of danger both to world peace and to its own national security. During these decades, each has voiced its faith in a historical outcome that would amount to victory, but each also has been moved by fear that the other might somehow prevail.

Although this competition has been the dominant reality of the two-way relationship during the postwar period, awareness of it came slowly for Americans. The intensity of this social competition was probably not realized until the launch of Sputnik in 1957. The Soviet Union, on the contrary, has for much of its existence measured itself by what it must do "to catch up with and surpass America." The rivalry with America has long been an enduring leitmotiv of the Soviet rulers, infusing the Soviet people with the consciousness of a permanent race with the dominant Western democracy. In that respect, for the Soviets at least, the emergence of the cold war between the two superpowers was a normal development, inherent in both ideology and history. Not so for the United States. The wartime alliance seemed to many Americans an augury of a peaceful and cooperative postwar relationship. Walter Lippmann doubtless spoke for most Americans when he voiced the hope in a column in the New York *Herald Tribune* in February 1945, right after the Yalta Conference, that Churchill, Stalin, and Roosevelt "have checked and reversed the normal tendency of a victorious coalition to dissolve as the war, which called it into being, approaches its end. . . . The military alliance is proving itself to be no transitory thing, good only in the presence of a common enemy, but in truth the nucleus and core of a new international order."

In fact, Yalta's continuing historical significance lies in what it reveals about Russia's enduring ambitions toward Europe as a whole. Yalta was the last gasp of carefully calibrated Soviet diplomacy designed to obtain Anglo-American acquiescence to a preponderant Soviet role in all of Europe. At Yalta, in addition to timidly reopening the issue of Eastern Europe, the West also deflected, but again in a vague and timorous fashion, Soviet aspirations for a dominant position in the western extremity of the Eurasian landmass.

It is, therefore, a myth that at Yalta the West accepted the division of Europe. The fact is that Eastern Europe had been conceded de facto to Joseph Stalin by Franklin D. Roosevelt and Winston Churchill as early as the Tehran Conference (in November–December 1943), and at Yalta the British and American leaders had some halfhearted second thoughts about that concession. They then made a last-ditch but ineffective effort to fashion some arrangements to assure at least a modicum of freedom for Eastern Europe, in keeping with Anglo-American hopes for democracy on the European continent as a whole. The Western statesmen failed, however, to face up to the ruthlessness of the emerging postwar Soviet might, and in the ensuing clash between Stalinist power and Western naïveté, power prevailed.

The American-Soviet collision thus came as a shock to most Americans. But even then it came as a rude awakening, not to the natural order of things, but to what seemed to them to be an unnatural and temporary condition that ought to be soon resolved. The ensuing cold war, even though it lit doctrinal passions in the hearts of many Americans, was still viewed as something of an aberration to be ended somehow in a great act of reconciliation. Hence the periodic bursts of hope in anticipation of U.S.–Soviet summits and even following in their wake. Hence also the painful and disturbing shifts in public mood from euphoria about détente to hysteria about the cold war.

By now it is becoming evident to more Americans — though this reality is still painfully and reluctantly assimilated — that the American-Soviet relationship is, indeed, a historical conflict. There is a growing appreciation that this rivalry is a struggle with many causes, one that is not susceptible to broad and quick resolution, one that will have to be waged patiently but with national determination for many decades to come.

This struggle is not just one of ideas or for "the hearts and minds" of people. To be sure, ideological competition plays a role, but this dimension of the collision has faded in recent years with the decline in Soviet revolutionary fervor and ideological appeal. The conflict is expressed predominantly through the extension of power and influence over territory and people and through the acquisition of military might designed to intimidate or contain the opponent. It is geopolitical and strategic considerations that are critical in determining the focus, the substance, and eventually the outcome of this historical conflict.

The conflict arose as a natural consequence of the collapse during World War II of the Europe-based international system. Dominated politically and financially by Great Britain, the prewar interstate system involved maintaining a precarious global balance among two large empires (the British and the French), several smaller European empires, an emerging Japanese empire, and two large continental states (Germany and Russia). The United States was essentially on the periphery of world affairs in the wake of the self-imposed isolation that resulted from the U.S. Senate's rejection of membership in the League of Nations.

That world died in World War II. From the ashes of the old Europe-dominated world, a new distribution of power emerged. It involved only two major states, both essentially non-European. America already exercised global influence, and the Soviet Union dominated the world's largest continent and historically and ideologically aspired to global status. The Soviet Union quite naturally viewed the United States as the principal obstacle to its quest for greatness and for ideological fulfillment, even if initially the United States perceived the Soviet Union only as a security threat to its allies, a threat to be dealt with by a carefully calibrated policy of military containment. Thus there came to pass the historical conflict predicted a century and a half ago with remarkable confidence by a twenty-six-year-old Frenchman, Alexis de Toqueville, with each country eventually possessing the power "to sway the destinies" of the globe.

Yet though the conflict involved new participants, it was still the legatee of the old, almost traditional, and certainly geopolitical clash between the great oceanic powers and the dominant land powers. The United States was in this sense the successor to Great Britain (and, earlier, Spain or Holland) and the Soviet Union to Nazi Germany (and, earlier, Imperial Germany or Napoleonic France). The seafaring states projected their power by exploiting the accessible ocean routes to establish transoceanic enclaves of political and economic influence. The land powers sought continental domination as a point of departure for challenging the hegemony of the transoceanic intruder. History teaches that such conflicts tend to be protracted, and not to be as susceptible to quick solution, either by victory or accommodation, as head-on collisions between seafaring nations or between territorial powers.

Geopolitical factors might have been cause enough by themselves to propel the two major postwar powers into a collision. But added to them was the fact that, to a greater extent than any previous historical rivals, America and the Soviet Union differed profoundly. The gulf between them may be characterized in ten different ways:

(*1*) *In the imperatives of their respective geopolitical situations,* as just noted.

(*2*) *In the historical experience that shaped each nation's political subconscious.* The United States was an open, freely expanding society of voluntary immigrants, who did not share a common past, but aspired to a shared future. The Soviet Union was a society always subordinated to the state, regimented by it, and expanding through organized military conquest and penal settlements directed from the center.

(3) In the philosophical values that either shape the national outlook or are formalized through an ideology. The United States stresses the primacy of the individual, enshrined in the Bill of Rights. The Soviet Union has institutionalized the concept and practice of the subordination of the individual to the state.

(4) In the political organization and political culture that determine how decisions are discussed, made, and reviewed. The United States has a system of open political competition, reinforced by free mass media and formalized through the secret ballot, free elections, and a deliberate separation of powers into the executive, legislative, and judicial. The Soviet Union has concentrated such powers in a monopolistic fashion under a closed and disciplined leadership that is self-selective and self-perpetuating, exercising total censorship on the mass media and emphasizing the deliberate political indoctrination of the people.

(5) In the relationship of the spiritual to the political, which helps to define the inner content of the human being. The United States has a deliberate separation of church and state designed to maximize the freedom of religious choice and to minimize the spiritual role of the state. The Soviet Union has subordinated the church to the state, not for the sake of instilling formal religious values but in order to promote state-sponsored atheism and to confine strictly the scope of religious practice.

(6) In economic organization. The United States has a system that, however imperfectly, provides economic opportunity and encourages personal initiative, private ownership, risk taking, and the profit motive, and it has generated a high standard of living for the majority of the people. In the Soviet Union the political leadership is in charge of directing all economic activity, with the predominant means of production centralized

through state ownership, and with free initiative and private ownership deliberately limited, all in a setting of continued economic deprivation and relative backwardness.

(7) In life-styles, which express the personal quest for self-fulfillment. The United States has a fluid, consumer-oriented, highly mobile society, with a somewhat crass mass culture that is given to changing fads and frequent artistic experimentation. It has a tendency to undergo sudden shifts of mood, with a perhaps inadequate sense of civic obligation that permits the state to levy few formal demands on the individual, as demonstrated by the absence of a military draft. The Soviet Union promotes a more formal, confined, and controlled existence within an officially decreed culture, from which citizens take refuge in deeper and perhaps more binding family ties and group friendships than are found in America, but all of whose lives are subject to the heavy demands of formal socialist patriotism and also to the militarization even of early education.

(8) In the external ideological appeal of the two systems that defines how they are perceived throughout the world. The United States has a society that influences the world through communications and mass media, "Americanizing" the youth culture in particular and creating an exaggerated "Dallas"-like perception of America. The Soviet Union appeals to the world's poor countries as an example of allegedly just social self-development. It presents itself as the spearhead of a world revolution, though this picture is increasingly being overtaken by a growing global awareness of Soviet social stagnation, economic inefficiency, and political bureaucratization.

(9) In the historical cycles that these great nations experienced as they rose, peaked, and declined in vitality and power. The United States is a nation clearly at its peak — some would argue already past it — but it is still the world's prime power. The Soviet Union is a nation still historically aspiring to be the Third Rome, and thus perhaps more motivated in seeking su-

premacy and more prepared than its rival to make the necessary sacrifices.

(10) In the definition of historical victory, which indirectly affects the shaping of immediate goals. The United States has a vague yearning for "a world of peace" and for worldwide democracy, as well as a patriotic and doubtless self-serving tendency to associate this global condition with continued American primacy. The Soviet Union has a more focused desire to "surpass America," to become the center of a world of increasingly like-minded socialist states and of a Eurasian continent from which its rival will have been explicitly excluded.

Never has there been a contest between two powers so fundamentally different. Even the war with Nazi Germany did not involve all these stark contrasts. Yet never has such a conflict been managed with such caution. Rivalries of this range and scale — especially those with animosities intensified by systemic differences — have historically resulted in war. Even taking into account the fact that conflicts between oceanic and territorial powers tend to be protracted, the United States and the Soviet Union by all previous standards should have gone to war against each other on many occasions. *Prudently, they have not.* The nearest they have come is indirect war, as in Korea. Their remarkable restraint is directly attributable to the destructiveness of the nuclear weaponry that both sides possess. It negates the traditional benefits of a military victory. This new factor in the relationship induces restraint, but it also helps to perpetuate the contest. Hostility is mixed with extraordinary insecurity. Each side has to do whatever is necessary to ensure that the other does not gain a decisive military edge, for in the nuclear age there is no time to recover and recoup after war begins. The advent of nuclear weapons has tempered the struggle but enhanced its enduring, historical nature.

An Imperial Contest

The American-Soviet contest is not only between two nations. It is between two empires. Both nations had acquired imperial attributes even before their post–World War II collision, but that collision has heightened the strategic importance of their respective imperial assets and has intensified their imperial growth. Some might say that this view is tantamount to asserting that there is a kind of "moral equivalence" between the Soviet Union and the United States. I do not suggest that. I use the term "empire" as morally neutral to describe a hierarchical system of political relationships, radiating from a center. Such an empire's morality is defined by how its imperial power is wielded, with what degree of consent on the part of those within its scope, and to what ends. This is where the distinctions between the American and the Soviet imperial systems are the sharpest.

Moscow's empire has three layers. First, there is the Great Russian empire. About 135 million Great Russians dominate as imperial subjects about 140 million people from a variety of non-Russian nations, including approximately 50 million central Asian Muslims and 50 million Ukrainians. Second, there is the Soviet empire. Moscow controls satellite states in which about 120 million East Europeans, 15 million Afghans, and 2 million Mongolians live. Third, there is Moscow's Communist empire. This includes its imperial clients, such as Cuba, Nicaragua, Vietnam, Angola, Ethiopia, Southern Yemen, and North Korea, that are dependent on Moscow for political guidance, military support, and economic aid and that have a total population of 130 million people. Thus, about 135 million Great Russians exercise political control over an imperial system that cumulatively encompasses, themselves included, approximately 545 millions spread throughout the Eurasian continent and in overseas dependencies.

It is, however, predominantly a territorially contiguous empire, the product of a sustained and unrelenting historical drive. Indeed, the distinctive character of the Russian imperial drive stems from the connection between the militaristic organization of Russian society and the territorial imperative of its instinct for survival. This has often been noted by both Russian and non-Russian historians. From time immemorial, Russian society expressed itself politically through a state that was mobilized and regimented along military lines, with the security dimension serving as the central organizing impulse. The absence of clearly definable national boundaries made territorial expansion the obvious way of assuring security, with such expansion then breeding new conflicts, new threats, and thus a further expansionary drive. A relentless historical cycle was set in motion: insecurity generated expansionism; expansionism bred insecurity; insecurity, in turn, fueled further expansionism.

Russian history is, consequently, a history of sustained territorial expansionism. This expansion from the northeast plains and forests of Muscovy has lasted — almost on a continuous basis — for more than three hundred years. It has involved a push westward against major power rivals, resulting in the eventual expulsion of Sweden from east of the Baltic and in the partition of the Polish-Lithuanian republic. It has involved a persistent drive southward, culminating in the wake of defeats inflicted on the Ottoman Empire in the subordination of the Ukrainian cossacks and the Crimean Tatars and in the absorption of several Caucasian nations and Muslim central Asia. It has involved a steady stream of settlers, penal colonists, and military explorers moving eastward, along the rim of the Chinese empire, all the way to Kamchatka. Both in scale and in duration such territorial expansion is doubtless one of the most ambitious examples of a relentless imperial drive in known history. It has for some two centuries meant the subordination to Moscow every year of territory equivalent to a Holland or a Vermont!

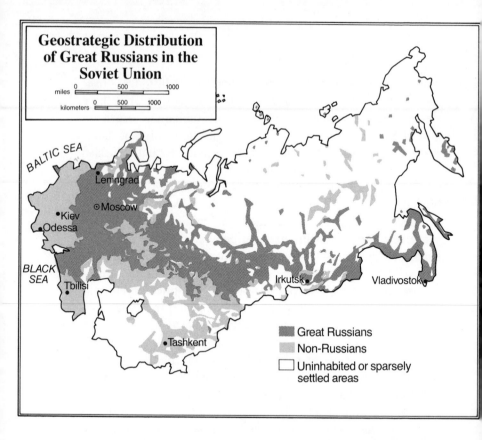

Geostrategic Distribution
of Great Russians in the
Soviet Union

The Russians have come in this manner to control the world's largest piece of real estate. They do so by inhabiting relatively densely its inner core — the large area known as European Russia — and by settling in smaller but still politically significant numbers in strategically significant colonial outposts in the Baltic region (including Kaliningrad), parts of Byelorussia, the eastern Ukraine, the northeast shore of the Black Sea, large parts of Kazakhstan, and along a long security belt spanning the Trans-Siberian Railroad all the way to the Soviet Far East. The empty vastness of Siberia has thus been effectively sealed off and remains available for gradual colonization.

During and after World War II, Moscow's domination expanded to almost all of Eastern Europe. This, too, was largely a matter of military conquest, reinforced by an ideological transformation of the subordinate societies. A dependent cast of local Communist functionaries came to exercise power on Moscow's behalf, while acquiring a vested interest in their positions and privilege. The association was formalized through the Warsaw Pact and buttressed also by an economic organization, the Council of Mutual Economic Assistance, that by the 1980s was increasingly used by Moscow to achieve tighter economic integration of Eastern Europe with the Soviet Union.

The Russian imperial system — with its mixture of elite co-optation, strategic settlement, and national subordination — thus emerged in a manner that differs profoundly from the experience of other recent empires. Naval expansion to remote lands, followed by limited settling, was not the method. It was much more organic. It was a process of steady seepage into contiguous territory, with the atavistic instinct of survival dictating the felt need to acquire more land. "Insecurity" was translated into persistent expansion. As a result, Russia historically was not so much a victim of frequent aggression as the persistent aggressor itself, pressing from the center in this or that direction whenever opportunity beckoned.

Any list of aggressions committed in the last two centuries against Russia would be dwarfed by a parallel list of Russian expansionist moves against its neighbors. The predatory character of Great Russian imperialism is undeniable. The vaunted Russian sense of insecurity does exist — not because Russia was so frequently the victim, but because its organic expansion has prompted, and was prompted by, territorial acquisitiveness, and this has inevitably produced antagonistic reactions.

Two authors make rather pertinent comments on this issue. Richard Pipes writes in his book *Survival Is Not Enough* (1984),

Common sense, of course, might suggest even to those who lack knowledge of the facts that a country can no more become the world's most spacious as a result of suffering constant invasions than an individual can gain wealth from being repeatedly robbed. . . . In the 1890s, the Russian General Staff carried out a comprehensive study of the history of Russian warfare since the foundations of the state. In the summary volume, the editor told his readers that they could take pride in their country's military record and face the future with confidence — between 1700 and 1870, Russia had spent 106 years fighting 38 military campaigns, of which 36 had been "offensive" and a mere 2 defensive.

Max Singer argues in Aaron Wildavsky's book *Beyond Containment* (1983),

The Soviet Union is best understood as *insatiably* defensive. There are those who argue, with substantial basis, that the Soviets are committed to an offensive policy — although probably an extremely cautious and patient one — because of ideology or the desire for imperial aggrandizement. However, since their policy, and the danger to us, may be essentially the same regardless of whether their motivation is defensive or offensive, I see no point in insisting on the assertion that their motivation is offensive. Perhaps it is, but we are no better off if it is not. The insatiability of their self-perceived defensive requirements takes all the relief out of seeing the Soviet Union as a defensive power. This insatiability follows from the fact that they cannot make their fundamental objective — preservation of the empire — truly secure so long as our strength lasts. Therefore they cannot be satisfied as long as we are capable of resisting their demands.

An additional and enduring consequence of such relentless territorial expansion has been the emergence of an imperial consciousness among the Great Russian people. The notion of "imperial consciousness" may be difficult to define, but the fact that an idea is difficult to define does not negate it. There is something strikingly imperial in the way the Russians insist on describing themselves as the "Big Brother" of the dominated peoples. This imperial attitude is also visible in the spontaneous determination to build huge Russian Orthodox cathedrals in the very centers of dominated capitals, as was done in Helsinki and Warsaw during the nineteenth century. And it was not a coincidence that Moscow replaced the Warsaw *So-*

bor, which the newly emancipated Poles had blown up in 1919, with the monumental Stalin "Palace of Culture" thirty years later. There is a deeply rooted feeling among Great Russians that Moscow must retain the non-Russian nations of the Soviet Union and Eastern Europe as part of Mother Russia's special domain. For a firsthand insight into imperial and hierarchical relations, one should read the account of the former Polish ambassador to Washington, Romuald Spasowski, who resigned after the imposition of martial law in December 1981.

Great Russian imperial consciousness is a complex web of religious messianism that has long associated Moscow with the Third Rome; of nationalistic instincts of survival and power; and of more recent universalistic ideological zeal. Insecurity produced by territorial expansion is also part of this consciousness, and its paranoiac attitudes toward the outside world have been reinforced by the Communist obsession with internal and external enemies. In contrast to the American outlook, which stresses diversity as normal, the ideological component of the Soviet worldview emphasizes the notion that all of humanity is governed by certain "iron laws of history" that only the Soviet leaders have decoded correctly. Doctrinal self-righteousness thus makes the Soviet leaders view all those in the outside world who do not share their view, and especially America, as inherently hostile. In brief, in the American outlook, differences are normal; in the Russian, they are symptoms of conflict.

In the modern era this complex web of motivations has helped to generate and sustain a world outlook in which the drive to global preeminence, for decades measured by competition with the United States, has become the central energizing impulse. This continuation of Russian territorial expansiveness and Soviet Communist ideology, the historical successor to the concept of the Third Rome, was bound to collide with the power that in the meantime had reached across the oceans to contain Moscow at both the western and eastern extremities of the Eurasian continent. And that transoceanic power was in many respects also imperial in character.

Initially, American expansionism bore some striking resemblances to the Russian experience. This was especially true of the American conquest during the nineteenth century of territories once held by Mexico. Otherwise, American expansionism, especially during the phase of "Manifest Destiny" at the turn of this century, tended to reflect the oceanic character of American power. American naval might expanded U.S. political domination into Cuba and the Caribbean, into Central America, and beyond Hawaii almost to the coast of Asia through the acquisition by war of the Philippine islands. This overt imperialism was justified ideologically on the grounds of democratic universalism, capitalizing at the same time on the intrinsic appeal of America as a free and relatively rich land.

The American imperial system emerged full-blown only after World War II. It was also largely an accidental empire. By virtue of emerging from World War II unscathed, the United States was the world's preeminent power, with its GNP accounting for more than half the world economy. That de facto status transformed the United States into an empire. For both international and domestic reasons, it could no longer be indifferent to developments in virtually all of the world's regions. The political and military ties that can be said to have codified the American empire grew out of the emerging cold war. An initial inclination to disengage from Western Europe had to be reversed because of the growing threat from the Soviet Union. A constricted definition of the American security perimeter in the Far East had to be redrawn after the outbreak of the Korean War. A later strategy to protect American interests in south Asia through regional powers had to be abandoned after the internal collapse of Iran and the Soviet invasion of Afghanistan.

Like the Soviet Union, the United States faced geopolitical imperatives. Whoever controlled Eurasia dominated the globe.

If the Soviet Union captured the peripheries of this landmass — Western Europe, the Far East, and southern Asia — it would not only win control of vast human, economic, and military resources, but also gain access to the geostrategic approaches to the Western Hemisphere — the Atlantic and Pacific oceans. It is not a fluke of history that the geostrategic lines have been so drawn. Just as the Kremlin leaders must view the American presence on the Eurasian continent as the key obstacle to achieving their geopolitical aspirations, the United States must view its transoceanic positions as the forward lines of defense that spare it from having to mount a defense of North America.

Although the United States undertook its imperial role with some degree of reluctance, and without thinking of itself as imperial, its foreign policy debates today center on how best to protect and manage its imperial domain — and both ends of the political spectrum employ what can only be described as imperial arguments. This is most evident in debates about American policy in the third world, particularly toward such states as Iran under the Shah or the Philippines under Ferdinand Marcos. It is a scenario that has been replayed often: American economic and military aid goes to a strategically situated, pro-Western third world state. This state has an authoritarian government and comes under attack from internal forces that are hostile to the United States. On the right, it is argued that the national interest requires the United States to keep the friendly regime in power. On the left, it is asserted that the United States should use the leverage of its assistance programs to induce the government to reform or even to abdicate. U.S. power and influence is to be used in the first case to maintain the American position and in the second to force internal changes on a sovereign state. Both views, however, consider it to be the right of the United States to use its power to affect the internal affairs of another nation.

Unlike the Soviet empire, the American one is territorially

noncontiguous, relatively porous, and held together through indirect ties. Though formalized through treaty arrangements — which in effect acknowledge the status of Western Europe, Japan, and South Korea as American protectorates — the U.S.-dominated imperial system is much more a mosaic of shared interests and also of informal ethnic and business ties. America's democratic inclination toward consensual decision making has mitigated its political, economic, and military domination. The most important protected allies are Western Europe, Canada, Japan, and South Korea. But America also has dependent clients in the Middle East (Israel and Egypt), southwest Asia (Pakistan), and Southeast Asia (Thailand and the Philippines). The entire imperial system embraces more than 780 million people by comparison with the Soviet empire's population of 545 million, but lacks the ideological homogeneity, the political centralization, and the territorial contiguity of the Soviet rival. The American empire is therefore not as easy to delineate precisely.

Initially both imperial systems started as duopolies. The Anglo-American alliance, personalized by Roosevelt and Churchill, gave favored status within the Western alliance to Great Britain, and the special relationship gave British leaders unparalleled influence in Washington. It was manifested very directly in the restraining role London exercised on Washington during the Korean War. For a while, too, Communist China was a junior partner in an enormous Sino-Soviet bloc, dependent on Soviet help but far from being subordinate; Mao Zedong's deference to Stalin was manifestly quite restrained. However, unlike Great Britain, a power in decline whose special status gradually faded, China was on the ascendancy, and this eventually produced a decisive rupture with the Kremlin. Moscow's undisputed imperial leadership within the now strictly Soviet empire was thus purchased at a high geopolitical cost.

America owes the flexibility of its imperial system to external and internal influences. Externally there was the defensive reaction that shaped the initial American security ties with Western Europe and the Far East, and the generous economic recovery plans for the war-devastated protectorates that soon followed. Internally there was the multiethnic character of U.S. society itself. In contrast to the Soviet Union, where multiethnicity is subordinated to the predominant nation and could eventually prompt a dangerous internal implosion, American multiethnicity has produced a reverse cultural "explosion," influencing the countries whence many Americans originated. It reaches beyond the obvious ties with Great Britain. The deep-seated popularity of America in many countries, such as Italy, Ireland, and Poland, is derived directly from the impact on their populations of the many millions of relatives who have become Americans. It reinforces the positive, attractive appeal of the American way of life and creates political sympathies that further cement the formal relationships. It also permits the United States more deliberately to exploit this advantage through the deployment in foreign service or business positions of Americans with particular foreign affinities. As the number of Asian-Americans grows, the same process is beginning to be repeated in relation to Korea, Japan, China, India, and Southeast Asia.

Finally, political ties of the American imperial system are reinforced by the dynamic and highly creative character of socioeconomic change in America. It provides a model for political and economic development, and it prompts the voluntary flow to America of hundreds of thousands of foreign students. All of this spins a web of relationships at least as important as the initial extension abroad of American military power.

As a result of these factors — but particularly of the transoceanic character of U.S. power — America's dependencies do tend to view themselves as genuine allies, and in fact they are such allies. This is not to ignore the reality of political differences and economic conflicts with the United States, but such dissension occurs within a framework of predominantly shared interests, with geographical distance creating political attraction. (The neighbor of my neighbor is my friend but not my neighbor!)

In contrast, the contiguous territorial character of the Soviet empire means that Moscow is seen by its neighbors as inherently threatening and dominating. Hence, even its formal allies are in many respects resentful and potentially unreliable. Communist China and Yugoslavia, both geographically proximate to the Soviet Union, broke with the Kremlin. The split with Yugoslavia set a dangerous precedent for Eastern Europe, and the rupture with China was especially damaging to the Soviet quest for continental predominance. Not surprisingly, Moscow's most genuine friends have been such geographically distant countries as Cuba and Vietnam.

The imperial conflict between Washington and Moscow highlights basic differences of attitude and practice toward wider international arrangements. It also provides an important insight into what the historical success of one or the other would portend for the global condition.

A Global Contest

The collision between America and Russia is now global in scope. But it did not begin in this way. The cold war started as a contest between a maritime power and a continental power over the remnants of Europe. After the war, the Soviet side clearly expected the United States to withdraw its forces from Europe — not least because President Roosevelt explicitly pledged to Stalin that the United States would do this. With all major European powers either destroyed or exhausted, the presence of the Red Army in the heart of Europe would have had decisive geopolitical consequences. If America had withdrawn from Europe, Western Europe would have had to defer to Moscow.

Yet America quickly concluded that it could not abandon

Western Europe. The United States was linked to these countries by the Atlantic Ocean and was part of a joint community culturally and politically. As the American engagement in Europe grew, America and Russia discovered that they could not attain their goals without seeking, paradoxically, each to become to some extent like the other. America had to become a territorial power. It did so by shaping a transcontinental alliance, deploying large American ground forces in Europe, and backing these up with its naval and air power and a nuclear guarantee. This nuclear threat compensated in the early years for the relative weakness of these American conventional forces.

In contrast, the Soviet Union, contained in Europe and initially intimidated by the U.S. nuclear monopoly, had to acquire not only a nuclear capacity but also a maritime capability to break out of the U.S.-engineered European containment. By the late 1950s, the Soviet Union was able to acquire both of these in sufficient strength to begin to break out of the containment, projecting its political, ideological, and military presence to areas far outside of Europe. It established a lasting presence in Cuba and Indochina. It had temporary footholds in Indonesia, Africa, and the Middle East. In the 1970s, it went on a geopolitical offensive in the third world, spreading its influence over South Vietnam, Cambodia (Kampuchea), Laos, Ethiopia, Southern Yemen, Angola, Mozambique, Afghanistan, and Nicaragua and increasing its presence in still more countries. In the 1980s, Soviet military presence was being projected worldwide, even though the Soviet Union remains still predominantly a continental power. Today, pro-Soviet regimes are scattered throughout the world.

The global rivalry between America and Russia is new. Never before have two powers competed on such a broad front. Moreover, never before would the eclipse of one of the major rival powers have given to the other effective global preponderance. Not even World War II, which in any case ended with a U.S.–Soviet duopoly, could have produced such a one-sided outcome. A German-Japanese victory would have led to a division of global spoils, though the Western Hemisphere for a while at least would have remained largely outside of direct German-Japanese hegemony.

Earlier major historical rivalries were even more regionally confined. World War I was primarily a European war, waged by Allied powers to deny Germany continental domination. Two noncontinental maritime powers, Great Britain and the United States, made the decisive contribution to the outcome, but its consequences were largely confined to Europe. Similarly, the Napoleonic Wars involved an effort to construct a continental system — one designed to challenge Great Britain — and the failure of this challenge did give London international primacy. But even this was far from effective global preponderance. Much of Europe and large parts of Asia and the Western Hemisphere remained beyond the influence of British power.

The global scope of the current contest results not only from the unprecedented collision between a transoceanic power and a transcontinental power, each supported by its own imperial system, but also from developments in both weaponry and mass communications. Modern weaponry, in terms of both range and destructiveness, gives substance to the concept of a genuinely global war and reality to the threat of global devastation. Competition for the control of outer space — or at least the denial of monopoly to the rival — is today also part of the struggle for the globe.

At the same time, the combination of mass communications and mass literacy also makes the political-ideological contest geographically unlimited. No continent is unaffected by conflicting appeals and competing social models. Much of the global discourse is dominated by American and Soviet concepts of the future and profoundly differing philosophical assessments of the human condition.

All of the foregoing contributes to making the American-

Soviet conflict *a protracted contest of historical attrition.* In that contest, periodic changes in diplomatic atmospherics are to be expected. The détente of the 1970s might well be reproduced in a new form in the late 1980s. But occasional tactical accommodations cannot obscure the enduring and underlying competitive character of the relationship. Conflict — produced by geopolitical realities and reinforced by ideological and systemic differences — will continue to be the central motif in the relationship. But for the first time in history, prudence — induced by the sheer destructiveness of nuclear weaponry — places a high premium on a long-term strategy for a global contest in which the outcome, also for the first time, is not likely to be determined by a direct clash of arms.

II

The Struggle for Eurasia

THOUGH global in scope, the American-Soviet contest has a central priority: Eurasia. This landmass is the contest's geostrategic focus and its geopolitical prize. The struggle for Eurasia is a comprehensive one, waged on three central strategic fronts, the far western, the far eastern, and the southwestern.

For the United States, the prevention of Soviet domination over Eurasia is the precondition of achieving an acceptable outcome to the contest. For the Soviet Union, expelling America from Eurasia through a political or a military breakthrough on the three central strategic fronts remains the precondition of decisive success in the historical conflict.

The struggle on the three central fronts principally involves a political competition buttressed by military power. Nonetheless, on each front at different times, there have been direct tests of will using force or the threat of it. Political will and military power are thus intertwined in the contest for the globe's central continent.

Russia and Eurasia

The exclusion from Eurasia of any powerful external force and the subordination to itself of any other continental power is for Russia both a geopolitical goal and an expression of historical ambition. Russia's geographical situation is paradoxical. The Great Russian empire is clearly militarily dominant on a huge continent that contains most of the world's people, territory, and wealth, and that occupies the central strategic location in relation to the other continents. At the same time, as the map highlights, Russia is subject to a peculiar isolation, or even encirclement. Despite the country's enormous continental size — it is by far the biggest state in the world — it is in effect landlocked. It does not have a truly open access to the world. At one end, Western Europe effectively blocks entry to the Mediterranean Sea and to the Atlantic Ocean. Russia's outreach to the Atlantic and beyond is contained by strategic choke points, such as the Dardanelles Straits between the Black Sea and the Mediterranean, the Kattegat and Skagerrak narrows linking the Baltic Sea to the North Sea, and the passage running between Norway and Spitsbergen (which in any case leads out from Soviet ports that are forced to close during winter).

To the south, access to the Persian Gulf and to the Indian Ocean is denied by a rim of states, starting with Turkey, including Iran, Pakistan, and India, and finishing with China. The Chinese frontier also becomes the limit of the Soviet empire in the Far East, with South Korea and offshore Japan as the final confining outposts. Here, too, the Soviet Union is effectively landlocked. Access to the Pacific Ocean is limited to a narrow strip of the Soviet Far East, with the port of Vladivostok vulnerable to a choke point at the Strait of Tsushima leading out of the Sea of Japan. Finally, the north is blockaded by an almost permanent ice barrier, and is unnavigable.

Tsarist and Soviet statesmen have this in common: both have by unremitting expansionism persistently sought certain key strategic goals designed to alter decisively their country's geographical situation, gaining thereby continental preponderance. This is not a matter of surmise, or of anti-Russian suspicions, but of historical record.

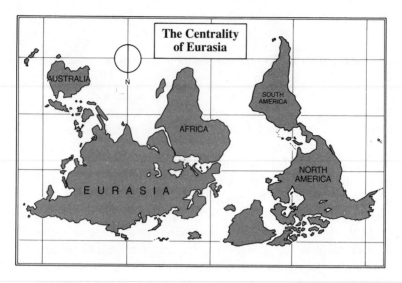

The global map simply inverted from the traditional perspective dramatizes the geostrategic centrality of Eurasia. The table summarizes the wealth of the continent that Russia seeks to dominate.

Even prior to World War I, the tsarist empire through its Far Eastern expansion sought to impose on China arrangements that would have gained for Russia effective control of Manchuria and access, through control of Port Arthur, to the Yellow Sea. Russia's defeat in the Russo-Japanese War of 1905 temporarily set back these efforts and also prompted the loss to Japan of the southern part of the strategically located Sakhalin Island. As a result, the barrier to the Pacific Ocean was reinforced. Similarly, prior to and during World War I, Russia expressed the consistent desire for direct access to the Mediterranean Sea. Moscow's protracted struggle with the Ottoman Empire even produced a brief collision during the Crimean War (1853–1856) with a Franco-British coalition determined to keep Russia out of the Mediterranean. The same objective was later explicitly articulated in the official tsarist war aims formulated shortly after the outbreak of World War I. Russia's second most important goal, as stated in a document prepared by a committee of the Tsar's Council of Ministers, was defined quite

Region	Population (millions) 1983	GNP ($U.S. billions) 1981	Land Area (square miles)
1. The World	4,714.3	12,392.2	52,240,371
2. Eurasia	3,390.1	7,429.0	19,829,447
USSR / Warsaw Pact	383.4	2,257.5	9,033,390
Far East	1,222.5	1,546.1	4,542,340
Western Europe	377.9	3,120.7	1,506,007
South Asia	859.6	184.3	1,424,403
Southwest Asia	151.6	109.8	1,195,737
Southeast Asia	395.1	210.6	2,127,570
3. Middle East	106.3	375.5	1,790,990
4. North America	259.0	3,223.4	8,225,629
5. Central America / South America	385.3	765.8	7,893,413
6. Africa	550.6	405.4	11,231,646
7. Pacific Group	23.0	193.1	3,269,246

(SOURCE: The World Bank and the Central Intelligence Agency)

succinctly: ''2) Realization of the historic tasks of Russia in the Black Sea by the annexation of Tsar'grad [Constantinople] and the Turkish Straits.''

The same document postulated Russian expansion westward. It called for the incorporation into Russian-controlled Poland of all Polish territory held by Germany and for the deliberate dismemberment of Germany. This would have undone Europe's strongest land power and ceded continental predominance to Russia. With the intent of keeping Russia engaged in fighting Germany, Franco-British leaders expressed sympathy for Moscow's aspirations in Poland, and in April 1915 they even agreed to the Russian annexation of Constantinople and the Turkish Straits. (It is no wonder that Stalin felt justified in asking later for just as much!) Had tsarist Russia attained these goals, the strategic consequences would have been far-reaching, anticipating in some respects the situation that emerged in 1945.

Soviet statesmen, though imbued with a revolutionary doctrine, still continued to share tsarist geopolitical aspirations. Control over Poland was proclaimed at the first Comintern Congress in 1920 as the central strategic objective because it would give Soviet Russia a direct link to the revolutionary fervor in Germany. That, in turn, was seen as part of a broader revolutionary upheaval throughout the world. The new Bolshevik leaders hoped that unrest even in Asia would play a critical role in undermining the dominant Western empires. Leon Trotsky, perhaps the most articulate strategist of the new Soviet regime, explained to the Central Committee as early as the summer of 1919 that "agitation in Asia" needed to be stepped up because "the international situation is evidently shaping in such a way that the road to Paris and London lies via the towns of Afghanistan, the Punjab and Bengal."

The next twenty years produced not Soviet expansion but some limited contraction of the old tsarist empire. Moscow lost Poland, Finland, and the Baltic states in the west. It failed to incorporate a section of northwestern Iran in the south. It lost special privileges in China in the Far East. But this was merely a historical pause. When World War II ushered in a new phase of global instability, Moscow's pursuit of its broader strategic goals was given a revived burst of vitality. Some goals were achieved unilaterally. Stalin struck a deal with Hitler to carve up Poland in 1939. Eastern Finland and the Baltic republics were conquered and annexed in 1940. Poland, Czechoslovakia, Hungary, Romania, Bulgaria, and East Germany were turned into satellite states in the immediate postwar years. North Korea was occupied in 1945.

Other central goals were claimed but not obtained — though again these claims reaffirmed the Eurasian scope of Moscow's strategic vision. Particularly revealing of Soviet ambitions were the brutally frank Nazi-Soviet discussions in late 1940 (fully transcribed in captured Nazi archives) regarding a collaborative division of the spoils in the wake of the expected Nazi victory. During this phase of active Nazi-Soviet collusion, Vyacheslav Molotov, Stalin's foreign minister (and Gromyko's mentor), visited Berlin at Hitler's invitation on November 12, 1940, to discuss the terms of Soviet adherence to the recently concluded Tripartite Pact between Nazi Germany, Fascist Italy, and Imperial Japan. Moscow was informed that the pact was "directed exclusively against American warmongers" and that the objective was to deter U.S. aid to Great Britain. Molotov was also encouraged to participate in a "delimitation of the interests on a worldwide scale" among the four principal beneficiaries of the anticipated British defeat.

In the course of prolonged discussions, Molotov, who stated that he was speaking personally for Stalin, quite explicitly endorsed Hitler's assertion that "the United States had no business either in Europe, in Africa, or in Asia." He also indicated general agreement with the proposition that the British Empire would be partitioned. But to the German suggestion that Russia seek "a natural outlet to the sea" in the south, Molotov responded evasively, asking innocently, "Which sea?" He refrained from providing a precise answer immediately as to what the broader Soviet postwar objectives might be, but Molotov quickly registered with the Nazi leaders the Soviet interest in obtaining a free outlet from the Black Sea and from the Baltic Sea.

Soviet ambitions, however, soon became explicit. The Nazis drafted protocols defining the proposed division of spheres of influence that would be secretly attached to the formal announcement of Soviet adherence to the Tripartite Pact. In keeping with Hitler's comments in Berlin, the Western Hemisphere was left alone on the periphery, with the proposed "worldwide delimitation" of interests of Nazi Germany, Fascist Italy, Imperial Japan, and Soviet Russia focused on Eurasia and Africa. For the Soviet Union, the German draft proposed the phrase "the Soviet Union declares that its territorial aspirations center south of the national territory of the Soviet Union in the direction of the Indian Ocean."

The formal Soviet response was provided two weeks later, and it was remarkably revealing. The Kremlin, indicating it was ready to join a four-power pact directed at America and Great Britain, demanded that the accord include the acknowledgment by Germany of Soviet preeminence in both Finland and Bulgaria, the establishment of a Soviet base in the Dardanelles, and the termination of Japanese privileges in northern Sakhalin that dated back to the aftermath of the 1905 war. Also, in two somewhat repetitive formulations Moscow requested that the German draft regarding major Soviet goals to the south be amended to the effect that "the center" and "the focal point of the aspirations of the Soviet Union" was to be "the area south of Batum and Baku in the general direction of the Persian Gulf."

The identification of these two cities as geographic points of reference, located respectively on the shores of the Black and Caspian seas, stood in sharp contrast to the vagueness of the German formulation. It indicated that the Soviet leaders had carefully considered the issue and were now prepared to register their specific objectives. The reference to areas south of Baku could have only meant Iran. Given the fact that the Soviets reaffirmed the German draft's language on maintaining the territorial integrity of Turkey, Moscow's reference to the territories south of Batum pointed at Iraq. Abadan and Basra, the Persian Gulf outlets nearest to the Soviet Union, were thus the probable eventual targets. The Soviets were clearly seeking, not only control over the area's vast oil resources, but also access to the Persian Gulf and a presence in the Middle East. It was the scope of these demands as well as the proposed strategic flanking of Germany in Scandinavia and in the Balkans that convinced Hitler that a permanent accommodation

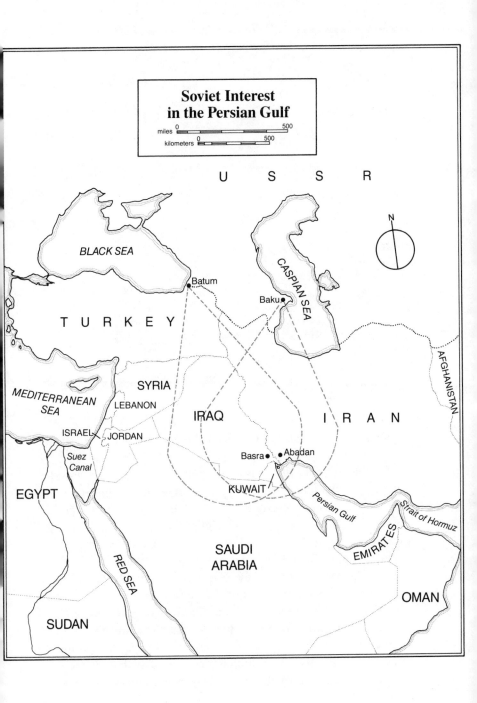

Soviet Interest in the Persian Gulf

miles 0   500
kilometers 0   500

U S S R

N

BLACK SEA

CASPIAN SEA

Batum

Baku

T U R K E Y

AFGHANISTAN

SYRIA

MEDITERRANEAN SEA

LEBANON

IRAQ

I R A N

ISRAEL

JORDAN

Suez Canal

Basra

Abadan

EGYPT

KUWAIT

Persian Gulf

Strait of Hormuz

SAUDI ARABIA

EMIRATES

RED SEA

OMAN

SUDAN

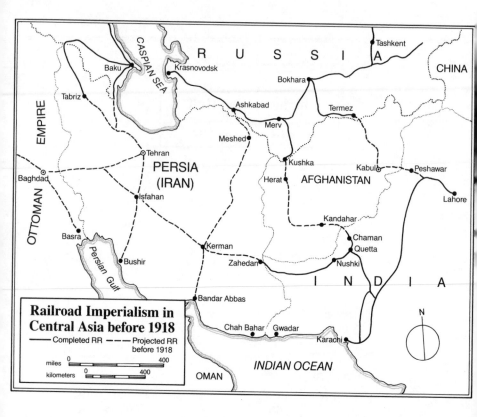

Railroad Imperialism in Central Asia before 1918
— Completed RR — — — Projected RR before 1918

with Stalin was not possible, and three weeks later he issued his famous Directive Number 21 — Operation Barbarossa.

It is noteworthy that Russian expansion to the south has always been dominated by strategic considerations, and Russian military theorists, prerevolutionary and Bolshevik, have openly written on the subject. In an excellent study published in the spring 1985 issue of the journal *Orbis* ("Seizing the Third Parallel: Geopolitics and the Soviet Advance into Central Asia"), Milan Hauner summarizes the conceptual underpinnings of that sustained drive and provides revealing examples of the Russian economic interest in the southward push. These include an effort to gain direct access to the Persian Gulf and the Indian Ocean through the construction of several strategic railroad trunk lines. The military-political consequences of such construction by a powerful state within relatively weak and economically backward countries would have been decisive. As the accompanying map illustrates, the Russian goal has been to establish two major railroads, one from Baku through Iran to Bushir on the Persian Gulf with a side connection to Baghdad and to the port of Basra; the other from Ashkabad in Russian central Asia to the Persian Gulf strategic choke point of Bandar Abbas. Additional connections were contemplated through Afghanistan, linking up with existing railroads leading south to the port of Karachi on the Indian Ocean. These projects, interrupted by World War I, doubtless loomed in the back of Stalin's mind as he pressed Hitler in 1940 for German acquiescence to Russia's renewed push to the south. Today's Soviet strategists cannot be ignorant of them.

During World War II, Soviet war aims were restated in various consultations with the new Anglo-American allies with varying degrees of specificity but with evident strategic consistency. In the west, while expressing the hope for American disengagement from Europe, Stalin tabled various schemes designed to ensure not only a weak Germany (as well as Soviet military presence in it) but the absence in Western Europe of any viable, major power. The Soviets also registered their interest in gaining control of Norwegian Spitsbergen and of the strategically located Bear Island between the Norwegian coast and Spitsbergen. At Potsdam in July 1945, when complimented on the Soviet conquest of Berlin, Stalin wistfully noted that Alexander I had occupied Paris, and Stalin then proceeded to demand for the Soviet Union a share of the Italian colonies in the Mediterranean. A year later, during the first audience with the newly appointed U.S. ambassador, General Walter Bedell Smith, Stalin reiterated the Soviet desire for a base in the Dardanelles as "a matter of our security." And in a conversation with Milovan Djilas, then Tito's closest associate, the Soviet leader mused sadly that the Soviet Union had failed to occupy all of Finland out of unfounded fears that this might precipitate a strong American reaction.

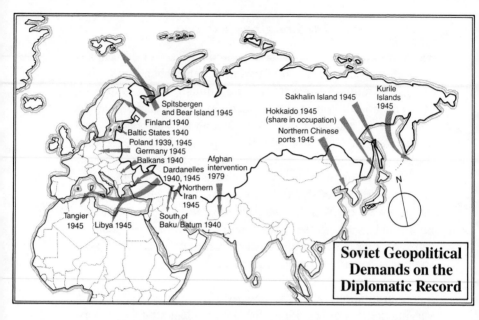

Soviet Geopolitical Demands on the Diplomatic Record

Spitsbergen and Bear Island 1945
Finland 1940
Baltic States 1940
Poland 1939, 1945
Germany 1945
Balkans 1940
Dardanelles 1940, 1945
Northern Iran 1945
Afghan intervention 1979
Tangier 1945
Libya 1945
South of Baku/Batum 1940
Sakhalin Island 1945
Hokkaido 1945 (share in occupation)
Northern Chinese ports 1945
Kurile Islands 1945

In May 1945, to an even greater extent than in February at Yalta, Stalin had tipped his hand regarding the Soviet ambitions in the Far East. When Harry Hopkins, President Roosevelt's emissary to Stalin, pressed the Soviet leader for an early intervention in the war against Japan, Stalin disarmingly observed that "the Russian people must have a good reason for going to war against Japan" and then proceeded to detail what that good reason might be. It would not come cheaply. To secure a Soviet intervention in the war, Stalin explained, the United States would have to commit itself to five conditions: (1) the continuation of the status quo in Mongolia — which was a euphemism for Soviet control; (2) the cession to the USSR of all of Sakhalin Island and the adjoining islands; (3) the internationalization of the Chinese port of Dairen — which was a polite way of claiming an extraterritorial presence — and the leasing to the Soviet Union of Port Arthur as a naval base; (4) the creation of a joint Soviet-Chinese railroad to provide for direct Soviet access to Dairen; and (5) the incorporation of the Kurile Islands into the USSR. It is striking to note that of these five demands, two were at the expense of Japan — which was the enemy — and *three* at the expense of China — which was an ally. But all were designed to enhance Soviet access to the Pacific and a dominant position vis-à-vis China. Viewed as a whole, the Soviet Union's postwar territorial demands reveal a three-pronged strategic thrust: westward through the heart of Europe, with a northwestern flanking reach for the Spitsbergen Islands and a southwestern try at the Dardanelles and even Tangier; eastward at the Kurile Islands and through Manchuria to the ports on the Yellow Sea; and southward through Iran and toward the Persian Gulf. There is remarkable historical consistency in these goals. And should the Soviet leaders ever succeed in attaining them, there will be one decisive effect: the Soviet Union will have achieved a dominant geopolitical position in Eurasia.

Three Central Strategic Fronts

The struggle between Russia and America was joined when it became clear that the United States would not disengage from Europe and that it was prepared to oppose any demands Moscow made in excess of what the Soviet Union effectively controlled by 1945. This opposition was a historical milestone. In effect, it represented the beginning of the latest phase in the age-old struggle for the domination of the world's most active continent — a struggle that had raged from the time of the collapse of the Mediterranean-centered Roman Empire, through successive attempts to organize a Holy Roman Empire encompassing all of Europe, to protracted conflicts between oceanic empires, like Great Britain, and predominantly land-based powers, like Napoleonic France, Nazi Germany, and Russia. Now this struggle put the two successful survivors of World War II — the dominant transoceanic power and the dominant power on the central landmass — on a collision course.

The initial point of impact was the far western "peninsula"

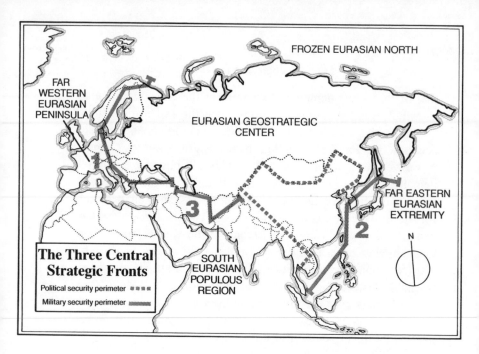

of the Eurasian continent. With the entire continent running
for almost 9,000 miles on an east-west axis, this far western
front sheltered only 1,150 miles outside of Soviet control. The
American enclave might have seemed geographically minus-
cule, but it was geopolitically critical. It included the vital section of industrial Europe that possessed the principal outlets to
the Atlantic Ocean.

The first strategic front emerged out of the twin dangers to
Greece and Turkey and to Berlin. In both cases the Soviets
tried to alter the post-1945 status quo with potentially far-
reaching consequences. Success with either Greece or Turkey
would have injected Soviet power into the Mediterranean at a
time of considerable turmoil in the region. Italy was beset with
ideological conflicts. Britain was embroiled with the future of
Palestine. The United States was not yet even present in the
region militarily. A success in Turkey — which would have
also included acquiescence to Soviet territorial demands just
south of Batum — would have opened the way to Iraq. This
would have put added pressure on Iran at a time of great po-

litical uncertainty. Radio Moscow suddenly announced in December 1945 that two new republics had been set up in Iran by revolutionary forces, the Autonomous Republic of Azerbaijan and the Kurdish People's Republic. Strong U.S. backing for Iran's territorial integrity, which included allusions to the existence of nuclear weapons, brought about a Soviet pullback in early 1946. This crisis was the first major skirmish between the two powers.

If the Soviets had succeeded in ejecting the Western powers from Berlin or in subordinating their status, the strategic consequences would have been decisive. Such a victory in a very overt and dramatic test of will would have demonstrated Soviet predominance over the United States at a very early stage of the evolving American political and economic commitment to Western Europe. The effects would have been more than symbolic. They might well have tipped the political balance in Germany by creating a crisis of confidence in the United States. The effects would also have reverberated through France at a moment when Communist electoral strength was peaking.

The decisions of President Harry S Truman were thus historical in consequence. He signed the Truman Doctrine into law on May 22, 1947, thereby engaging the United States in the defense of Greece and Turkey, and responded firmly with an airlift to break the Berlin blockade of April 1948. With these actions, Truman not only directly involved the United States in resisting Soviet political expansion in Europe, but he also credibly committed it to military engagement in support of those pledges. This was a qualitative change from the merely political and rhetorical opposition that Britain and the United States had previously undertaken against Soviet expansion. For the first time, the United States drew a line and demonstrated, by overt commitments and military deployments, that crossing it would produce a military clash. The far western strategic front — which has held now for forty years — thus took shape.

This front has protected a relationship that over the years

has come to be seen as organic to American security itself. The Atlantic Community, a transoceanic web of cultural, economic, and political relations, has become for the United States an extension of its own existence. At the same time, it has become for Moscow a major political-military barrier to the attainment of a predominant position in one of the two most economically vital regions of the Eurasian continent and a continuing source of external attraction for the Soviet-dominated countries of Eastern Europe. Thus, the very existence of the transoceanic far western community represents, not only a strategic impediment, but also a persisting political challenge to Moscow's empire. As a result, continued efforts to decouple the transatlantic political-military relationship have dominated the East-West political competition in Europe.

The second central strategic front in the historically new American-Soviet contest soon followed the first. Initially, the prospect for collision in the Far East seemed remote. The United States, largely on the personal initiative of the strategically minded U.S. supreme commander in the Far East, General Douglas MacArthur, succeeded in containing and then rebuffing the Soviet efforts to obtain a direct military foothold on the Japanese islands. The undertakings of Yalta and Potsdam did yield to the Soviet Union control over southern Sakhalin and the Kurile Islands, and the Soviets unilaterally seized additional Japanese islands off northern Hokkaido. But these were relatively small gains. The Soviet Union and the United States moved preemptively to seize as much of Korea as was possible, but this competition was resolved by an agreement fixing the demarcation line on the thirty-eighth parallel. Initially China was seen as moving into the American orbit, though the Soviet occupation of Manchuria and quiet assistance to Communist Chinese forces was complicating the reestablishment of effective Chinese Nationalist authority.

Nonetheless, even as late as 1949, with the far western confrontation sharply delineated, an American-Soviet Far Eastern contest still seemed unlikely. The United States was distressed by the Communist Chinese victory but powerless to alter it. Washington's strategic inclination soon shifted to avoiding a collision on the mainland of Asia with the emerging Sino-Soviet bloc. This attitude led to the famous statement of Secretary of State Dean Acheson in January 1950 that defined the U.S. strategic interests in the Far East as essentially offshore and focused on Japan. Not mentioning Korea, Acheson quite precisely outlined the U.S. "defensive perimeter" as running "along the Aleutians to Japan and then . . . to the Ryukus . . . to the Philippine Islands." The Korean War changed all that. That direct and overt character of the Communist aggression in midsummer of 1950, which was made possible by large-scale supply of Soviet arms, left President Truman with little choice. He now faced a situation in the Far East in which the failure to respond could have jeopardized American stakes in a Japan that was just beginning to recover from the war. This, in turn, could have pushed America out of the Far East altogether.

Truman's decision to respond militarily created the second central strategic front in the American-Soviet struggle, this time at the far eastern extremity of the Eurasian continent. Through the three-year Korean War, the United States succeeded in holding on to South Korea and thereby expanded the perimeter of its vital strategic interests. This now included Japan, South Korea, Taiwan, and the Philippines. In the early 1950s, it also came to include support for the French presence in Indochina and for the independent Indochinese states after the French withdrew. During the 1950s and 1960s, Washington considered these commitments to be directed at least as much against Communist China as the Soviet Union.

Indeed, it was this strongly anti-Chinese strategic orientation that subsequently contributed quite directly both to America's greatest setback of the entire cold war and to the most significant Soviet geopolitical loss. America's preoccupation with the expansionary drive of the Sino-Soviet bloc in the Far East generated the initial support for the French efforts to maintain their colonial possession of Indochina. It also later led the United States to intervene directly in the Vietnam War to prevent North Vietnam — which was wrongly considered to be a Chinese proxy — from conquering South Vietnam. American decision makers saw the Vietnam War largely as a replay of the Korean conflict, and felt that it necessitated a forceful U.S. response.

Paradoxically, the Vietnam War both crippled and enhanced the American position in the struggle with the Soviet Union. The damage was incalculable in terms of the ability of the United States to conduct an effective foreign policy. A post-Vietnam paralysis militated against boldness even in areas of vital importance and called into question the credibility of American security guarantees throughout the world. On the other hand, the fixation with halting Chinese expansion (which was seen as part of a larger Sino-Soviet design) contributed quite directly to the Sino-Soviet split, and that fundamentally altered the geopolitics of the Far East to the advantage of the United States.

The Sino-Soviet split took more than a decade to evolve, from the late 1950s until its eruption into open though limited violence in the late 1960s. Perhaps the conflict was inevitable, given the heavy-handed Soviet treatment of its new but not subordinate partner, but it was propelled forward by real differences in outlook and interests.

A major initial impulse for the split was the crisis over Quemoy and Matsu islands in 1958. The Chinese Communists initiated intense shelling of the offshore islands that protected the approaches from the Chinese mainland to the Kuomintang-held island of Taiwan. The United States responded with the threat of a military reaction. This precipitated, in turn, strong Chinese demands for Soviet assistance, including the provision to China of a nuclear capability. The Soviet leadership refused both demands, and this general caution unleashed a pent-up Chinese fury, sparking sharp, though at the time unpublicized, Sino-Soviet polemics and creating an enduring personal estrangement between the Soviet and Chinese leaders.

The Quemoy-Matsu confrontation, which the United States saw as a test of will with a combined Sino-Soviet bloc, was thus in fact a catalyst for the basic disintegration of that bloc. This led eventually to a Sino-American rapprochement in 1972 and even to some significant security cooperation by the late 1970s and early 1980s. Thus, over the course of the postwar period, the U.S. position in the far eastern central strategic front improved. Not only did it become more secure for the United States, but its geopolitical front lines were also tacitly pushed back from the edge of the Asian mainland to the Sino-Soviet frontier.

The Soviet Union, however, did gain one important geopolitical and geostrategic asset: Vietnam. The conflict between Moscow and Beijing precipitated their competition for control over Communist Hanoi. Geographical contiguity and therefore the related historical experience worked to China's disadvantage. China also could not match the Soviet Union's ability to supply vast amounts of arms, munitions, and sophisticated weaponry for North Vietnam's war effort. Thus, a pro-Soviet orientation in Hanoi easily gained the upper hand. As a result, the Soviet Union outflanked China. This intensified a Chinese resentment, already strong because of the Soviet domination of Mongolia. Moscow also obtained leverage on the United States. Its strategic bases in the newly united Vietnam could contest the U.S. naval and air domination of the sensitive maritime routes through the Strait of Malacca (through which passes about 65 percent of the oil consumed by Japan) and more generally the critical area spanned by Vietnam, the Philippines, south China, and Indonesian Borneo/Malaysia.

America's political and economic ties with the countries it protects along the far eastern front have come to be as important as those with the Atlantic Community. The spectacular

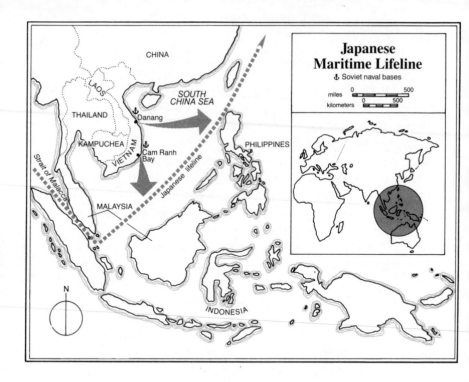

economic performance of Japan, South Korea, and the Association of Southeast Asian Nations (ASEAN) and the evolution of a Pacific Basin community have led to the emergence of an economic relationship that in trade already surpasses the transatlantic one. In fact, this is the world's fastest-growing economic region, which enhances its political and strategic significance to the United States. From the Soviet standpoint, diluting or severing these ties has gradually become as important as decoupling Western Europe.

Even more important, the trilateral relationship between the states of the Pacific Basin in the Far East, North America, and Western Europe has emerged as the basis for a new non-Eurocentric international system sponsored by the United States. Cooperation among these three economically vital and politically democratic regions has become central to the maintenance of international stability and to the development of the third world. Anything that would unhinge either the far eastern or the far western connection from the United States — particularly a Soviet political or military breakout — would contribute directly to the destabilization of these largely American-sponsored international arrangements.

The third central strategic front — the southwestern one — emerged much later. Indeed, for almost a quarter of a century following the Soviet pullback from Iran in 1946 and the promulgation of the Truman Doctrine in 1947, the region to the south of the Soviet Union did not involve a direct American-Soviet conflict. The Soviets did not cross the line running from the northeastern frontier of Turkey, the northern boundary of Iran, to the northwestern limits of Pakistan. Afghanistan was a genuinely neutral buffer state, which by bordering also on China sealed off Pakistan from a direct exposure to the Soviet Union. Turkey, Iran, and — to a lesser extent — Pakistan were politically and militarily closely connected with the United States, while the British naval and air presence in the Persian Gulf provided for more direct Western security support.

The lull ended in the 1970s. The British pullout "east of Suez" in the second half of the 1960s created a security vacuum in the Persian Gulf. Washington tried to fill it by buttressing two pillars of regional security, Saudi Arabia and Iran. This arrangement, though contested from within the Middle East by the new Soviet-supported revolutionary regimes in Iraq and Syria, worked only as long as these countries remained internally stable. When the pro-U.S. regime in Iran disintegrated in 1978, this unstably balanced regional arrangement also collapsed.

Even prior to Iran's demise, however, the Soviet Union was making progress on the area's periphery. Moscow was not yet ready to test the United States by directly crossing the southern line. But in the late 1970s the Soviets were able to outflank it to some extent by establishing a political-military presence in Somalia and in Southern Yemen, then by reversing its commitment to Somalia in favor of a more ambitious military-

political presence in Ethiopia, including the deployment of Soviet proxy forces from Cuba. Thus, its clients stood astride the
choke point controlling access to the Red Sea and the Suez
Canal. By the end of the 1970s, the United States was con-
fronted by an arc of crisis on the edge of the Arabian Sea.

But even more dangerous strategically was the collapse of
the U.S.-supported Iranian government. Its fall ended the
American effort to promote Iran as the dominant regional power
and the pivot of the southern security belt. Iran's collapse,
without a doubt, made it possible for the Soviet Union to act
decisively regarding Afghanistan. That neutral buffer had in
the meantime undergone four major political upheavals: an an-
timonarchical coup in 1973, followed by a Communist takeover in 1978, followed by an intra-Communist upheaval that
produced an even more radical Communist regime in 1979, all
of which generated the outbreak of widespread opposition from
nationalists and Islamic fundamentalists. In late December 1979,
the Soviet Union exploited this situation to advance its own
military forces. For the first time since the inception of the
American-Soviet conflict it crossed the lines that emerged at
the conclusion of World War II.

The third front was thus joined. The United States responded on January 23, 1980, by formally proclaiming for the
Persian Gulf region the equivalent of the Truman Doctrine. In
the words of President Jimmy Carter (and his statement then
became known as the Carter Doctrine): "Any attempt by any
outside force to gain control of the Persian Gulf region will be
regarded as an assault on the vital interests of the United States
of America and such an assault will be repelled by any means
necessary, including military force." The United States thus
became directly engaged. It quickly expanded its air and naval
deployments to the region. It increased military aid to Pakistan. It explicitly reaffirmed the American guarantee of 1959
to protect Pakistan against a Soviet invasion. It became in-

volved in sustaining Afghan resistance to the Soviet occupation.

The American engagement was predicated on the strategic premise that, whatever might have been the subjective motives of the Soviet military move into Afghanistan, its objective consequences were profoundly threatening to the region, and could lead to regional Soviet domination. Moreover, a Soviet breakthrough on the third front would carry grave implications for the other two. A Soviet success on either the West European or the Far Eastern front would unhinge the international system, but even such a setback would still not deprive the United States of the capability of defending the other front. A Soviet success on this third central front, however, would automatically give the Soviet Union enormous leverage in the competition with the United States on the other two central fronts. This is still true despite the oil glut on world markets in the mid-1980s. With 56 percent of the world's proven oil reserves, the Persian Gulf states will continue to be a vital strategic interest of the West. Given Western Europe's and Japan's dependence on Middle Eastern oil, domination over this region would place the Soviet Union in a position to blackmail both Western Europe and the Far East into a political accommodation on terms favorable to Moscow.

The strategically decisive and catalytic nature of the stakes involved in this third front required an American engagement in spite of major disadvantages the United States faced in the region. To a greater extent than on the other two fronts, the third front offered little possibility of defense in depth and no fallback positions. Should the Soviet occupation of Afghanistan prove to be permanent, the political destabilization of Pakistan or Iran would become all the easier, and Moscow's ambitions — so explicitly stated in late 1940 — would become fulfilled. In addition, unlike its defense of Western Europe and Japan, the American engagement had to be undertaken here in

support of governments that were not democratic and whose
long-term stability was dubious. Indeed, the American undertaking to protect the Persian Gulf region implicitly included
Iran. The Iranian government, however, remained implacably
hostile to the United States — though it balanced that hostility
with its religious animus against the Soviet Union. All these
factors enhanced the difficulties in sustaining this front, maximized the longer-range prospects of Soviet success, and made
this front the most volatile and dangerous of the three.

Geopolitical Linchpin States

The political outcome of the contests on each of the three
central strategic fronts is likely to be determined largely by
who gains or retains control over several key countries that
have become the geopolitical linchpins in their respective regions. A linchpin state is one that is both intrinsically important and in some sense "up for grabs." The importance of a
linchpin state might stem from its geopolitical position radiating regional political and/or economic influence or a geostrategic location that makes it militarily significant. Its vulnerability raises the possibility that it may be susceptible to either
seduction or takeover, the latter in turn affecting its current
external affiliations. Other states may be equally or even more
important, but their firm anchorage in one or the other system
indicates that they are fixed points, not catalytic linchpins.

These linchpin states are Poland and Germany on the far
western front; South Korea and the Philippines on the far eastern front; and either Iran or the combination of Afghanistan
and Pakistan on the southwestern front. Soviet domination over
Poland is central to Moscow's control over Eastern Europe,
and the subordination or seduction of West Germany would tip
the balance in Europe in Russia's favor. Soviet domination
over South Korea and the Philippines would encircle China,
directly threaten Japan's security through Korea, and poten-

tially endanger Japan's main maritime lifeline from the Philippines. Soviet domination over either Iran or both Afghanistan and Pakistan would give Moscow control over access to the Persian Gulf or a presence on the Indian Ocean from which Soviet power could be projected at vulnerable areas to the southwest and southeast.

Conversely, the denial of at least West Germany to the Soviet Union assures continued independence of Western Europe, while diminution of Moscow's control over Poland would be tantamount to the eventual weakening of its hold over Eastern Europe. Access to South Korea and the Philippines enables the United States to maintain a political-military presence on the far eastern edge of the Eurasian mainland, securing Japan and permitting a wide entry to China. The denial of Iran or Afghanistan and Pakistan to the Soviet Union prevents Moscow from fulfilling its long-standing strategic goals "south of Batum and Baku," thereby protectively sealing off the Persian Gulf and the Middle East from a contiguous Soviet military-political presence.

Soviet domination over Poland is vital to Moscow's control over Eastern Europe. Indeed, controlling Poland has been a 250-year-long Russian objective, first attained late in the eighteenth century after a protracted struggle. The turning point in that conflict came three hundred years ago, in 1667, when Poland ceded sovereignty over the Ukraine to Russia. That seminal event marked the ascendancy of the emerging tsarist empire over its principal Slavic rival, the Polish-Lithuanian-Ruthenian commonwealth. With the Ukraine won, the expansion of the tsarist empire accelerated, with Poland fully subordinated by the 1790s. Since then, every Russian government has insisted on Russia's preponderance in Polish affairs.

That insistence was voiced in inter-Allied councils during World War I by the tsarist foreign minister, Sergei Sazonov, in terms almost identical to those used by Molotov with the Anglo-Saxon leaders during World War II. Control over Po-

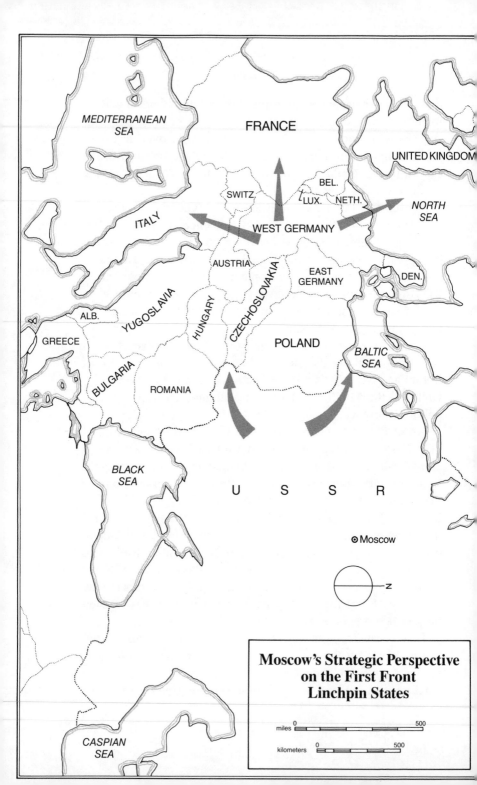

MEDITERRANEAN SEA

FRANCE

UNITED KINGDOM

BEL.

SWITZ.

LUX. NETH.

NORTH SEA

ITALY

WEST GERMANY

AUSTRIA

EAST GERMANY

DEN.

ALB.

YUGOSLAVIA

HUNGARY

CZECHOSLOVAKIA

POLAND

BALTIC SEA

GREECE

BULGARIA

ROMANIA

BLACK SEA

U   S   S   R

⊙ Moscow

z

CASPIAN SEA

Moscow's Strategic Perspective on the First Front Linchpin States

miles 0 — 500

kilometers 0 — 500

land was presented as central to Russia's security and as an *internal* Russian matter, not subject to serious negotiation with the West. Russia's World War I and World War II territorial goals were also remarkably similar: Poland was to be shifted westward at Germany's expense, thereby making permanent Poland's dependence on Russia against Germany, while control over Poland would be the bridge to a decisive Russian role in German affairs. The Soviet leaders were especially sensitive to the memory of the 1920 defeat of the Soviet armies by the resurrected Polish state, which in effect deprived the Red Army of access to a Germany then convulsed by revolutionary tensions.

Poland's geopolitical and geostrategic importance extends beyond the fact that it lies astride access to Germany. Moscow's domination of Poland also facilitates its control over Czechoslovakia and Hungary and seals off from Western influence the Western-oriented non-Russian nations of the Soviet Union. A more autonomous Poland would inevitably disrupt Soviet control over Lithuania and the Ukraine. Polish religious and historical ties with these countries are deeply rooted, and a Poland free of Moscow's control would be likely to galvanize secessionist attitudes to the detriment of Great Russian preponderance. Moreover, the history of post–World War II Poland indicates clearly that the Soviet-sponsored regime lacks popular support, while the Solidarity movement of the late 1970s demonstrated the vitality of Polish national and religious identity. Poland's 37 million people make it the largest Soviet-dominated East European state, and its armed forces constitute the largest non-Soviet army in the Warsaw Pact. It is a restless asset that may be costly for Moscow to control but too costly to forsake.

With Poland secured, the long-term competition for Germany can be pursued — and its outcome, in turn, is crucial to the future of an independent Western Europe associated with the United States. After World War II, the Soviet Union gained control of Poland and a third of Germany, subsequently reshaping the latter into a new state, the German Democratic Republic. This placed the Soviet Union in a position to compete for the rest of Germany, in the meantime reconstituted as a sovereign state, the Federal Republic of Germany. With a population of 62 million and a GNP of some $698 billion in 1983, the FRG has emerged as the strongest member of the West European community and also the single largest European contributor to common NATO defense.

West Germany's political orientation, not to speak of its formal links, is therefore critical to the political-military balance in Europe. The advent of a more "neutral" FRG that formally remained a member of NATO and the European Economic Community would weaken the cohesion of the Western alliance. Toward this end, the Soviet Union has been using as bait the inherent West German sense of concern for its brethren in the Soviet-dominated GDR. The danger is that a West Germany that Moscow succeeds in enticing into a special relationship with itself could become a lever for undermining the political unity of the Atlantic connection.

Both history and geography play a role here. On the German side, there has been a tradition of a strong pro-Russian orientation, particularly among the Prussians. Direct Soviet control over 17 million East Germans has strengthened the argument that Germany must be sensitive to Moscow's concerns. German banking and industrial circles have historically backed Russian economic development, and this connection is still strong in the German business community. West Germany is today the Soviet Union's most important Western economic partner, and the major West German subsidies to East Germany increase Bonn's importance.

On the Russian side, Russian foreign policy has had a strong German focus since Catherine the Great. The Russians admire German efficiency and are attracted by the notion of a collaborative relationship. Such collaboration was central to the par-

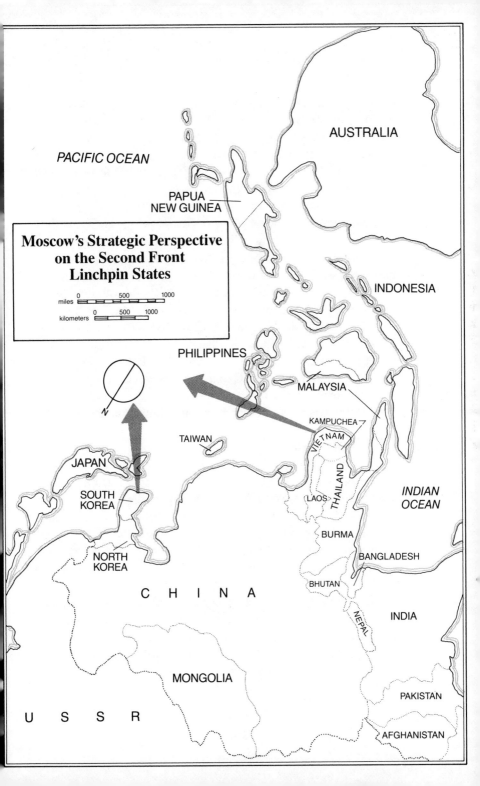

Moscow's Strategic Perspective on the Second Front Linchpin States

tition of Poland, and German reunification under Bismarck enjoyed benign Russian support. During the early Bolshevik era, Soviet leaders were obsessed by fervent hopes that a German revolution would join hands with the Russian one. In Stalin's more geopolitical vision, a Soviet presence in Germany was the prerequisite for precluding the emergence of any European rival to the Soviet Union. Thus, through much of the postwar era, the political-strategic focus of Soviet policy in Europe has been on Germany because the Soviets see it as the key to the question of who wields decisive power at the western end of the world's central landmass.

In the Far East, Japan's and China's relations with the United States present the major obstacle to the emergence of a dominant Soviet position. Here the linchpin states have become South Korea and the Philippines. Neither represents by itself an asset as vital regionally as West Germany. But both are critical to the security of Japan and China and represent major outposts of U.S. power at the far eastern end of Eurasia. Each is vulnerable to events — South Korea to military attack and the Philippines to political upheaval — that could alter their international allegiances.

The U.S. military presence in South Korea, though not large in comparison to its detachments in Western Europe, represents the single most important American deployment in the Far East. That presence is based on the recognition that South Korea's security is central to Japan's. It also reflects American determination to avoid any repetition of the ambiguity created in 1950 by Dean Acheson's exclusion of South Korea from the U.S. "defensive perimeter." From the Soviet standpoint, a successful North Korean takeover of South Korea would transform the strategic situation in the Far East. It would open up the East China Sea to Soviet naval access, drive the United States off the mainland, expose all the principal islands of Japan to a military threat, and outflank China's industrial northeast.

Such a takeover would also eliminate a growing ideological-national challenge to North Korea's stability. In recent years, South Korea has demonstrated a remarkable capacity for sustained economic growth. Its GNP exceeds $66 billion (in 1983), raising its per capita income to about $1,700. North Korea's economic achievements — a paltry $20-billion economy with a per capita income under $1,000 — stand in stark relief. Seoul's economic success has not only strengthened South Korea relative to North Korea. It has also increased the costs for the north in maintaining military forces capable of challenging the south. Given the likely rates of GNP growth, by the end of the century North Korea will have to spend six times as much of its GNP on the military as the south just to stay even in terms of expenditures. North Korea, as a result, will doubtless expect increased economic assistance from the Soviet Union. Moscow can begrudge it only at the risk of enhancing the rival influence of China within the leadership in Pyongyang.

Moreover, South Korean economic success is bound to have political-ideological consequences. Korean nationalism has not accommodated itself to the arbitrary division of the country. The partition is considered to be a historical injustice. (Unlike the Koreans, the Germans at least initially were prepared to accept the division of their country, as a historical penalty for having started the war.) This means the competition between the two Korean states has remained focused largely on the issue of whether the north or the south has a better claim to sponsor the country's eventual reunification. Reunification is still a live issue. An economically successful and socially attractive South Korea puts North Korea on the defensive. Pyongyang is no doubt conscious of the possibility that a major international upheaval that temporarily paralyzes both Communist China and the Soviet Union would open the doors to Korean reunification on non-Communist terms. That concern feeds back into the North Korean–Soviet relationship. It intensifies Soviet interest in a resolution of the Korean issue on terms favorable to the Soviet Union.

The other Far Eastern linchpin state, the Philippines, also has strong connections with the United States. But its vulnerability stems from its volatile politics. The Philippines is the location of two U.S. naval and air facilities, Subic Bay and Clark Field, manned by approximately fifteen thousand servicemen. They are important to the protection of free passage from the Indian Ocean to the Pacific Ocean. With the development of a countervailing and challenging Soviet air/naval presence at former American bases in Vietnam, the strategic significance of the U.S. military presence in the Philippines has intensified. Soviet access to the naval base of Cam Ranh Bay enables its warships to spend approximately 75 percent more time at sea than was possible when they were based at remote Vladivostok. The deployment of Soviet air power both to Cam Ranh Bay and to the Danang air base has created a significant flanking pressure on the expanded Far Eastern strategic front.

The Philippine islands, inhabited by 53 million people, represent a cultural-political anomaly in the Far East. Malayan in origin, with a strong overlay of Spanish influence created by almost 380 years of colonial rule and only partly supplanted by American traits acquired during the half century of U.S. rule, the Filipino people have a political and cultural life with some similarities to Central America, with its mixture of Spanish culture and American presence. Unlike any Asian country, about 90 percent of the people are Christian, of whom about 90 percent are Catholic. The relationship with the United States is both close and ambivalent. American influence is powerful in educational institutions, in the business community, and in the military. But it is also resented, for there are lingering memories of initial American suppression of Philippine aspirations for national independence.

The formal trappings of American democratic institutions have proven difficult to adapt to the Philippines, particularly because of its extreme disparities in social wealth and its massive poverty. The result has been turbulence since Filipino independence in 1945, with rising social dissatisfaction creating opportunities for revolutionary violence. Recent years have seen both the collapse of the personal dictatorship of President Ferdinand Marcos and the rise of a Communist-led New People's Army (NPA) that has engaged in increasingly effective revolutionary violence. The Soviet Union has not been oblivious to these developments. When China cut off its support to the NPA in 1975, Moscow took steps to replace Beijing. KGB defectors have testified that the Soviet Union not only took charge of shifting NPA strategy but also began providing money and perhaps arms. One shipment was intercepted coming through Southern Yemen from Eastern Europe. The country is porous. Its more than seven thousand islands spread over an eleven-hundred-mile-long archipelago afford rich opportunities to set up independent revolutionary bases for easy maritime supply from Vietnam.

Long-term instability in the Philippines has thus become a threatening prospect. Furthermore, in that setting, a nationalist-radical reaction to earlier dependence on the United States is to be expected, and it could express itself through efforts to compel the United States to withdraw from its military facilities in the Philippines. All this would constitute a signal U.S. setback, political as well as military. The Philippines represents an experiment in transplanted democracy, and its failure would reflect badly on the relevance of the democratic system. But the strategic consequences would be more severe, especially if in the wake of this U.S. defeat the Soviet Union projected its influence from Vietnam to the Philippine archipelago. Southeast Asia would be subject to a significant Soviet military reach and Japan's principal maritime trading route would pass through a zone of effective Soviet naval control.

The third set of geopolitical linchpin states encompasses either

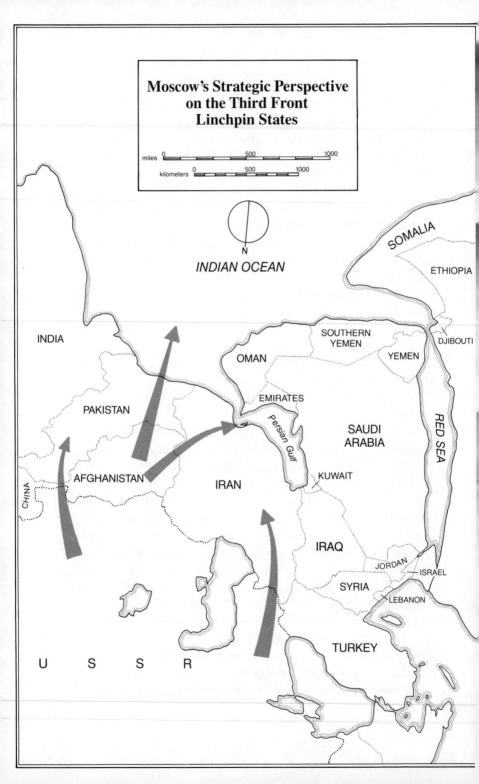

Iran, or Afghanistan and Pakistan. These countries are experiencing internal disorder or are susceptible to it. They are even more vulnerable to Soviet penetration — and therefore to Moscow-inspired upheaval — because they are territorially contiguous to the USSR or Soviet-occupied territory. Soviet ambitions regarding Iran, as already noted, have been both explicit and historically persistent. Already in 1908, Moscow obtained through the Anglo-Russian Convention a sphere of influence over half of Iran, and in 1921 the new Soviet regime claimed by an imposed treaty the right to interfere in Iranian affairs. Of Iran's almost 40 million people, about a third are not Farsi in origin, and the Soviets have more than once attempted to exploit Kurdish and Azerbaijani resentment over domination by Tehran. Moscow quite justifiably viewed the collapse in 1979 of the Shah's regime as a massive strategic setback for the United States and as a major political opportunity for the Soviet Union.

The Khomeini regime frustrated these hopes. It was soon depicting the Soviet Union as a "Satan" almost as evil as the United States. Soviet hopes hence faded that the fall of the Shah might generate a radical swing to the left that would eventually bring to power the pro-Soviet Tudeh party (a thinly veiled Communist-led movement). Indeed, the Khomeini regime proceeded to crush the Tudeh even more brutally than the Shah had done and to provide some assistance to the anti-Soviet *mujahideen* (of Shia dispensation) in Afghanistan.

Soviet hopes for Iran seem to have been set back, therefore, probably until the post-Khomeini phase of Iranian politics produces a new contest for power. At that point, the Soviet Union will be in a position either to exploit minority unrest to fragment Iran or to encourage and support a central seizure of power in Tehran. This does not exclude the possibility even of the deployment in Iran of some Soviet forces, with airborne detachments descending on Tehran and ground troops pushing into the north. The United States would then confront the ex-

traordinarily difficult decision of whether and how to respond.
At stake would be an oil-rich country that controls half the
coastline of the Persian Gulf and that is situated next to a string
of Gulf states of uncertain political stability and relatively weak
military capabilities. Geopolitically, the prize of success would
be colossal.

A Soviet success in Iran would dwarf anything the USSR
might achieve in Afghanistan or even in Pakistan. But seizing
control of these two states together would have geopolitical
consequences of the same gravity. The Soviet Union would
gain wide access to the Indian Ocean. More important, it would
gain a point of departure for developing greater political influence on the littoral of the Arabian Sea and the Indian Ocean.
A consolidation of Soviet control over Afghanistan would expose both Iran and Pakistan to Soviet pressure along a wide
front, and permanent Soviet control over Afghanistan would
generate enormous strains within Pakistan itself. This country,
which has become linked with the United States and China in
sustaining Afghan resistance to the Soviet occupation, has long
felt threatened by India's regional ambitions. An enduring Soviet presence on the northwest frontiers of Pakistan, matched
by a continuing threat from India on the eastern boundary,
would place Pakistan and its 93 million people in a strategic
vise. It would create an impossible security problem and it
would probably generate increased internal tensions. Under these
circumstances, a reluctant accommodation to Moscow's regional preeminence might become the only way of avoiding
internal fragmentation brought about by forces abetted deliberately by the Soviet Union, especially among dissident ethnic
minorities.

A fundamental reorientation of either Iran or Pakistan, placing one or even both states within the orbit of Moscow's strategic preponderance, would represent more than a regional Soviet success and a breakthrough on the third central strategic
front. Its long-term effects, at first felt only indirectly, would

radiate beyond the Persian Gulf. They would subtly affect the relations between the Soviet Union and both Western Europe and the Far East because of the importance of the Persian Gulf region to the economic viability of these two highly industrialized areas. In that sense, the linchpin states of the third central strategic front have a catalytic potential far beyond their regional geopolitical radius.

Soviet Geostrategy

In the broadest terms, Soviet strategy is focused on both a negative and a positive central goal. Defensively, it is to prevent the political and military encirclement of the Soviet Union by the United States and its allies. Moscow's greatest fear is a united Western Europe, militarily and politically revitalized, tied closely to the United States, and exercising a magnetic attraction on Eastern Europe; and a close U.S.–Japanese-Chinese connection, with China and Japan eventually capable of pressing hard on the relatively empty territories of Soviet Siberia. To prevent that from happening, however, a defensive posture does not suffice. To foreclose the possibility of such an encirclement, the Soviets must sever the connection with America at each end of the Eurasian continent. And that, in turn, would tip the global balance in Russia's favor.

The defensive and offensive elements of the strategy are thus inseparable. As a result, the debate about whether the Soviets are primarily insecure (defensive) or aggressive (offensive) is meaningless. In the Soviet geostrategic context, the two motivations produce the same results. Moreover, in pursuing this strategy, the Russians have been both persistent and patient. There is no sense of urgency in Moscow's behavior. Rather, it moves step by step, through gradual expansion, slow attrition of the adversary, careful consolidation of gains, and constant probing for openings. Space and depth give the Russians a sense of confidence that other land powers, such as Germany, lacked.

Moreover, as the Kremlin leaders see it, the contest for Eurasia is being waged in a geopolitical setting favorable to the Soviet Union. In the words of two Soviet strategists quoted by Richard Pipes in his *Survival Is Not Enough,* "the socialist camp enjoys an advantage over the imperialist camp in respect to territory and population. From the western borders of the German Democratic Republic and Czechoslovakia to the Pacific Ocean it constitutes a single mass. By contrast, the countries of the imperialist bloc form a chain of states occupying a narrow coastal rim of Europe and Asia, while their principal economic base — the United States — lies beyond the ocean. As a result, the lines of communication connecting these countries . . . are extremely extended and vulnerable. In time of war, such communications can be readily disrupted by nuclear missile weapons."

The reference to nuclear war, however, does not mean that the outcome of the struggle for Eurasia will be determined by the direct use of force. In fact, military means are viewed by the Soviet leaders largely as supportive of political moves — unless and until such a margin of military superiority should emerge that either intimidation or the direct use of force is likely to be effective and relatively safe.

The dichotomy of defensive versus offensive is not the only misleading cliché widely used in the Western discussion of Soviet policy. So is the frequent speculation on the internal debates that are said to take place in Moscow between those who advocate a broad accommodation with the United States — "the condominium strategy" — and those who seek to detach Western Europe and the Far East from the United States — "the decoupling strategy." In fact, neither of these is a strategy, but rather the tactical expression of the same strategic objective.

The condominium strategy does not have as its goal the perpetuation of the status quo in Eurasia, though it may be presented that way. Rather, it aims at an American-Soviet arrangement for the gradual retraction of U.S. influence, accelerated in part by the resulting West European resentment over a superpower accommodation, which would be perceived by the West Europeans as having been reached behind their backs and at their political expense. Every periodic American-Soviet flirtation has provoked such fears in Europe, stimulating thereby not only European resentments but also a neutralist reaction.

The decoupling strategy has the same goal as the condominium strategy, the only difference being that it is pursued more openly. Under the decoupling strategy, the Soviets seek to create the appearance that the interests of Europe or Japan and those of the United States are incompatible and that a U.S. connection produces a threat to the security of these countries. One or the other tactic has often been pursued by Moscow and, at times, even both have been pursued simultaneously — because their strategic goals are identical.

In the pursuit of this strategic objective — expelling the United States from the peripheries of the Eurasian continent — Soviet policy on each front has involved a mixture of diplomacy, military pressure, propaganda, and subversion. But the formula varies from one front to another. On the western front, in recent years, the Soviets have relied primarily on diplomacy and propaganda, backed by the steady buildup of the Warsaw Pact forces and reinforced by selective subversion. Overt military pressure has been used only twice: during the two Berlin crises of 1948 and 1959–1961. In both cases, the goal was to demonstrate the unreliability of Europe's security ties with the United States. The predominant Soviet pattern, however, has been to concentrate on diplomatic-propaganda campaigns, designed particularly to accentuate separate European interests, notably those of Germany, and to obstruct movement toward a political-military unification of Western Europe.

In the immediate postwar era, France was the special object of Soviet diplomatic attention. The cultivation of France, nurtured perhaps by hopes that its powerful Communist party might even come to power, exploited French nationalism to impede European unification and to limit American influence. In recent years, Moscow's focus has shifted to Germany. German nationalism and neutralism have been encouraged. Moscow has little hope at this stage of detaching Germany from NATO. The play has been to the West German desire to keep alive all-German links and the subliminal desire of reviving the traditional German fascination with a special relationship with Russia. These, it is hoped, might be exploited to transform West Germany into a neutral member of NATO. Should these tactics succeed, West Germany would formally still belong to the alliance but would be practically neutral on the central East-West issues.

Selective subversion has also been used on the western front, mostly on the southern flank. There is evidence that Bulgaria and Czechoslovakia supported terrorism aimed in the 1970s at the destabilization of both Turkey and Italy. In Turkey particularly, the campaign reached massive proportions, with weaponry valued at over $2 billion being made available largely through Bulgaria to various terrorist groups. Italy, too, has been a major target. A clandestine radio station operating out of Prague, for example, provided ideological-political support to Marxist terrorists seeking to destabilize Italian democracy.

Broadly speaking, the strategy pursued toward Europe can best be described as that of political attrition. It is designed to weaken Western Europe's connection with the United States, without precipitating either massive West European anxieties or strong American reactions to the progressive and piecemeal neutralization of Western Europe. The steady and very substantial buildup of the Warsaw Pact forces, while doubtless designed to pose a potential military threat to Western Europe through a blitzkrieg-like military invasion, serves as an important source of political intimidation. It creates an atmosphere in which the Europeans are more inclined to pressure the United

States to make East-West concessions for the sake of a "relaxation of tensions" than to oppose the Soviet Union either for its arms buildup or for regional aggression outside Europe. Moreover, Moscow's buildup has necessitated a West European response that has imposed social strains on its societies, even though their military spending remains considerably below the level of that of the United States. These domestic tensions, in turn, have fed neutralist and even anti-American sentiments. In brief, conscious that Western Europe continues to suffer from historical fatigue, Moscow hopes to suborn rather than to conquer.

On the eastern front, the Soviet Union has relied even more on diplomacy and propaganda, and rather less on military pressure or subversion. The Korean War was waged by proxy forces, and Moscow probably learned in its aftermath that in fact it served to consolidate a closer and more enduring U.S.–Japanese connection. Similarly, Soviet military pressure on China in the late 1960s precipitated the initial Sino-American rapprochement, skillfully brought about by President Richard Nixon in the early 1970s and boldly consummated by President Carter in 1978. As a result, the Soviets have put more emphasis in recent years on seeking better economic ties with Japan and a gradual normalization of relations with China. These efforts, however, have been handicapped by recurrent Soviet heavy-handedness and Moscow's curious inability to relate effectively to its oriental neighbors, a product of both cultural distance and geopolitical fear.

As a result, Soviet standing in Japan plummeted during the 1970s. The Japanese resented the occasional Soviet threats and remained mindful of the fact that the Soviets are occupiers of Japanese soil. Several islands just north of Hokkaido that Moscow seized in 1945 are still held as well as the Kurile chain, conceded to the Soviet Union as its reward for participating in the Pacific war. Furthermore, the buildup of Soviet air and naval power, both in the bases on the Sea of Japan and in

Vietnam, has reinforced Japanese public acceptance of the need for a closer U.S.–Japanese security connection.

The long-term Soviet concern in the Far East goes beyond the region's continuing connection with America. The specter of a rapidly modernizing China — benefiting from American and Japanese high technology and industrial cooperation — is bound to be profoundly disturbing to Soviet strategists. It creates the prospect of another major power center emerging on the Eurasian landmass, a condition absent since World War II. Moreover, the specter of China has long haunted the Russian popular consciousness, with its deeply ingrained preoccupation with "the yellow peril."

It is revealing to note that this fear was apparent as early as the turn of this century in the most popular "futurological" book in Russia, the work of a Russian historian-philosopher, V. S. Soloviev, which speculated on the likely state of affairs by the year 2000. In his *War and Christianity: From the Russian Point of View, Three Conversations* (1902), Soloviev predicted that the Japanese would assimilate Western values and techniques, that they would eventually forge an alliance with the Chinese, and that sometime toward the end of the twentieth century China and Japan, by then both highly industrialized, would jointly sweep westward across all of Russia.

To forestall such a development, the Soviet leaders are probably counting on internal upheavals within China. Deng Xiaoping has both spearheaded the modernization drive that has reoriented China toward the United States and Japan and has firmly consolidated China's independence from the Soviet Union. They hope that when he has gone new openings may arise. Continued links doubtless exist between Moscow and some of the Soviet-trained Chinese leaders, who are now in their late fifties and early sixties. If a period of political turmoil develops after Deng's departure, the Soviets might well expect a reorientation in Chinese policies, stimulated by party bureaucrats fearful of the political consequences of economic decentralization and privatization. Indeed, from the Soviet point of view, the derailment of China's ambitious modernization program is much to be desired. It would diminish the prospect of a powerful and modern state emerging on the Soviet Union's eastern frontier.

A relatively weak China, friendly to the Soviet Union, is the ultimate Russian preference. But to win the friendship of even a weak China, Moscow would have to accommodate China's desire for the termination of the Soviet Union's military presence and political preeminence in Mongolia, a part of the Chinese empire historically and a Russian satellite since the early 1920s. Moscow's control over Mongolia gives the Soviet Union enormous strategic advantage in any clash with China, exposing China's vital industrial regions and capital to a direct Soviet threat. It is therefore very improbable that the Soviets will be prepared to satisfy Chinese concerns on this point, and the issue of Mongolia will continue to symbolize the deeper and ultimately insoluble suspicions between these two large, contiguous, but ultimately very different peoples.

Japan is the other major Soviet worry. Moscow no doubt hopes that the intensifying tensions in U.S.–Japanese economic relations will eventually spill over into political relations, thereby weakening the American-Japanese connection. The Soviets must be aware of the rising tide of anti-Japanese sentiment in America. They are bound to seek to exploit any vulnerabilities in the currently solid American–Japanese axis. Moscow may even be counting on the remote prospect that an economic rift might sharply alienate Washington and Tokyo. The Kremlin might then offer to return the disputed northern offshore islands to Japan so as to generate Japanese neutralism in exchange for major economic cooperation with the Soviet Union.

Should a gradual improvement in Soviet-Japanese and Sino-Soviet relations be accompanied by more basic upheavals in the Philippines, or even South Korea, the overall geopolitical situation in the Far East would be altered significantly in the Soviet Union's favor. In neither case, however, is Moscow likely to intervene directly with military forces or to become heavily involved in supporting hostilities. A new conflict on the Korean peninsula would be unpredictable in its consequences for both Sino-Soviet and Japanese-Soviet relations, not to speak of U.S. military involvement. Soviet engagement in the Philippine insurgency would also be likely to stimulate strong American countermoves. Thus, the achievement of the Soviet Union's optimal goals on the eastern front remains remote. For now, Soviet diplomatic and propaganda efforts in the region are likely to yield only limited and incremental gains, while remaining focused on the central strategic objective of preventing the emergence of a Sino-Japanese coalition closely linked with the United States.

The prospects are much better, from the Soviet point of view, to the south of the Soviet Union. Here the policy mix is quite different. Military pressure, subversion, diplomacy, and propaganda — in that order — are the instruments of Soviet policy. Military pressure has been applied directly through the occupation of Afghanistan, and indirectly through threats directed at Pakistan. The Soviets presumably calculate that over the long haul such military pressure on Pakistan may begin to weaken Pakistani will and develop internal political demands for a reorientation of Pakistan's policy. That, in turn, will serve to reduce the American inclination both to provide massive support to Islamabad and to stand by the security guarantee explicitly given to Pakistan by the United States. Soviet military involvement at some point in the internal affairs of Iran cannot be excluded, as I have noted, though in all probability it would not take the form of as direct and massive an intrusion as the invasion of Afghanistan. More likely, it would involve military support, either for secessionist activities or for an internal coup in Tehran by pro-Soviet elements as a reaction to the failures of the fundamentalist Khomeini regime.

In any case, military pressure is likely to be aided and even spearheaded by sustained efforts at subverting the internal stability both of Pakistan and of Iran. Ethnic conflicts, social tensions, and political instability all create ripe conditions for a policy designed to undermine the internal stability of these two geopolitically critical countries. Iran's population is 63 percent Persian, 19 percent Turk or Baluchi, 4 percent Arab, and 3 percent Kurd. Since the fall of the Shah, a few minorities have sought to exploit the chaos to loosen Tehran's control over their regions. The post-Shah economic stagnation and the interminable war with Iraq — support for which Tehran increasingly seeks through the appeal of *Persian* nationalism — will only serve to bolster separatism and reduce the central government's ability to cope with it. Similar problems exist in Pakistan, whose population is 66 percent Punjabi, 13 percent Sindhi, 8 percent Pushtun, 7 percent Urdu, and 3 percent Baluchi. Unlike Iran, Pakistan is a new state, founded only in 1947, and its various ethnic groups have not yet developed a national political consciousness. They are united only by a common religion. All the minority groups resent the rule of the central government, especially when the military is in power, because both are dominated by and are perceived to favor the Punjabis. In 1971, such tensions led East Pakistan to break away to form Bangladesh. Soviet leaders can be expected to try to exploit this separatism if it is to their advantage. Such a policy involves relatively low risks and the potential for high yield, while presenting the United States with limited opportunities for effective counters.

All these efforts — the push to decouple Western Europe and Japan from the United States and the attempt to expand Soviet influence in southern Asia — are directed toward one overarching Soviet objective: to achieve dominance on the world's central landmass by eliminating its rival's influence from the continent's western, eastern, and southern peripheries. The Soviet Union in recent years has become more overt

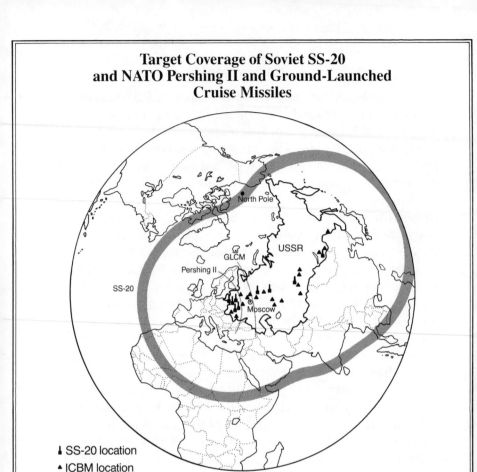

Target Coverage of Soviet SS-20 and NATO Pershing II and Ground-Launched Cruise Missiles

in these efforts. It was not until the 1970s that the Soviet Union could feel reasonably confident that it enjoyed at least strategic parity with the United States, and that this parity in turn could begin to inhibit American freedom of action in regional conflicts. The ambitious program to deploy, on a truly massive scale, the SS-20 missile involves nothing less than an attempt to create a situation of military vulnerability of the entire Eurasian landmass. It places the entire continent within Moscow's strategic reach. With the radius of this truly Eurasian weapon of mass destruction — which can cover targets throughout all of Western Europe, the Middle East, south Asia, and most of the Far East — the scope of Soviet strategic power exeeeds the current limits of Soviet political control. But Soviet leaders might well calculate that this will change as the political effects of this new military reality gradually make themselves felt.

III

Peripheral Zones of Special Vulnerability

THE two global contestants each dominate nearby regions that are geopolitical time bombs. Revolutionary activity in one case and political resistance in the other challenge the two dominant powers. But because such regional unrest occurs so close to the imperial centers themselves, the major rivals are careful not to be overprovocative to each other. The two dominated but vulnerable regions are Central America and Eastern Europe.

Prudence and thousands of miles of ocean compel the Kremlin to regard the Central American conflict as peripheral and diversionary. Its stakes are dwarfed in geopolitical significance by those of any one of Eurasia's three central strategic fronts, and any direct collision in Central America would put the Soviet Union at a massive disadvantage. Eastern Europe is peripheral for Washington because of prudence and also because American policy in Europe has been largely defensive. Nonetheless, Soviet regional vulnerability is great and there is a close connection between Eastern Europe's future and the outcome of the contest for Europe as a whole. Indeed, American awareness of the Soviet Union's vulnerability has heightened

Washington's self-restraint, lest some regional spark generate a more widespread European explosion.

Unstable Imperial Domains

The parallels between U.S. preponderance over Central America and Soviet domination over Eastern Europe are striking. For more than a century the United States has exercised direct and indirect influence on the region immediately to its south. There has, at different times, been political control, territorial expansion, economic exploitation, and military occupation. Still, there are also important differences. The United States, after a period of conflict with Mexico and of intervention in Mexican affairs, has come to accommodate itself to a Mexico that is independent in internal affairs and cautiously critical of the United States in external affairs. It has also started to dismantle its more overt forms of domination over Central America. The Panama Canal Treaties of 1978 were an explicit affirmation of a widespread American inclination to terminate the more obnoxious manifestations of its regional preponderance.

The Soviet domination of Eastern Europe is much more direct, assertive, even brutal. The Soviet Union does not tolerate regimes in Eastern Europe that deviate far from the dominant and externally imposed ideological pattern of a Marxist-Leninist state. Moscow also insists on close economic and military integration of the region with the USSR. In recent years it has tried to tighten the bonds that tie Eastern Europe to the Soviet Union. Despite the differences between U.S. and Soviet predominance, the relations in each region remain essentially imperial. Since World War II, the United States has felt that its national and regional security justified intervention in the internal affairs of Guatemala in 1954, Cuba in 1961, the Dominican Republic in 1965, Grenada in 1983, and Nicaragua today. There were strong precedents for such activism running back more than a century. It was in 1856 that an American, William Walker, inaugurated himself, with the help of a small army of fellow soldiers of fortune, as the president of Nicaragua. During this century there have been numerous military expeditions into Mexico, Haiti, and Central America. These interventions have reflected the view that the region and the related Caribbean region are central to the security of the southeastern coastal arc of the United States. In addition, the Panama Canal has enhanced the U.S. capacity for naval domination of the Pacific and Atlantic oceans.

The Monroe Doctrine, proclaimed as early as 1823, thus expressed a sentiment with powerful domestic political appeal in the United States. Originally, it simply stated that the United States would intervene to prevent an external power from imposing its form of government on any of the newly independent American states. But what might be called the "spirit of the Monroe Doctrine" evolved to mean regional hegemony. Both the Spanish-American War of 1898 and the near U.S.–British naval collision in Venezuela in 1895 reflected the high priority Washington assigned to its military monopoly in the region — and its insistence on that monopoly was quite open. U.S. Secretary of State Richard Olney justified American naval threats against Great Britain during the 1895 crisis by invoking the Monroe Doctrine, adding with striking frankness that "the U.S. is practically sovereign on this continent, and its fiat is law. . . ."

The political substance of this claim, however, has gradually changed over the last fifty years. Increasingly, the American public and government have come to the view that regional stability requires greater American sensitivity to local aspirations and greater respect for more genuinely equal relations. Malign neglect has gradually given way to benign concern. Unfortunately for the United States, this gradual shift has coincided with two threatening developments: an internal crisis of the region's antiquated social and political structures, surfacing in the process latent anti-American feelings, and the entrance into the region of an alien ideological power.

The watershed was the emergence of a Communist Cuba — and America's incapacity either to come to terms with it or to crush it. The nadir was 1961 when the newly installed President John F. Kennedy sanctioned a CIA-backed invasion of Cuba from Florida by armed Cuban émigrés. The Bay of Pigs fiasco that followed demonstrated that the United States no longer exercised a monopoly of power in a region contiguous to itself. This failure also revealed an extraordinary degree of cowardice and strategic shortsightedness on the part of American decision makers. The abandonment of several thousand Cubans, who believed that they were embarking on a mission to liberate their country from communism with the active support of the United States, reflected badly on American integrity, especially because Latin Americans traditionally attach a high value to honor and chivalry. Even more damaging was the widespread presumption that this abandonment was motivated by fear of the Soviet Union, at a time when the United States still enjoyed a considerable advantage in nuclear weapons. In any case, the Monroe Doctrine was punctured.

Henceforth, Central America was no longer an exclusive U.S. preserve. Though initial Cuban efforts to export the revolution failed badly (notably in Bolivia and Venezuela), the fact remained that such efforts could now be attempted. Moreover, Cuba and the Soviet Union gradually became bolder and more overt in their political and military cooperation. Moscow used Cuba as a training ground for revolutionaries in the 1960s, employed Cuban ports to extend the reach of the Soviet navy, and deployed Cuban troops as Soviet proxies in Africa in the late 1970s.

America's position in the region deteriorated further with the collapse of the Somoza regime in Nicaragua in 1979 and its replacement by an increasingly radical Sandinista revolutionary government. Nicaragua emerged as the first mainland

Western Hemispheric outpost of Soviet influence — though Moscow was still careful to project that relationship mainly through Cuba or its East European satellites. By 1981, the expansion of Soviet influence to Nicaragua was no longer the main issue for the United States. Instead, Washington's problem was finding a way to contain its further spread to El Salvador, not to speak of perhaps Panama later and throughout Central America still farther down the road.

The dilemma the United States faced was all the more complex because it involved the confluence of four major trends: (1) the American inclination to reorder its relations with the region on a more equitable basis; (2) a Central American popular political awakening with more intense national consciousness and social radicalism; (3) a demographic explosion accentuating internal poverty and inequality; (4) the emergence of a defiant Cuba, effectively backed by the Soviet Union, eager to exploit regional developments inimical to the United States.

This combination of factors, in turn, compelled at least a partial reversal of American disengagement from the region. American efforts to buttress El Salvador against internal revolutionary violence involved growing military assistance, as well as the deployment of American forces in nearby Central American states, in part as a contingency for possible action against Nicaragua and in part as a source of pressure both on Nicaragua and on Cuba. Moreover, after a comprehensive study of the region's problems, a special presidential commission chaired by Henry Kissinger reported that social stability would be attained only if, in addition to political pacification, the United States was prepared to undertake a massive economic aid program, requiring the commitment of no less than $9 billion. Thus, a more equitable relationship with the region was not to be had by quiet disengagement. It required a significant and multifaceted reengagement.

In contrast, the Soviet position in Eastern Europe was much more firmly asserted. During the years immediately following its entrance into Eastern Europe in the mid-1940s, the Soviet Union sponsored quite literally the physical liquidation of the region's political elite. Several tens of thousands of Poles, Czechs, Hungarians, Romanians, and Bulgarians were executed because of opposition, even peaceful, to the imposition of a political system modeled on that of the Soviet Union. The ruthlessness and bloodshed of the Stalinist purges of 1936–1938 were reproduced in countless trials and in still more unannounced executions. And on three major occasions the Soviet Union used its military power to reassert the crumbling authority of the East European Communist regimes, in East Germany in 1953, Hungary in 1956, and Czechoslovakia in 1968. It also threatened to intervene in Poland during 1980 and 1981, when the Solidarity movement seemed to be gaining the upper hand.

The Soviet determination to control east central Europe was codified in the "Brezhnev Doctrine" of 1968, announced publicly in conjunction with the crushing by Soviet military forces of the "Czechoslovak spring." The Brezhnev Doctrine postulated the right of the Soviet Union to intervene in any Communist country to prevent the evolution of its regime into a more popularly accepted form of government. The doctrine reflected the centrality of the Soviet interest in east central Europe — a region viewed by Moscow as its natural sphere of domination and a necessary springboard for political-military pressure on Western Europe.

But the Brezhnev Doctrine was also an important historical admission. It reflected the truth that to this day most of the East European regimes are artificial. The phenomenon of organic rejection of an alien political tradition has manifested itself in varying degrees throughout the region, most acutely in Poland. The Soviet system, which reflects a long-standing subordination of Russian society to the Russian state, is simply not in keeping with the more pluralistic east central European political culture. Every public opinion sampling taken in Eastern Europe indicates that the overwhelming majority would prefer either a Social-Democratic or a Christian-Democratic government to the current Communist rule.

The failure of the Communist ideology to take hold of the popular mind in spite of forty years of intense indoctrination is dramatically, and also humorously, illustrated by a series of interviews that Radio Budapest conducted at random on Budapest's Marx Square on the occasion of the May 1, 1985, celebrations. In each case, the passerby was asked who Karl Marx was. The replies, as actually broadcast by Radio Budapest, were as follows. First passerby: "Oh, don't ask me such things." Radio Budapest: "Not even just a few words?" Answer: "I would rather not, all right?" RB: "Why not?" Answer: "The truth is, I have no time to study such things." RB: "But surely you must have heard something about him in school." Answer: "I was absent a lot." Second passerby: "He was a Soviet philosopher; Engels was his friend. Well, what else can I say. He died at an old age." Third passerby, a woman: "Of course, a politician. And he was, you know, what's his name's — Lenin's, Lenin, Lenin's works — well, he translated them into Hungarian." A fourth passerby, also a woman: "It was mandatory to study him so that we would know." RB: "Then how about a few words?" Answer: "Come on now, don't make me take an exam of my eighth-grade study. That's where we had to know it. He was German. He was a politician and . . . I believe he was executed."

Despite forty years of enforced indoctrination, all the Communist regimes in Eastern Europe remain in power through heavy reliance on severe internal police control, reinforced by the potential threat of Soviet intervention — and by Soviet troops on the ground in Poland, East Germany, Czechoslovakia, and Hungary. It is clear that the only doctrine that shapes the political reality of these countries is not Marxist doctrine but the Brezhnev Doctrine.

Ideological and political difficulties are intensified by persistent economic failures. Modeled to a significant degree on the Soviet experience, these centrally controlled command economies simply have not worked well in Eastern Europe. Though Poland is the most glaring example, even the relatively successful East German economy still has not been able to prevent significant social discontent, with 3 percent of the total population officially applying for emigration from the country and with 30,000 leaving legally in 1984. All the East European economies continue to suffer from structural rigidities and an inability to satisfy consumer demand. No wonder these countries are eager to widen their economic relations with Western Europe. Yet the Soviet Union is bent on their tighter integration with the Soviet economy, a recipe for making things worse.

At the same time, Moscow is determined to restrict the scope of East European independence in foreign affairs, even when attempts to widen such autonomy are made by highly loyal Communist regimes and allegedly for the sake of enhancing East-West cooperation. In 1983 and 1984, East Germany and Hungary cautiously expressed the view that they could be helpful in bridging gaps between the East and the West. They were rebuffed. After Mikhail Gorbachev's accession to power, these points of view were vigorously denounced, with *Pravda* asking in a major article (June 21, 1985), "What question can there be of any mediation by particular Socialist countries in resolving disagreements between the USSR and the USA if on key international questions the foreign policy of the USSR and of the Marxist-Leninist nucleus of world socialism is identical?" At the first Warsaw Pact meeting held under Gorbachev's chairmanship, the principle of tight coordination of foreign policy under the Kremlin's direction was firmly reasserted.

All these efforts reflect Moscow's realization that its control over Eastern Europe continues to meet with widespread and spontaneous opposition. But this inherent instability is intensified by a condition that is unique in the history of imperial regimes: the absence of a social or cultural magnetism on the part of the dominant power.

All past empires were based to a degree on the perceived cultural superiority of the dominant nation, typically reflected in a combination of more widespread intellectual attainments, higher literacy, greater philosophical or religious vigor, as well as a better standard of living and technological capability. In varying degrees, the Roman Empire and the various European empires possessed these advantages. Indeed, at times the greatest ambition of a subject was to be accepted as a true Roman citizen, or to be seen as a fully culturally assimilated Frenchman. The American way of life similarly exercises a significant attraction for many Central Americans, not to speak of the economic motivation to emigrate to the United States because it has a per capita standard of living ten times as high and a GNP twenty times as great as those of Central America.

None of this is so with the Russian domination over Eastern Europe. East Europeans, especially Poles, Hungarians, and Czechs, consider the Russians (rightly or wrongly) to be culturally inferior and quasi-barbarous. These feelings have been reinforced by the absence of some of the more objective criteria of cultural superiority, such as a high standard of living or a spontaneous attraction for immigration. In fact, the opposite is true. No one ever wishes to emigrate to the Soviet Union. The East European per capita standard of living is about one and a half times as high as that of the Soviet Union. To make matters more difficult for Moscow, Eastern Europe still sees itself as part of Europe — and most East Europeans do not see Russia as an integral part of the European civilization. That strong cultural-political pull westward continues to work against the stability of Soviet control, thereby making the region less of a secure imperial domain than might appear on the surface.

Historical Enmity and Geopolitical Necessity

Both Washington and Moscow face a fractious neighbor within their unstable contiguous domains. That neighbor, though accommodating itself to the geopolitical necessity of deference to the interests of the major power next door, remains motivated by an intense historical memory that keeps alive feelings of antagonism and of inflicted injustice, despite the thin veneer of officially professed friendship. As a result, the formal reality of the prevailing relationship is at odds with widespread social sentiments and with latent popular political impulses. This condition, in turn, creates tempting openings for each of the major rivals — not so much to alter the basic geopolitical realities, but rather to maximize the political difficulties of the other in its particular sphere of preponderance.

The parallels between American-Mexican and Russian-Polish relations are many. In both cases, the weaker partner today was once a very major power, in some respects dwarfing its now-giant neighbor. These neighbors expanded by gobbling up territories that were Mexican or Polish, respectively, and they did so by guile and force of arms. As a result, for every Mexican or Polish schoolchild, history is the story of how his country shrank while his neighbor's expanded. Of course, the notion of a great Mexico, embracing much of California and of the U.S. Southwest, or of a large Polish-Lithuanian Commonwealth, stretching from east of Smolensk through much of the Ukraine to the Black Sea, seems a fantasy in today's world. But that is irrelevant to how political-national attitudes tend to be shaped. Patriotic romanticism and national resentment blend to fuel an attitude of historical enmity that may be latent because of geopolitical necessity but that can become explosive given a sudden opportunity.

Vivid memories of inflicted injustice and national humiliation intensify these Mexican and Polish attitudes. U.S. interventions in Mexican affairs did not match the protracted Rus-

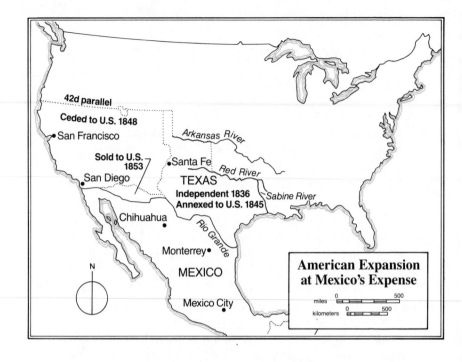

sian domination of Poland during the three partitions in the seventeenth and eighteenth centuries. Nor is there an American equivalent to the truly brutal Russian effort during the nineteenth century actually to Russify the Poles, which was carried even to the point of banishing the Polish language, or to the mass murder in Katyn and elsewhere in 1940 of much of the Polish military elite. But American interventions in Mexico left a strong memory of outrage that subsequent U.S. efforts to place the relationship on a more equitable basis have not fully erased. Mexicans remain acutely sensitive to any hint of U.S. intervention in their affairs. Keeping a certain distance from the United States on foreign policy issues is a condition of national self-respect.

Today, with Poland transparently subordinate to Moscow, the proclaimed relationship between the two countries is one of friendship. Yet even in that enforced setting, enmity keeps surfacing. A food riot will begin with slogans about bread, then shift into cries for freedom, and before long the memory

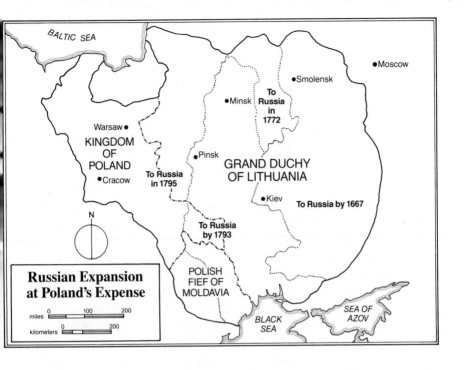

Russian Expansion at Poland's Expense

BALTIC SEA

Moscow

Smolensk

To Russia in 1772

Minsk

Warsaw

KINGDOM OF POLAND

Cracow

Pinsk

GRAND DUCHY OF LITHUANIA

To Russia in 1795

Kiev

To Russia by 1667

To Russia by 1793

POLISH FIEF OF MOLDAVIA

BLACK SEA

SEA OF AZOV

miles 0 100 200
kilometers 0 200

of Katyn is invoked. The Polish-Soviet animosity is not one-way. To a greater extent than in the American-Mexican relationship, the underlying antagonism is reciprocated by popular attitudes within the stronger power. Most Americans tend to be either indifferent about Mexicans or ignorant about Mexican historical grievances, but the antagonism between the Poles and the Russians is reciprocal and mutually recognized. Russian attitudes toward the Poles tend to mirror Polish attitudes toward the Russians, but with the Russians especially resentful of the fact that the Poles instinctively associate themselves with the culture of the West rather than with the Russian-led Slavic brotherhood.

This cultural gap is an important aspect of the difficulties plaguing the Polish-Russian relationship. While Mexico's national identity was defined through an authentic revolution, Poland's current institutions were established by an artificial revolution imposed from without. But the Polish national identity is defined by the Catholic Church, with its presence and institutions facilitating resistance to Soviet occupation. For centuries, the Poles even perceived themselves as the eastern bastion of Christendom, thus implying that any country farther east, such as Russia, was not truly Christian and certainly not European. Their antagonism toward the Russians is mixed with a strong dose of cultural superiority. The Russians sense and naturally resent it. There is a deep psychological-cultural gap between the two peoples, one that doubtless has hurt their relations and one that has contributed to the difficulty of placing them on a stable and equitable footing.

To a degree, a cultural gap also separates the United States and Mexico. Mexicans, especially the more educated and wealthier classes, have a certain ambivalence toward American culture. They see it as predominantly Anglo-Saxon and Protestant, and commercial and pragmatic in its values. American efficiency and technological attainments are admired, but America is also viewed as vulgar, overmaterialistic, and excessively driven by the profit motive. Spanish and Catholic traditions and an altogether different language lead Mexicans to see the preservation of their country against the danger of Americanization as an important cultural value. Unlike Poland-Russia, however, economic conditions are such that emigration to the United States is for many poorer Mexicans the only opportunity for personal advancement and upward mobility.

Within both Poland and Mexico there is a widespread predisposition to blame internal economic difficulties on the powerful neighbor. ''Exploitation'' is the standard explanation for the grave economic problems that each country has had to confront in recent years; highly visible economic dependence on the major power next door simply intensifies national bitterness.

For all this, both the Mexican and Polish peoples recognize that geopolitical necessity dictates some accommodation. The Poles resent their loss of independence, but they also realize that Russian power allows Poland to retain its western territories. Without Soviet support in 1945, Poland would not have obtained the economically rich region just east of the Oder-Neisse frontier in compensation for the incorporation of eastern Poland into the Soviet Union. Neither the United States nor Great Britain was initially inclined to support such a westward shift of Poland, even though both were prepared to endorse the Soviet Union's westward expansion at Poland's expense. Thus, a security link between Poland and Russia remains for Poland the sine qua non of its territorial integrity.

Mexico, too, has come to terms with its situation. American-Mexican relations in recent years have been in fact solid and generally cooperative. The United States has shown a requisite sensitivity to Mexico's economic problems, and it has not overreacted on those foreign policy issues on which the Mexicans have deliberately distanced themselves. Even Mexico's relatively cordial relations with Cuba have not been permitted to disturb the practical accommodation that has characterized U.S.–Mexican relations in recent years.

Nonetheless, the longer-term prognosis in both cases is for continued and probably increased difficulties. The issue for the Soviet Union is whether to accept eventually a Poland that is more like Finland or to insist on continued ideological-political subordination. Moscow's inclination has been to opt for the latter. Yet that choice intensifies Polish resentments, thereby making Poland more susceptible to external attraction from the West, especially from the United States. The lasting impact of the Solidarity phenomenon of the late 1970s and early 1980s has demonstrated the utter failure of the indoctrination efforts of the preceding forty years, and it has also given Polish nationalism a new boost of vitality.

Consequently, Poland poses a profound dilemma for the Soviet Union. The Communist regime formally continues to enjoy its monopoly of power. But there also exists a quasi-independent society, with its own values and activities, especially in the area of political education and history. A genuinely widespread underground press produces hundreds of illegal books and journals, which are widely circulated and read. This is reinforced by U.S.-supported broadcasts from Radio Free Europe, with the result that the Communist monopoly over the means of communication has been broken. The national dialogue on key domestic and international issues is dominated by dissent. And this uncontrolled dialogue receives crucial support from the Catholic Church, an institution that commands the allegiance of the vast majority of the overwhelmingly Catholic Poles.

Common sense might dictate that the right course for the Soviet Union would be to adjust to this reality. It could exploit the Poles' recognition of their geopolitical interest while permitting the gradual emergence of a more pluralistic political system limited only by the acceptance of Moscow's external preponderance. Such a development would certainly help to stabilize Poland and reduce the attraction of the West. Yet such a policy would require a colossal change in Russia's ideological-historical attitudes toward Poland. Moreover, it would require acceptance of a reform that might prove contagious throughout Moscow's East European imperial domain. In effect, the Kremlin rulers cannot place the Polish-Russian relationship on a healthier basis without a more profound reassessment of overall Soviet regional hegemony. The prospect is thus for continued tension in the Soviet Union's control of its most troublesome neighbor, but with no fundamental change in the nature of that control.

For the United States, the threat is that internal economic and political failures of the Mexican regime might galvanize latent anti-American sentiments and merge them with the wider crisis in Central America. Mexico's population, almost 80 million today, will by the end of this century grow to more than 120 million. Its capital city alone will swell to approximately 31 million, with two-thirds of its inhabitants beset by massive unemployment and living under less than minimal hygienic and nutritional standards. This socioeconomic crisis might coincide with the fragmentation of its one-party, mildly authoritarian political system — a system that, despite its radical and nationalist rhetoric, has managed the relationship with the United States quite responsibly. As the existing political system loses the capacity to cope with domestic problems, radical elements might demagogically exploit historical grievances against the powerful neighbor to the north. This could also become acute because of the massive pressures from Mexico's unemployed millions for access to the American labor market.

The management of the potentially explosive American-Mexican relationship is further complicated by the rapid growth in the number of Mexicans who have settled in recent years on the American side of the border. Approximately 12 million U.S. residents originate from Mexico, and this number continues to grow with the inflow of illegal immigrants. According to one estimate, 25 million Mexican-Americans will be residing in the United States by the end of the century. With their Spanish language kept alive by the bilingual education policies unwisely adopted in the United States with respect to Hispanic-Americans and with their homeland territorially contiguous, their assimilation and integration into U.S. society may prove to be slower than those of other immigrant groups. Intensified political and social conflicts within Mexico — especially if they produce tension in the American-Mexican relationship — could make this large community the object of nationalist passions. The two-thousand-mile-long, largely artificial, and currently quite porous U.S. southern border could even become the focus of major violence.

Given the prospects for political unrest in Poland and for socioeconomic tensions in Mexico, it is unlikely that these enduring historical enmities will soon fade. The dilemma will persist for both major powers. American cultivation of Poland and Soviet courtship of Mexico will offer opportunities for disruptive tactical probes, as well as for even more significant strategic gains.

Stakes and Policies

Both superpowers have been cautious in exploiting each other's regional difficulties. This derives from a mutual understanding that each has a vital interest at stake in its contiguous region. For Washington or Moscow, the costs of a regional setback from intrusion by the rival power would be extremely high. As a result, each feels justified in adopting extreme measures to protect its preponderance, and each feels that it can afford to be patient in probing the other's domain.

For the United States, a major political defeat in Central America would have immediate strategic consequences, whereas for the Soviet Union a loss in Central America would represent only a tactical setback. In Eastern Europe, the situation is reversed: a major Soviet setback would entail strategic consequences, whereas an American failure to penetrate Eastern Europe would represent only a tactical disappointment.

Accordingly, American policy toward Eastern Europe has been extremely restrained, both substantively and rhetorically. Except for a brief period in the early 1950s, when the "rollback" of Soviet influence and "liberation" of the area was the proclaimed goal of U.S. policy, the United States has stated that it favors the evolution of the region's political systems into more pluralistic forms and the gradual enhancement of the external freedom of the East European countries. These objectives, U.S. officials have stressed, do not involve turning the region against the Soviet Union. Several successive U.S. administrations have been consistent in this regard, whether the goal has been defined as seeking "peaceful engagement" in Eastern Europe's future, or as striving to "build bridges" to Eastern Europe, or as pursuing "a policy of differentiation," or as trying to undo "the artificial division of Europe."

The United States has been careful not to contest the Soviet Union even when Moscow faced the prospect that one or another of its East European Communist systems might collapse. When the East German regime was being overthrown in 1953 the same U.S. administration that had proclaimed a policy of "liberation" for Eastern Europe did nothing to deter the Soviet Union militarily. Nor did it when the Hungarians actually did overthrow their Soviet-sponsored rulers and proclaimed their country to be a neutral state in 1956. Twelve years later, the United States remained similarly passive when it obtained advance intelligence that a Soviet military move into Czechoslovakia was imminent. Only in late 1980, when it appeared that the Soviet Union was about to invade Poland, did the United States act to preempt the Soviet Union. Unlike the response in 1968, the Carter administration deliberately publicized Moscow's preparations for the intervention; organized concerted international pressure on the Kremlin to desist, both from U.S. allies and even from Moscow's friends (such as Prime Minister Indira Gandhi of India); warned Solidarity leaders to take precautions; even considered initiating arms sales to China; and quietly warned Moscow of the "grave" consequences of any such action. The credibility of such moves was probably strengthened by the energetic American reaction to the Soviet invasion of Afghanistan a year earlier.

Apart from this, the United States has concentrated its efforts in Eastern Europe on a strategy of indirect intrusion, designed over the long haul to dilute the effectiveness of Soviet control. The prime and central instrument of that effort has been the U.S.-sponsored Radio Free Europe. For more than three and a half decades it has broken the Soviet monopoly on the information reaching East Europeans. Though it is impossible to measure Radio Free Europe's effect precisely, on a number of occasions, notably in the case of Poland, Hungary, and Czechoslovakia, its exposure of Stalinist-type secret police brutality has contributed directly to political upheavals within ruling circles and to more sustained and informal domestic pressure for systemic reform. Without Radio Free Europe, and the several associated information and exchange programs, East Europeans would surely have become politically more pliant.

The United States has also pursued a policy of differentiation among the East European countries. It has granted limited economic benefits to, and promoted more extensive exchanges and political contacts with, those East European regimes that have adopted more moderate domestic policies or demonstrated greater foreign policy independence from Moscow. Poland before the declaration of martial law and Hungary benefited from this policy of differentiation because of internal reforms, and Romania and genuinely independent Yugoslavia did so because of their foreign policies. All became the targets of special U.S. political cultivation and more privileged economic treatment.

Nonetheless, the overall U.S. approach has been not to contest directly Soviet primacy in the region and even to avoid increasing Soviet anxieties. For some U.S. policymakers, at least, the region has also been of secondary and essentially expedient interest. Some have favored not ruffling Soviet sensitivities and have placed a much higher value on an eventual U.S.–Soviet accommodation. Others, stressing the primary importance of Germany, have taken this a step farther even by urging actions that would have pushed Eastern Europe into Soviet arms. The extreme manifestation of this viewpoint appeared in the early 1950s in a secret U.S. planning memorandum regarding a post–World War III settlement. In these contingency plans, policymakers considered a revitalized, reunified, and rearmed Germany to be pivotal to U.S. interests — a consideration that, if it had become publicly known, would have greatly facilitated Soviet domination over Poland and Czechoslovakia. But in general American leaders have viewed Eastern Europe as a region of peripheral geopolitical interest, significant only in relation to the central (and defensive) struggle against Soviet domination over Western Europe.

In contrast, Soviet policy in Central America and the Caribbean has been tactically bolder, though in a larger sense it has also been strategically cautious. The Soviet Union did not itself produce the Communist regime in Cuba, but once it had emerged Moscow did not hesitate to support it. The Bay of Pigs was the watershed. The spectacle of the American president and his advisers acting with such timidity in an area of immediate proximity to the continental United States could have conveyed only one vital strategic message: provided it did not provoke the United States into some rash overreaction, Moscow could with little risk gradually expand its links with the increasingly Communist Cuba. The limits of such expanding ties were drawn with greater precision a year and a half later during the Cuban missile crisis of 1962. This time it was Moscow that had to pull back. And it was seen as a U.S. triumph. But there was a price: a guarantee that Cuba's pro-Soviet regime would not be overthrown. Thus, the United States acquiesced to a Soviet foothold in the Western Hemisphere, provided Moscow itself did not exploit it in a militarily significant way.

On balance, therefore, the longer-range net result of the Cuban missile crisis was a tactical victory for the United States and a strategic success for the Soviet Union. The Soviet missiles in Cuba were gone, but a pro-Soviet regime endured. Within less than ten years, the intermediate-range missiles that Moscow had tried to slip into Cuba were more than replaced in military value by Soviet ICBMs, while Cuba became both a regional and an international Soviet asset. Cuban military forces acted as Soviet proxies in Africa, and Cuba later contributed to the Central American revolutionary turmoil. Soviet confidence that Cuba was immune to American intervention gradually grew, and Moscow became bolder both in establishing a military presence on the island and in defining Cuba as "a constituent part of the world system of socialism," to quote Brezhnev's words of June 1972. Yet the Kremlin has continued to refrain from making the ultimate commitment to Cuba's security. Though East Germany and Vietnam, both presumably acting with Moscow's blessings and on its behalf, concluded political-military treaties with Cuba in the early 1980s, no formal security treaty between Moscow and Havana has been signed.

Kremlin leaders are likely to remain cautious in Central America, especially in light of the outcome of the 1984 U.S. presidential election. Early in 1985 Soviet apprehension that Washington would step up its pressure against Nicaragua was manifest. During the Reagan administration's first term, the U.S. military intervention in Grenada in 1983 demonstrated a renewed U.S. willingness to use force in the region. During this time the Soviet involvement in Nicaragua had grown, with Eastern bloc military equipment deliveries rising from $6 million to $112 million a year and with Cuban military advisers topping 3,000. After the 1984 election, however, Moscow deliberately downgraded the ideological status of the Nicaraguan regime, describing it merely as a "progressive" government rather than as one with "a socialist orientation." More generally, the Soviet Union started a propaganda campaign designed to prevent U.S. military action against Nicaragua, while softpedaling revolutionary rhetoric about a wider revolution in Central America. Moscow's posture made it clear that an American invasion of Nicaragua would precipitate a rhetorically violent Soviet propaganda campaign — but no more than that. Soviet leaders must have realized that logistical and geographical factors ordained that the United States would succeed in any determined military action and that Nicaragua itself was not worth at this time a direct American-Soviet collision.

Moscow and Havana clearly differed on how to handle this issue. Their differences reflected the gap between Cuba's intensely ideological approach to the promotion of Marxist revolution in Latin America and the Soviet Union's longer-range geostrategic perspective. Cuba not only spearheaded the moves to consolidate and radicalize the new Nicaraguan regime, but also led the effort to identify Managua closely with the pro-Soviet camp. Furthermore, Cuban statements indicated a higher degree of revolutionary optimism than the Soviet Union's did. Havana favored greater activism and naturally assigned a higher priority to the Western Hemisphere. Moscow stressed the importance of consolidating revolutionary gains in Nicaragua, as it had done previously in the case of Cuba, and argued that in a head-on confrontation with the United States these revolutionary gains could be lost.

More dispassionate in perspective than its ally, Moscow must have realized that geographically, logistically, and economically even a conflagration throughout all of Central America would not become another Vietnam for the United States. The United States, if it needed to, could blockade Central America while rapidly applying massive military force. In addition, the region's 25 million people (not counting the far more numerous Mexicans) were far from united in opposition to the United States, with local antipathies and even growing anti-Communist sentiments increasingly tending to isolate Nicaragua. The Kremlin leaders therefore concluded that the wiser policy was to expand the base of revolutionary activity gradually, counting on its progressive expansion into adjoining countries as internal crises within them ripened, festered, and finally exploded.

In Latin America as a whole, moreover, the Soviet leaders saw the U.S. position as entering a phase of general crisis. The Soviet Union can encourage this process, taking advantage of economic and social tensions to fan anti-American nationalist feelings and supplying arms to Cuba and Nicaragua, but the Soviet Union cannot at this stage become directly involved in contesting the paramount position of the United States in the Western Hemisphere. Soviet leaders, while preaching that true revolutionaries must never allow themselves to be intimidated by ''geographic fatalism,'' are very conscious of the practical limits that geography imposes on policy. Consequently, they consider revolutionary upheavals in Latin America and the eventual elimination of U.S. preponderance in the region as one of the final phases of the historical contest.

Thus, as a result of historical timing and geography, Central America specifically as well as Latin America more generally is a theater of secondary operations for Moscow. Of course, Soviet tactical successes in Central America can have an important effect: they can divert American attention from the three central strategic fronts. Soviet tactical boldness can help to undermine the U.S. determination needed to sustain American global involvement. Tactical gains, consolidated into strategic outposts, can provide support for the proposition that the global balance is shifting from one superpower to the other. But in the final analysis the region is not foreseeably an arena for a Soviet strategic test of American will.

The temptation for the Soviet Union will grow if the internal problems of Central America should merge with a much larger domestic explosion in Mexico, which, in turn, could inflame the American-Mexican relationship. The possession by Moscow of strategic outposts in the Caribbean and/or Central America would provide the Soviet Union with staging areas for logistical and other support for the fullest political exploitation of any U.S.–Mexican conflicts, capitalizing on the inevitably intense passions that such disputes would generate. By the end of this century, especially if in the meantime the United States remains largely on the geopolitical defensive, it is quite possible that a fourth central strategic front may be opening up on the Rio Grande.

IV

The One-Dimensional Rival: A Threat Assessment

A LONG-TERM U.S. policy for dealing effectively with the Soviet Union must be based on a realistic appraisal both of Soviet intentions and of Soviet capabilities. Soviet intentions are not primarily a matter of the subjective inclination of this or that Kremlin leader. They are the product of deep-rooted historical-geographical drives, reinforced by the doctrinal perspectives embedded in the institutions of political power and diffused throughout the ruling political elite. They do not change dramatically, except on the most superficial and largely tactical level, and these shifts are often deliberately designed to exploit the propensity of the American mass media to interpret atmospheric changes as basic strategic shifts.

Soviet intentions derive from the historical Russian desire to achieve a preeminent global standing. The central strategic precondition for reaching that objective is the severance of the American connection with the extremities of the Eurasian continent. But such aspirations are significant only if backed by sufficient capabilities. The American policymaker must therefore carefully monitor changes in these capabilities and scrupulously assess their overall potential. This is both a sensitive and a critically significant undertaking. An underassessment of Soviet power could be fatal. But an exaggeration of Soviet capabilities could produce a serious problem of morale and needless and wasteful reactions, weakening America's capacity to endure a protracted competition. Thus, a prudent assessment requires taking stock of several aspects of national power — notably the socioeconomic one, for this factor can be central to the successful conduct of the rivalry unless it is at some point terminally resolved by a direct military collision.

Soviet Military Capabilities

The military dimension, nonetheless, must be the point of departure. If one side were to gain such overwhelming military superiority as to predetermine the outcome of a test of arms, or if a military conflict were to arise because of miscalculation, then all the other nonmilitary aspects of national power would become irrelevant. That is the stark and inescapable reality of international affairs, and it makes the estimate of relative military might the central consideration in a policy-oriented assessment.

The centrality of military power is not simply a matter of relative numbers and destructive capabilities. Even more important is its impact on the political conduct of the rivals, especially regarding their freedom to pursue unilateral policies under the mutually paralyzing protection of the nuclear deterrent. The danger inherent in the acquisition of comprehensive military power by the Soviet Union was recognized by U.S. policy planners at a relatively early stage in the U.S.–Soviet nuclear competition, when the United States still enjoyed a marked strategic superiority and could even afford to base its containment policies on the public threat of massive nuclear retaliation.

On October 30, 1953, the administration of President Dwight D. Eisenhower concluded a wide-ranging and very systematic six-month review of U.S. "Basic National Security Policy."

Both the president and his principal National Security Council advisers took a very active part in this exercise. The resulting formal NSC statement of policy, classified at the time as top secret, focused first of all on the implications for the United States of the growth of Soviet military power. Several key paragraphs deserve full citation, because of their foresight and continued relevance:

When both the USSR and the United States reach a stage of atomic plenty and ample means of delivery, each will have the probable capacity to inflict critical damage on the other, but is not likely to be able to prevent major atomic retaliations. This could create a stalemate, with both sides reluctant to initiate general warfare; although if the Soviets believed that initial surprise held the prospect of destroying the capacity for retaliation they might be tempted into attacking.

Although Soviet fear of atomic reaction should still inhibit local aggression, increasing Soviet atomic capability may tend to diminish the deterrent effect of U.S. atomic power against peripheral Soviet aggression. It may also sharpen the reaction of the USSR to what it considers provocative acts of the United States. If either side should miscalculate the strength of the other's reaction, such local conflicts could grow into general war, even though neither seeks nor desires it. To avoid this, it will in general be desirable for the United States to make clear to the USSR the kind of actions which will be almost certain to lead to this result, recognizing, however, that as a general war becomes more devastating for both sides the threat to resort to it becomes less available as a sanction against local aggression.

The USSR will continue to rely heavily on tactics of division and subversion to weaken the Free World's alliances and will to resist the Soviet power. Using both the fear of atomic warfare and the hope of peace, such political warfare will seek to exploit differences among members of the Free World, neutralist attitudes, and anticolonial and nationalist sentiments in underdeveloped areas. For these purposes, Communist parties and other cooperating elements will be used to manipulate opinion and control governments wherever possible. This aspect of the Soviet threat is likely to continue indefinitely and to grow in intensity.

The three most vital questions of contemporary significance, foreshadowed by the 1953 NSC document, are: (1) whether the military balance and the resulting nuclear deterrence between the two powers is becoming threatened by the possibility of effective strategic preemption through a disarming first strike; (2) whether local conflicts are likely to grow into a general war because the superpowers may be more inclined to escalate in response to apparent provocations; and (3) whether the nuclear stalemate can create openings for a greater assertion of Soviet conventional power on any one of the three critically important central strategic fronts. In other words, the central issue is not how much relative military power the Soviet Union possesses but to what strategically or politically significant uses it can apply that power. Accordingly, the intellectual challenge in a politically relevant threat assessment is not merely to count weapons, and to determine on that basis the relative ratio of force, but to analyze the possible circumstances in which Soviet military power might be most effectively (and dangerously) applied.

That Soviet military power has grown most impressively during the last two decades hardly needs documentation. The three tables summarize the scale of the Soviet effort and the comparative status of strategic forces. Even this summary shows that the Soviet Union has not only gained strategic parity with the United States but has also outstripped the United States in the momentum of the arms buildup. These massive Soviet efforts have created a situation in which the United States and the Soviet Union can be seen as roughly equal in strategic power, with neither side at this stage entitled to a high degree of confidence regarding the outcome of a nuclear exchange, either through a surprise attack or by fully generated forces. In that respect, it can be said that a situation of ambiguous strategic equivalence exists today.

That assertion may be challenged by those who argue that the Soviet Union already enjoys strategic superiority. In terms

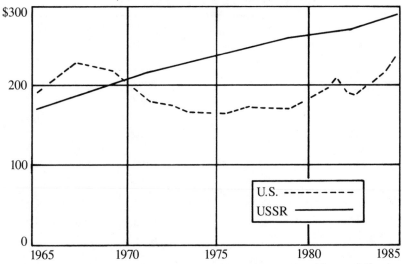

U.S. and Soviet Military Outlays
(in billions of constant FY 1985 dollars)

Source: Congressional Research Service

U.S. Strategic Forces, April 1985*

Systems	Launchers	Warheads	Yield/wh (kt)	CEP (nm)
Titan II @ 1 RV	26	26	9,000	0.80
Minuteman II @ 1 RV	450	450	1,200	0.34
Minuteman III @ 3 RVs	550	1,650	170–335	0.12
Total ICBM RVs		2,126		
Poseidon C-3 @ 10 RVs	304	3,040	40	0.25
Trident C-4 @ 8 RVs	312	2,496	100	0.25
Total SLBM RVs		5,536		
B-52G	167	1,822†		
B-52H	96	1,260†		
Deployed ALCMs		1,080		
Total Bomber Weapons		3,072†		
Total Ballistic Missile RVs		7,662		
Total Ballistic Missile RVs and ALCMs		8,742		

*Information derived from *Soviet Military Power* (1985), U.S. Military Posture Statement (FY '86).
† Figures derived from John M. Collins, *U.S.–Soviet Military Balance, 1980–1985.*

Soviet Strategic Forces, April 1985*

Systems	Launchers	Warheads	Yield/wh (kt)	CEP (nm)
SS-11	520		1,000	0.76
Mod 1 @ 1 RV	100	100		
Mod 2 @ 1 RV ⎫ Mod 3 @ 3 MRVs ⎭	420	≥420		
SS-13			600	1.00
Mod 2 @ 1 RV	60	60		
SS-17				
Mod 3 @ 4 MIRVs	150	600	500	0.20
SS-18				
Mod 4 @ 10 MIRVs	308	3,080	500	0.14
SS-19				
Mod 3 @ 6 MIRVs	360	2,160	550	0.15
Total ICBM RVs		6,420		
SS-N-5	42	42	1,000	1.50
SS-N-6	336	≥336	1,000	0.50
Mod 1 @ 1 RV				
Mod 2 @ 1 RV				
Mod 3 @ 2 MRVs				
SS-N-8	292	292	1,000	0.50
Mod 1 @ 1 RV				
Mod 2 @ 1 RV				
SS-N-17 @ 1 RV	12	12	500	0.75
SS-N-18	224	≤1,568	500	0.50
Mod 1 @ 3 MIRVs				
Mod 2 @ 1 RV				
Mod 3 @ 7 MIRVs				
SS-N-20 @ 6–9 RVs	60	360–540	100	0.30
SS-NX-23 @ >7 RVs	16	>112	—	—
Total SLBM RVs		2,722–2,902		
Bear Bombers	125	600†		
Bison Bombers	48	192†		
Backfire Bombers	250	260†		
Deployed ALCMs		200†		
Total Bomber Weapons		1,052		
Total Ballistic Missile RVs		9,142–9,322		

*Information derived from *Soviet Military Power* (1985). Warhead numbers reflect maximum tested counting type rules.

†Figures derived from John M. Collins, *U.S.–Soviet Military Balance, 1980–1985.*

U.S. AND SOVIET WEAPON PRODUCTION

	UNITED STATES		SOVIET UNION	
	1984 Production	*New Types Since 1970*	*1984 Production*	*New Types Since 1970*
ICBMs	0	0	150	4
SLBMs	80	1	200	4
Tanks	770	1	3,000	3
Field Artillery*	260	4	3,300	13
Cruisers	1	3	1	3
Destroyers/Frigates	7	3	6	5
Submarines				
Ballistic missile	2	1	2	7
Attack	5	1	6	5
Medium Bombers†				
Air force	0	0	35	1
Navy	0	0	0	0
Tactical Combat Aircraft‡	250	4	640	7
Surface-to-Air Missiles§	800	2	26,000	5
Transport Aircraft‖	11	0	250	1

*Self-propelled/towed artillery, mortars, and rocket launchers.
†One new medium bomber, the Backfire, serves air force and navy.
‡Includes interceptors, plus fighter/attack aircraft. U.S. Air Force, Navy, and Marine Corps all count.
§Excludes man-portable missiles, includes shipboard SAMs.
‖Excludes cargo helicopters; Soviet military and Aeroflot figures are inseparable.

of numbers of nuclear delivery systems and of throwweight (their potential destructive capacity), the Soviet Union does hold an advantage. But this is offset by an American lead in warheads if the nuclear bombs and air-launched cruise missiles (ALCMs) carried by B-52 and B-1 bombers are counted. Under prevailing conditions, it is unlikely that any Soviet military planner could confidently expect that a Soviet nuclear attack would so disarm the United States as to prevent an extremely damaging retaliatory response. Except for the SS-18s and perhaps the SS-19s, existing Soviet strategic systems are not sufficiently accurate to execute a genuinely effective surgical strike against existing U.S. strategic forces. With approximately 50 percent of the U.S. submarine-launched ballistic missiles (SLBMs) out at sea, and even with only a very small percentage of U.S. intercontinental ballistic missiles (ICBMs) and bombers perhaps surviving a Soviet first strike, an otherwise highly successful Soviet first strike would still leave Soviet

COMPARATIVE FIRST-STRIKE WARHEADS*

		Soviet Union	United States	
1985	SS-18	3,080	Pershing II (Europe)	108
	SS-19	2,160	Minuteman III, Mk 12A	900
	Total	5,240	Total	1,008
1995	New SS-18	8,000–10,500 combined	Pershing II (Europe)	108
	SS-24		MX	500
	SS-25		Minuteman III, Mk 12A	900
			Trident II, D-5	1,920
			Midgetman	?
	Total	8,000–10,500	Total	3,428

*Assumptions:
  1. Minuteman IIIs remain in place through 1995 or are replaced with comparable weapon.
  2. Current 50-missile MX deployment plan is fulfilled.
  3. Scale of Midgetman deployment is unknown.
  4. No Soviet SLBMs achieve first-strike accuracy comparable to U.S. D-5.

ESTIMATE OF COMPARATIVE FIRST-STRIKE TARGETS

TARGETS: Strategic Launchers (Silos and Subs), Strategic Bomber Bases, Launch-Control Centers, Command Bunkers, Leadership Shelters, Principal Communications Systems

	Soviet Union	United States
1985	4,500	1,500
1995	6,000–7,000	2,500

NOTE: A first strike, to be genuinely effective, must not only destroy most of the adversary's retaliatory capability but also so disrupt his command and control and communications as to preclude any response by any surviving weapons. Hence, the target list for a first strike has to be considerably larger than the number of strategic launchers targeted in such an attack.

society vulnerable to a destructive U.S. counterattack — though such a counterattack would be suicidal for the United States.

The key question for the future is whether a continued Soviet arms buildup and technological improvements might dramatically alter this situation to the disadvantage of the United States. Of special concern from the standpoint of strategic stability is the increasing precision of nuclear delivery systems and the growing capacity of central command to control the use of such accuracy in actual conflict. This is measured by the "circular error probability," or CEP — the radius within which targeted warheads will land. It has been diminishing through each new generation of missiles. A Soviet SS-19 has a missile CEP of 1,200 feet; an SS-18, 850 feet; a Minuteman III, 700 feet; an MX, 300 feet; and a Pershing II with terminal guidance, less than 100 feet. The latest Soviet missiles, the SS-24 and SS-25, are likely to be more accurate than their predecessors. The fact is that modern nuclear weapons are becoming the means, not only to inflict mass destruction, but also to strike precisely enough to disarm the opponent. As Albert Wohlstetter observed in *Commentary* in 1983, the revolution in precision is "in some ways more revolutionary than the transition from conventional to fission explosives or even fusion weapons" because an improvement in accuracy "by a factor of 100 improves blast effectiveness against a small, hard military target about as much as multiplying the energy released a million times."

The scope of projected Soviet strategic deployments is also daunting. Intelligence estimates suggest that by the mid-1990s nearly all of the Soviet Union's present strategic systems will be renewed. To replace the SS-17s and SS-19s, the more accurate SS-24 with ten warheads will be deployed in silos in 1986 and on mobile launchers in 1987. To retire the SS-11s, the single-warhead, mobile SS-25 was being introduced into operation in 1985, with seventy launchers deployed by April 1986. In addition, over the next five years flight tests will be-

gin of a new version of the SS-24, an improved model of the
SS-25, possibly with multiple independently targeted ·warheads,
and a new silo-based heavy ICBM to replace the SS-18s.

With these programs, the Soviet Union could expand its inventory of nuclear warheads to between 16,000 and 21,000 by
the mid-1990s. About half of those will have a first-strike capability and will be deployed in reloadable silos or launchers.
That number will be sufficient to explode more than three Soviet warheads on every land-based U.S. delivery system. Moscow would still have an impressive 10,000-warhead reserve
capability for a follow-up attack on the U.S. population in the
event of any U.S. nuclear response. Given the Soviet concentration on more accurate ICBM delivery systems, by the mid-
1990s all U.S. land-based strategic systems will be even more
vulnerable to a Soviet first strike. So will command centers
and communications. Only U.S. sea-based systems will still
remain relatively safe, though even this cannot be taken for
granted indefinitely. With improved Soviet tracking, U.S.
SLBMs could become increasingly vulnerable, while a massive Soviet attack on American strategic systems and command structure could also disrupt effective communications with
any surviving submarines. With the Soviets poised to launch a
massive second strike against American cities, the threat of a
spasmodic retaliation by surviving U.S. SLBMs against Soviet
urban targets might not be credible.

A partial counterattack would, in any case, be subject to
attrition by Soviet strategic defenses. It is the combination of
the large increase in Soviet first-strike systems with the steady
expansion of Soviet defenses that makes the Soviet strategic
threat potentially so serious. Although it launched a loud public campaign against President Reagan's proposal for strategic
defenses, Moscow has been surreptitiously enhancing its ability rapidly to deploy a comprehensive antiballistic-missile system. By the early 1990s, the Soviets will have a new network

of large phased-array radars that will be able to support battle management for a widespread ABM system. In their modernization of the Moscow ABM system, they have already developed other major components, such as an aboveground launcher and a high-acceleration missile. They are also planning to deploy a new mobile surface-to-air missile, the SA-X-12, that has some of the operational capabilities of an ABM system, for it can shoot down not only aircraft and cruise missiles but also tactical ballistic missiles. As a mobile antiaircraft weapon the SA-X-12 is technically not a violation of the ABM treaty. Yet through a gradual creep-out deployment, and with the radars in place and with production lines for other components available, it could give the Kremlin (in spite of the ABM treaty) a strategic defense that would protect key targets in the western Soviet Union and east of the Ural Mountains by the early 1990s.

There is also ample evidence to suggest that Soviet research into advanced laser-based or particle-beam strategic defenses has been extensive and amply funded, and is likely to have military applications by the early 1990s. Intelligence estimates put the cost of the laser weapon program alone at about $1 billion. Also, over the last decade, the Soviet Union has invested heavily in an elaborate nuclear shelter system designated to protect, even from a nuclear attack, much of its political elite. Shelters on between 800 and 1,500 sites are constructed in enormous complexes and are easily accessible from major Soviet cities through special transportation. (In some places they even have a separate subway system.) They could, according to some estimates, protect approximately 175,000 officials of the ruling party, KGB, and armed forces. This defense would be especially valuable in a more protracted but less than total nuclear exchange.

It would be escapist, therefore, to assume that Soviet military planners would *never* consider the option of a first strike.

They must know that the United States is more vulnerable to a surgical first strike because the precise location of key U.S. assets is much more easily ascertained and can be more effectively targeted than those of the Soviet Union. In brief, the troubling reality is that increasingly numerous and accurate nuclear weapons are making it possible for the first time for strategic planners to design an attack that would leave the opponent crippled, capable of only a spasmodic, disorganized, and strategically aimless response — or even none at all. This still does not make a first strike attractive from a moral or even a political point of view. But the truth is that given the growing Soviet capacity for strategic offensive preemption and defensive attrition, the military feasibility of this option — even if not its political attractiveness — is increasing.

Military feasibility is not to be mechanically translated into probability. Even in the context of wider strategic asymmetry, there are still good reasons to assume that the Soviet leaders would be unlikely to initiate a first strike, though one must be on guard against the possibility. The execution of a first strike would be such a complicated undertaking, with so many operational uncertainties and such enormous risks, that it is improbable that in the near future any Soviet leadership would embark on this course in cold blood. Even a partial American retaliation could still be quite destructive.

The central dilemma confronting the United States is more nuanced, and yet menacing. In the course of about a decade, the continuing Soviet buildup of strategic weapons and the covert expansion of Soviet strategic defenses could create a more unbalanced and inherently insecure situation. Indeed, the main danger is not that of a first strike as such but rather that the increased U.S. vulnerability to such a strike would give the Soviet Union greater flexibility for the use of both its strategic and conventional military power while inducing geostrategic paralysis on the American side. This would bode ill for the stability of our political relationships.

Such a state of heightened strategic insecurity would be the consequence of the fundamental difference between the U.S. and the Soviet strategic postures. The Soviet Union has been developing a nuclear war–fighting capability at several levels of intensity and potentially for protracted periods of time, and through its procurements over the last decade it has begun to realize such a capability operationally. In contrast, the United States has concentrated essentially on maintaining a nuclear war–deterring capability. Although its declaratory doctrine has been evolving toward giving decision makers greater targeting flexibility and although it has recently deployed some weapons with a first-strike capability, the United States still relies heavily on maintaining the threat of a massive retaliatory response. The growing asymmetry between these U.S. and Soviet strategic postures and doctrines is bound to heighten U.S. insecurity, and it could also embolden the Soviet Union to act more assertively to expand its influence through the use of conventional or even strategic military power.

This danger can only be offset by timely U.S. strategic programs or effective arms control. Lead times for strategic weapons are long, often stretching past a decade. Hence the danger — which may become critical in as little as a decade — requires not only early recognition, but also a prompt programmatic response. It follows that unless the threat of one-sided vulnerability is alleviated by a comprehensive arms control agreement, the key issues for the near future are in what mix and numbers U.S. strategic offensive forces must be deployed so that a survivable U.S. second-strike capability credibly deters a Soviet first strike; and/or what kind of strategic defenses the United States should also deploy so that a Soviet first strike is rendered militarily pointless.

The Soviet leaders are not sentimentalists when it comes to the uses of power. One cannot improve here on the warnings George Kennan wrote from Moscow in 1945, when he was exposed daily to the Soviet mentality. In a report to the secretary of state, Kennan did not mince words:

> I have no hesitation in saying quite categorically, in the light of some eleven years' experience with Russian matters, that it would be highly dangerous to our security if the Russians were to develop the use of atomic energy, or any other radical and far-reaching means of destruction, along lines of which we were unaware and against which we might be defenseless if taken by surprise. There is nothing — I repeat nothing — in the history of the Soviet regime which could justify us in assuming that the men who are now in power in Russia, or even those who have chances of assuming power in the foreseeable future, would hesitate for a moment to apply this power against us if by doing so they thought that they might materially improve their own power position in the world.

Beyond the strategic dilemma, the buildup in Soviet military capabilities is producing an additional problem that the United States previously has not had to face: a growing Soviet capability to project its forces far beyond its borders. Since the early 1970s, there has been a sharp increase in the Soviet Union's ability to project forces beyond the regions contiguous to its central landmass. Soviet air- and sea-lift capabilities have grown to the point that Moscow may soon be tempted not only to deploy proxy military forces (such as the Cubans in Ethiopia and Angola) but also to use its own troops so as to stage a demonstration of force or to establish a political presence in a distant region. This is something the Soviet Union has not been able to do during the forty years of the cold war with the United States.

The Middle East and southern Africa are the globe's most incendiary regions. The United States runs the risk of political isolation in each region because of its support for Israel and (in a much more ambiguous fashion) for South Africa. Intensifying racial conflicts in southern Africa could at some point tempt Moscow to involve itself more directly. It would expect local gains, but also the generation of widespread pro-Soviet feelings throughout the African continent. The Soviet Union is certainly also sensitive to the geopolitical importance of South Africa to the West, both as a source of strategically vital minerals and as a geostrategic control point for maritime trade.

Even more likely is Soviet involvement in the Middle East, especially if the Arab-Israeli conflict erupts into renewed hostilities. Already in the October 1973 war, the Soviet Union was tempted to intervene on Egypt's behalf but backed off in the face of U.S. warnings. At that time, the United States still held a margin of advantage in strategic weapons. In a setting of ambiguous strategic parity — and especially if this is compounded by asymmetrical American vulnerability — the Soviet Union may be bolder next time. It may simply act, deploying its airborne forces on the side of an Arab protagonist, and leave it to the United States to decide whether to respond or not.

The danger that a U.S. response could lead to an outright U.S. military defeat is, however, mitigated by the development since 1979 of the Rapid Deployment Force. This force, based on a U.S. air- and sea-lift capability that is still considerably larger than that of the Soviet Union, does have the capacity to more than offset any likely long-range Soviet deployments during the next decade. Because of the energetic efforts initiated by the Carter administration and carried farther by the Reagan administration, the forces dedicated to the RDF and its supporting airlift now have a significant capability for prompt power projection. Several light divisions, supported by tactical air power, can be deployed quickly in areas remote from the United States, at a faster pace and in a greater volume than the Soviets can achieve. The Soviet Union would therefore be risking a local defeat if it became engaged in a long-distance collision with the United States — though there is the inherently uncertain factor of the degree to which a precarious and perhaps asymmetrical nuclear balance would deter the United

States from using the Rapid Deployment Force directly against Soviet forces.

In a remote local collision that does not escalate into a central war, the Soviet Union would also be at a disadvantage because of superior U.S. naval capabilities. The Soviet fleet, despite the momentum of its growth in recent years, is still inferior. It also suffers from two other disadvantages. First, it is widely dispersed. Its three components — the northern fleet based at Murmansk and in the Baltic Sea, the Black Sea fleet, and the Far Eastern fleet — have to operate separately, and each has to pass through choke points on the way to open oceans. These choke points could be interdicted by the United States even with conventional munitions, though such a step would constitute an American escalation of a conflict. Second, the Soviet navy lacks distant facilities for refueling, logistical support, and air cover. The relatively few distant bases available to the Soviet fleet from pro-Soviet countries are highly vulnerable to rapid U.S. attrition, while the absence of long-range air cover exposes Soviet naval units to American air attacks from carrier-based jets.

This is not to deny the military significance of the Soviet naval buildup. Rather, it is to argue that its effect would be greatest in a protracted conventional war on one of the three central strategic fronts. The Soviet navy, as currently constituted, has the capacity to interfere significantly with U.S. sea control. It can disrupt — though not interdict — the American ability to sustain any protracted engagement on the Eurasian continent. This gives the Soviet Union an important negative capability — one that can be extremely damaging in a middle-level engagement, greater than a brush fire but less than a conflagration. In a central war, the most important Soviet strategic nuclear weapons are still largely land-based, with Soviet SLBMs merely playing a supportive role. In a remote local conflict, the Soviet navy deployed far from port is vulnerable to direct air attack and to interdiction of its supply lines. Thus, for some

Overall NATO–Warsaw Pact Balance of Conventional Forces

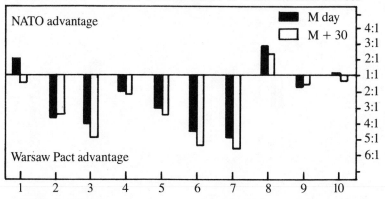

1. All military personnel on active duty
2. Total main battle tanks
3. Other armored vehicles
4. Artillery tubes, multiple rocket launchers, and surface-to-surface missiles
5. Antitank weapons
6. Launchers for surface-to-air missiles
7. Antiaircraft guns
8. Total helicopters
9. Total combat aircraft (fighters/interceptors/bombers)
10. Other aircraft

M day is the day the two sides begin to mobilize their forces; M + 30 is thirty days later

NATO–Warsaw Pact Conventional Balance—Southern Region

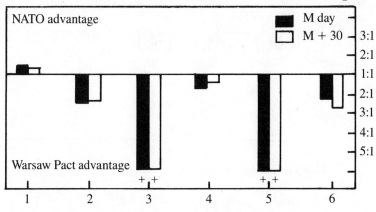

1. Personnel
2. Tanks
3. Other armored vehicles
4. Artillery and multiple rocket launchers
5. Antitank weapons
6. Combat aircraft

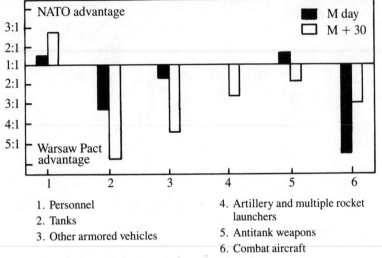

NATO–Warsaw Pact Conventional Balance — Northern Region

NATO advantage

■ M day
□ M + 30

3:1
2:1
1:1
2:1
3:1
4:1
5:1

Warsaw Pact advantage

1 2 3 4 5 6

1. Personnel
2. Tanks
3. Other armored vehicles
4. Artillery and multiple rocket launchers
5. Antitank weapons
6. Combat aircraft

M day is the day the two sides begin to mobilize their forces; M + 30 is thirty days later

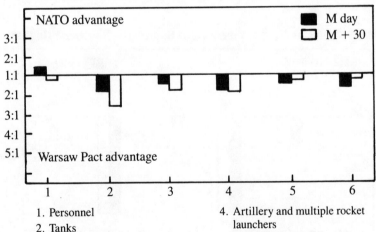

NATO–Warsaw Pact Conventional Balance — Central Region

NATO advantage

■ M day
□ M + 30

3:1
2:1
1:1
2:1
3:1
4:1
5:1

Warsaw Pact advantage

1 2 3 4 5 6

1. Personnel
2. Tanks
3. Other armored vehicles
4. Artillery and multiple rocket launchers
5. Antitank weapons
6. Combat aircraft

1983 Production of Ground Forces Matériel

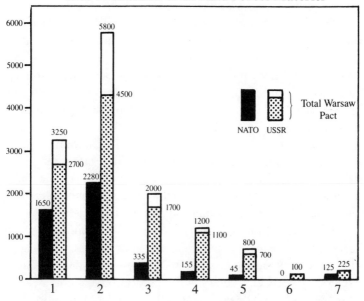

1. Tanks
2. Other armored fighting vehicles
3. Towed field artillery
4. Self-propelled field artillery
5. Multiple rocket launchers
6. Self-propelled AA artillery
7. Towed AA artillery

Source: Information in Department of Defense, *Soviet Military Power 1984*, p. 98

time to come any Soviet forces engaged in a remote local conflict will have to fight at a very decisive logistical disadvantage.

So much for Soviet reach. Soviet clout in conventional forces is manifest along two of the three central strategic fronts. The Far East is relatively secure, barring any unforeseeable developments in South Korea or the Philippines. But on the first and third fronts — Europe and southwest Asia — the balance is shifting gradually in favor of the Soviet Union. At some stage this could invite a more direct use of Soviet power.

On the first front, almost all indicators of military power show a significant Warsaw Pact advantage over NATO in conventional forces. Quite revealing of Moscow's confidence, and possibly its intentions, is the fact that the Warsaw Pact conducts its field maneuvers in an offensive mode, in contrast to NATO, which stresses defensive exercises. The Warsaw Pact enjoys a significant margin of superiority in several key dimensions of conventional power. In 1984, on the central front, the Warsaw Pact led NATO in divisions by 61 to 38; in tanks by 16,020 to 8,050; in artillery and mortars by 16,270 to 4,400; and in fighter-bombers by 1,555 to 1,345. Moreover, Moscow's newly deployed SS-20 missiles have a target range that can cover all Western Europe and the Middle East. The charts summarize the current balance numerically, though obviously such data provide only a most superficial analysis.

The combination of a Soviet conventional military advantage and increasingly capable Soviet strategic forces has given rise to a truly ominous shift in Moscow's military doctrine. Previously, Soviet military writings on conventional warfare have stressed "strategic operations" of relatively short duration, that either quickly terminated or escalated into nuclear conflict. By the early 1980s, however, Soviet military theorists had focused their attention on a "general conventional war" waged on a broad front, and lasting for a protracted period until a Soviet victory without the use of nuclear weapons by either side.

This development highlights an important fact. The key deterrent to a massive Soviet breakthrough is still the nuclear one. It is the danger that a conventional regional war would rapidly escalate into a central strategic engagement that acts as the ultimate restraint on Moscow. Peace still depends on the strategic balance.

Should it deteriorate, the penalty is not necessarily a nuclear war but a higher probability of a conventional one. That could happen in Europe, but it is more likely to occur on the southwestern central strategic front. There, both permanent geographical and transitional political factors could favor the Soviet Union. Political unrest in Iran or Pakistan could even provide openings for an internationally ambiguous intrusion of Soviet forces from close at hand.

In contrast, a U.S. response would have to overcome enormous logistical difficulties, geographical distance, and the probability of inadequate or tenuous political support from adjoining countries. Unlike the first or even the second front, on the third front the United States cannot count on any significant coalition to provide major conventional backing for American efforts to halt a Soviet advance. Some Defense Department studies indicate that in the event of a Soviet attack on Iran the United States could prevent the complete occupation of the country by using the RDF to hold the south and to interdict access routes through the central Zagros mountain range. But the fact remains that in any protracted conventional engagement the Soviet Union would enjoy a considerable advantage. Moreover, the U.S. nuclear deterrent is a less effective restraint in southwestern Asia than in Western Europe. U.S. nuclear forces are already deployed in Europe and their potential use is fully integrated into NATO operational planning. On the third front Soviet military and political planners might calculate that the United States would not dare to escalate a conventional conflict into a nuclear engagement. They might therefore gamble that they could undertake conventional aggression with impunity.

Accordingly, the long-range trend inherent in the growth of overall Soviet military capabilities is toward increased flexibility in the use of its conventional military power in support of its political objectives. Though the West has been preoccupied with Soviet military power during most of the cold war, the fact is that Moscow has been restrained from using it in areas outside of its direct control until the invasion of Afghanistan in 1979. Instead, it has tended to probe with military proxies while refraining from direct engagement itself. That situation is now clearly changing.

In summary form, assuming a continuation of current trends

in U.S. and Soviet defense spending and weapons deployment, Soviet military capabilities today and in ten years can be characterized as follows:

SOVIET MILITARY CAPABILITIES

Strategic Forces

1986	*1996*
No assurance that the United States would be unable to inflict massive destruction on the Soviet Union in the event of a Soviet first strike	A reasonable possibility that a Soviet first strike might be able to disarm the United States to such a degree that a retaliatory response would be fragmentary

Conventional Ground Forces on the Three Central Strategic Fronts

Probability of Soviet success in a purely conventional engagement on the first and third fronts, offset by the possibility of nuclear escalation	Probability of Soviet success with a higher degree of assurance, and a lower likelihood of U.S. nuclear escalation

Conventional Ground Forces in Long-range Force Projection

High vulnerability to conventional attrition by U.S. RDF because of inadequate logistics and vulnerable supply lines	Progressive improvement in capabilities, but probably continued inferiority to U.S. RDF

Naval Forces in Strategic Conflict

Secondary role in strategic conflict	Gradual shift to a significant strategic SLBM and SLCM capability

Naval Forces in Central Conventional Conflict

Soviet capacity for serious, but not conclusive, disruption of U.S. ocean control and of U.S. sustaining efforts on behalf of U.S. forces engaged in conventional conflicts on any one of the three main fronts	No basic change

Naval Forces in Remote Local Conflict

Soviets unable to sustain long-range deployment of ground forces in the event of limited conventional naval collision with the United States	No basic change but progressive expansion in radius of Soviet capability

The answer to the vital questions posed at the outset of this chapter is therefore that during the next ten years the most ominous change for the United States could occur as a consequence of shifts on the strategic level. A deterioration of the strategic balance might affect the American willingness and capacity to deter the use of Soviet conventional forces in geopolitically critical areas proximate to the Soviet Union. American determination to use tactical nuclear weapons in response to a major conventional attack would be undermined if the Soviet Union held a significant advantage in strategic weapons. A decision to escalate to the level of tactical nuclear weapons would depend on whether or not the United States could stop there. That, in turn, would depend on whether or not Washington had the capability to respond effectively to any Soviet nuclear counterescalation without fear of a Soviet first strike on the strategic level. An overall strategic imbalance can thus filter down to undermine the credibility of nuclear escalation as the deterrent of conventional aggression.

In the past, U.S. strategic superiority had the effect of counterbalancing Soviet conventional superiority. The growing U.S. vulnerability to a disarming Soviet strategic first strike changes that. There is now a risk that the nuclear deterrent might no longer dissuade Moscow from launching a conventional aggression in some area contiguous to the Soviet Union. At the very least, there is more probability of successful Soviet political intimidation. At the worst, there is the danger of outright military action. On the wider global scale, however, the Soviet Union will continue to lack the means for assertively projecting its power without regard to a possible U.S. response.

Thus, the principal political effects of the Soviet military buildup are still likely to be felt on the Eurasian landmass, while the main operational military consequence is likely to be greater Soviet flexibility in the use of conventional forces.

Socioeconomic Liabilities

Military power is the *sole* basis for the Soviet Union's status as a global power. In all other respects, the Soviet Union lacks the attributes for that exalted ranking, and in most respects it is not even a truly competitive rival of the United States. In 1960, Nikita Khrushchev, in issuing a ringing challenge to the United States, proclaimed, "We will bury you." Although the U.S. public seized upon this ominous phrase as a menacing forecast of America's destruction, Khrushchev's challenge was based on the belief that in the next two decades the Soviet Union would surpass the United States in social productivity. Indeed, the Soviet leadership was so certain of its imminent historical triumph that it included the forecast of a Soviet economic victory by 1970 as an integral part of the official program of the ruling Communist party — a document meant to provide programmatic guidance for all Soviet Communists.

In the two and a half decades following Khrushchev's prediction, nothing even remotely resembling it came to pass. The gap between the gross national products of the United States and the Soviet Union remained approximately the same in relative terms and increased in absolute terms. The divergence in the per capita standard of living of the two countries also increased. The symbolic race to put a man on the moon — a contest meant to highlight the Soviet claim to technological leadership — ended in an unqualified American victory. Perhaps most important of all, the already yawning qualitative gap in scientific-technological innovation widened still further to America's advantage. By the mid-1980s, the United States, followed closely by Japan, was plunging headlong into the technetronic age, while the Soviet Union was still struggling to make its relatively conventional industrial economy more efficient and modern. In 1960, the Soviet Union seemed to the world to be poised to challenge America's global economic-technological leadership. By 1985, the Soviet Union was widely perceived to be nothing more than one of the most advanced of the world's developing societies.

That perception was magnified by the continued inefficiency of the highly centralized and massively bureaucratized Soviet economy. That system literally required an explicit political decision at the highest Politburo level for any nonmilitary, primarily consumer-oriented product to be produced economically and with a degree of respect for quality. For example, in the spring of 1985, the Soviet mass media publicized a Politburo directive to the effect that shoes for the Soviet public ought to meet minimum standards for wear and tear as well as style. Such incredible overconcentration of authority created bottlenecks that all periodic reform drives and all calls for higher efficiency seemed helpless to overcome.

The global awareness of these kinds of systemic shortcomings certainly detracted from the Soviet Union's status as America's principal rival. Even more troubling for the Kremlin was the growing recognition that these shortcomings were deeply embedded in the Soviet system, with communism clearly failing to provide a historical shortcut to socioeconomic success. Still worse, it was more generally recognized that Soviet performance over the years required social sacrifice altogether disproportionate to the system's actual achievements. Perhaps never before in history has such a gifted people, in control of such abundant resources, labored so hard for so long to produce so little.

Comparative studies of socioeconomic development, such as Professor Cyril Black's "Soviet Society: A Comparative View" (1968), show that after fifty years of communism the Soviet Union was no higher in the world rankings of social and economic indexes than it was at the beginning of this century. Black's conclusion was that:

In the perspective of fifty years, the comparative rankings of the USSR in composite economic and social indices per capita has probably not changed significantly. So far as the rather limited available evidence permits a judgment, the USSR has not overtaken or surpassed any country on a per capita basis since 1917 with the possible exception of Italy, and the nineteen or twenty countries that rank higher than Russia today in this regard also ranked higher in 1900 and 1919. The per capita gross national product of Italy, which is just below that of the USSR today, was probably somewhat higher fifty years ago.

In fact, in recent years Italy also has outstripped the Soviet Union in most per capita indicators. Other studies have produced similarly grim findings. In a 1981 report, Professor Gertrude Schroeder of the University of Virginia concluded that the Soviet consumption standard "in many respects conforms to that in the less developed countries, and remarkably little progress toward a more modern pattern has been made in recent decades."

In other words, the sustained social deprivation that every Soviet citizen has experienced yielded results at best merely comparable to those achieved by other societies at much smaller social cost. The Soviet Union, moreover, would have been expected to grow comparatively faster after World War II because it had the initial statistical advantage of recovering from an artificially low plateau generated by wartime devastation. In 1950, the Soviet GNP accounted for about 11 percent of the world economy; three decades later it still constitutes 11 percent. It is no wonder that Soviet propagandists now prefer not to recall Khrushchev's challenge of 1960 "to surpass the United States" in absolute production by 1970 and in relative per capita production by 1980.

The picture is just as bleak in the social and cultural dimensions of Soviet life. Recent studies point to a globally unprecedented decline in Soviet male longevity from 66 years in 1965 to approximately 62 years in 1982. Soviet infant mortality has also dramatically worsened, reaching the level of 40 per 1,000 births, a figure three times as high as that of the West and comparable to those of the less-developed countries. Mortality from heart disease doubled between 1960 and 1980. In recent years, Soviet consumers have been spending approximately 17 percent of their household money on alcohol, in contrast to between 1 and 6 percent in the United States and other Western countries. In 1985, the Soviet government initiated a massive antialcoholism campaign, but it is doubtful that it will be able to overcome deeply inbred habits as well as the related absence of satisfying social outlets. Over the last several decades, intellectual and artistic life has been stifled, and spontaneous social innovation has been shackled by bureaucratic inertia.

The overall result is both ideological decay at home and the loss of revolutionary appeal abroad. Internally, the Soviet Union has become characterized by rote and doctrine expressed through the endless repetition of slogans. Ideological cynicism and political opportunism have become rampant. Dedication to shaping a more just society has come to be replaced by self-serving official mendacity; the rigidities of the system are oiled in daily life by a pervasive corruption that permeates the entire ruling bureaucracy. If faith in the future can be said to have characterized Soviet Communists under Lenin, and if Spartan dedication generated by massive fear can be said to have been the dominant feature under Stalin, the Soviet officialdom in recent years has become largely motivated by the quest for personal privilege, with political power the principal avenue to a discreetly camouflaged good life. As a consequence, the Soviet Union no longer projects worldwide an appealing image, a condition essential to the exercise of global leadership.

To the world at large, the Soviet Union is no longer the model it has been at times for some countries and for many revolutionary movements on several continents. There was a time when revolutionaries saw in the Soviet Union a truly successful experiment embodying a tested method for achieving both modernity and social justice. By the 1980s, there literally was no revolutionary movement around the world that proclaimed in its program that it intended to emulate the Soviet Union. Worse than that, some foreign Communist parties deliberately disassociated themselves from the Soviet experience, realizing that not to do so would be costly in popular support. Political leaders most hostile to the United States, such as Libya's Colonel Muammar Qaddafi, have become allied with the Soviet Union, not because of shared ideology or because the Soviet Union provides an attractive model, but simply because they think Soviet power is helpful in offsetting the United States. Permanent ideological affiliation has given way to transient political convenience as the principal motive for friendship with the Soviet Union.

Worse still for the Kremlin, the prospects of the Soviet leadership being able to overcome this handicap in the foreseeable future are relatively slim. Three interrelated conditions serve to perpetuate the negative aspects of the Soviet system. There is, first, the multinational character of the Soviet state. It is based on Great Russian preponderance and is, in effect, a Russian state. Although the official myth is that Russia is only one of the constituent Soviet republics, in an unguarded moment even the top Soviet leader, Mikhail Gorbachev, revealed the true feelings of the dominant Russian elite when in June 1985 he blurted out in a public meeting in the Ukrainian capital city of Kiev, "For all people who are striving for good, Russia, I mean the Soviet Union, I mean — that is what we call it now, and what it is in fact — for them it is a bulwark."

To decentralize an empire is to dismantle it. The Russian elite instinctively senses that any significant decentralization, even if initially confined to the economic realm, would strengthen the potentially separatist aspirations of the non-Russians inhabiting the Soviet Union. Economic decentralization would inevitably mean political decentralization, and political decentralization could become the stepping-stone to national emancipation. Russian anxieties on this score must be heightened by demographic trends. They indicate a decline in the dominant position of the Great Russians. During the 1970s the Russians ceased being the majority of the Soviet people, and a further shrinking of the Russian plurality is inevitable. In 1980 Soviet eighteen-year-olds were 48 percent Russian, 19 percent other Slavic, 13 percent Muslim, with 20 percent listed as "other." The projection for 1990 is that the figures will be 43 percent Russian, 18 percent other Slavic, 20 percent Muslim, and 19 percent "other."

In the longer run, the political aspirations of the non-Russians represent the Achilles' heel of the Soviet Union. The very existence of these non-Russian nations prevents a positive evolution of the Soviet Union toward a more modern system. And the non-Russians could over time become politically more active, especially if encouraged by the outside world. To the Muslims, the existence today of independent Islamic nations, some of them undergoing an intensive religious revival, is bound to be infectious. To the Ukrainians, who number about 50 million and whose country would rank high among European nations if it were independent, their continued submission to Moscow must be a source of increasing frustration. Yet to the Russians a genuinely far-reaching decentralization of the Soviet system, even if only economic, would pose a mortal danger to their imperial control. After all, what does "only economic" decentralization mean in political terms insofar as the Soviet Union is concerned? It would have to mean a greater degree of autonomy for the non-Russians, who would then be in a position to translate greater economic self-determination into growing political self-determination.

To most Great Russians, that is a highly threatening prospect. Any significant national self-assertion on the part of the non-Russians constitutes a challenge to Russian territorial preeminence and could possibly even pose a biological threat to Great Russian national survival. Where would genuine Soviet decentralization, the acceptance of more democratic norms, the institutionalization of pluralism, eventually lead? Where, indeed, could one even draw proper lines between the Great Russians and the others, given the intermingling of the recent decades? Tensions would escalate. Head-on conflicts might erupt in a variety of areas — in some of the Baltic republics heavily settled by unwelcome Great Russians, in the culturally commingled areas of Byelorussia and the Ukraine, and certainly on the fringes of the Caucasian and central Asian republics.

The dismantling of the overseas British and French empires did not have to mean the end of either Britain or France. The dismantling of the territorially contiguous Great Russian empire would threaten Russia itself, given the absence of natural frontiers. The difficulties the French faced in Algeria would be dwarfed on the peripheries of the purely Great Russian lands. Any attempted disentangling along national lines would be messy and bloody. Awareness of that prospect makes almost every Great Russian instinctively wary of tolerating any significant devolution of Moscow's central control. The instinct for survival gives the autocratic, highly centralized, and imperial Soviet system unusual staying power. It neutralizes the kind of inner self-doubt and imperial fatigue that induced the British and French to accede to the dismantling of their empires. But it also perpetuates an inefficient and a wasteful and socially stultifying system of dictatorship.

There is a second influence reinforcing the Great Russian inclination to maintain the centralized, even if inefficient, system: the progressive militarization of the Soviet state and society. As ideology wanes, the military ethos, with its traditional Russian nationalism, becomes the major political cement holding the country together. With military power providing the primary claim to Soviet global status, the military elite is in a favored position to make its claim felt, and the military favors a centralized state. Only such a state can provide for the needs of the military and justify the massive expenditures on the military's behalf.

These expenditures are socially destructive, especially if maintained at the high levels of the last two decades. For a still deprived and relatively backward society, annual military expenditures that consume approximately 15 percent of the GNP are an enormous burden. Moreover, Soviet cost accounting, based on an arbitrary price structure, favors the military sector so greatly that in fact the social costs of military expenditures may be considerably higher. (Since the percentage of Soviet GNP devoted to military expenditure is a little more than twice that of the U.S. and the Soviet GNP is only slightly more than half that of the U.S., the military burden for the Soviet citizenry is approximately four times as heavy as for the considerably richer Americans.)

The high priority assigned to military power not only reinforces centralism. It also induces a society-wide emphasis on military training and military indoctrination. This is corrosive. As Arnold Toynbee wrote in *A Study of History* (1947), "militarism . . . has been by far the commonest cause of the breakdowns of civilizations during the last four or five millennia which have witnessed the score or so of breakdowns that are on record up to the present date. Militarism breaks a civilization down by causing the local states into which the society is articulated to collide with one another in destructive fratricidal conflicts. In this suicidal process the entire social fabric becomes fuel to feed the devouring flame in the brazen bosom of Moloch."

The third factor perpetuating socioeconomic liabilities is the Communist tradition itself. Over the years, that tradition has become a web of vested interests, all with a stake in a centralized and bureaucratized system. Indeed, had the Soviet Union not been Communist, it is quite likely that the country's socioeconomic development might have been more substantial, more balanced, and more beneficial to the public. Studies in comparative development, including some on Russia's rates of growth prior to the Bolshevik Revolution, certainly suggest this.

It was the Stalinist collectivization that ruined Soviet agriculture. It was the Leninist-Stalinist concept of the dictatorship of the proletariat that resulted in the mass murder of several million of the most able Soviet citizens. It is the Leninist-Stalinist legacy that continues to choke Soviet social creativity today.

Yet in the long run, unless military means prove historically decisive, it is social creativity that will determine the outcome of the American-Soviet contest. The scientific and technological capacity of the two systems, including military power, is ultimately based on creative innovation. This in turn is a function of social and political organization rather than of individual talent. Both countries have talent in quantity. It is the use that is made of it that is crucial. In a paradoxical sense, for America, communism in Russia has been a historical blessing because it has locked the immensely gifted and patient Russian people into a system that stifles, squanders, and sacrifices their great potential.

A World Power of a New Type

The Communist experience has thus made the Soviet Union into a world power of a new type: its might is one-dimensional. The result is that the Soviet Union is essentially incapable of sustaining effective global dominance. It is neither a genuine economic rival to the United States nor — as once was the case — even a source of a globally interesting ideological experiment. This condition imposes a decisive limitation on the Soviet capability to act in a manner traditional to world powers or claimants to the status of a world power.

Traditionally, both the dominant world military power and its principal rival have possessed comparable political and socioeconomic systems, each with the capability for sustained and comprehensive preeminence. From the late Middle Ages, naval power has been the central instrument for exercising global military reach. To the extent that such global reach can be said to have existed in the age of slow communications and limited weaponry, the powers exercising it and their principal rivals were — broadly speaking — Portugal and Spain during much of the sixteenth century; the Netherlands and France during the seventeenth century; Britain, then France, and later Germany during the eighteenth, nineteenth, and part of the twentieth centuries; and finally the United States and the Soviet Union during the second half of the twentieth century. In all cases except the most recent one, the contest was between powers at a comparable level of development. The rival was quite capable of supplementing a military challenge with commercial and political leadership; it could offer leadership that was equally comprehensive. The Soviet Union offers only a military challenge.

The picture for Moscow is even more bleak if the performance of the Soviet Union and its bloc is compared with that of the United States and its principal friends. Neither the Soviet Union nor its bloc even comes close to matching the socioeconomic capacity of the United States alone, so the industrialized democracies are a bonus. In almost every quantifiable indicator of socioeconomic development, the Soviet camp is simply dwarfed in absolute terms and even more so when it comes to qualitative and innovative aspects.

The combined GNP of the United States, the European Economic Community, and Japan in 1983 came to approximately $7,094 billion, while that of the Soviet Union and Eastern Europe was only $2,566 billion. This absolute gap has widened since 1975, when the figures were $5,431 billion and $2,185 billion, respectively. Moreover, in terms of more specific indicators of socioeconomic development, the Soviet world remains strikingly retarded in comparison to the technologically advanced democracies, as the following table shows.

SOCIOECONOMIC INDEXES, 1983

	U.S.	EEC	Japan	USSR	E. Eur.
Per Capita GNP	14,120	8,450	9,700	6,765	6,520
INDUSTRY					
Primary energy (million b/d oil equivalent)	30.8	11.4	1.2	29.2	6.5
Electricity (billion kilowatt-hours)	2,459	1,260	603	1,416	445
Crude steel (million metric tons)	75.6	112	97.2	153	57.4
TRADE					
Exports (billion U.S. $)	200.5 (1981)	590 (1982)	147	91.6	96.2
Imports (billion U.S. $)	269.9	615.9 (1982)	126.4	80.4	91.0
INDICATORS OF LIVING STANDARDS					
Grain production (kilograms per capita)	890	460	120	715	760
Meat production (kilograms per capita)	107	83	27	59	92
Energy consumption (barrels of oil equivalent per capita, 1982)	55	25	21	32	28
Automobile registrations (units per 1,000 persons)	538 (1982)	321 (1981)	209 (1981)	35 (1981)	88 (1981)
Telephones in use (units per 1,000 persons)	791 (1979)	413 (1979)	476 (1979)	84 (1979)	115 (1978)

Even more revealing — and of even greater significance for the future — is the relative absence of innovation in Soviet industry. In computers and robotics, the Soviet Union and Eastern Europe are just not in the race.

The failure to develop and assimilate technologies on the cutting edge of scientific innovation is characteristic of the Soviet Union. Anthony C. Sutton, in his study *Western Technology and Soviet Economic Development,* examined seventy-six

HIGH TECH GAP
Computer Systems Installed (1983)

	U.S.	EEC	Japan	USSR	E. Eur.
Large/medium computers	96,500	23,400	16,900	3,040	n.a.
(per million pop.)	412	135	142	11	
Small computers	1,000,000	240,000	70,000	22,000	n.a.
(per million pop.)	4,273	1,387	588	80	
Industrial Robots (1981)*	44,700	51,877	67,435	3,000	890
(per million pop.)	196	201	571	11	17

*W. Germany, France, and U.K. only.
(SOURCE: Robot Institute of America)

key processes in fourteen major Soviet industrial sectors over three periods (1917–1930, 1930–1945, 1945–1965) and determined the national origin of each technology. He concluded that virtually all Soviet industrial technology is imported. From 1917 to 1930, there was no Soviet technological innovation to speak of. There were several attempts to produce innovations — synthetic rubber, tractors, and a few others — but these failed. From 1930 to 1945, the Soviets continued basic research but essentially abandoned industrial innovation. There were exceptions — particularly in weapons designs — but the Soviet economy was basically a copy of Western ones. From 1945 to 1965, the Soviets did come up with a few innovations, although, Sutton stated, "the hypothesis that there has been an absence of self-generated innovation is generally supported."

Sutton produced a table in which he detailed the origins of the technology the Soviets have been using in the seventy-six key industrial processes he studied. By recalculating what percentage came from which countries, one obtains the following results:

	1917–1930	1930–1945	1945–1965
Soviet Union	0	6	7
Tsarist Russia	7	1	0
United States	24	41	25
Germany	24	15	15
United Kingdom	6	7	11
France	2	2	7
Others	17	16	19
Not Available	20	12	16

A country that imports its technology must by necessity consistently lag behind those that export technology. This is the case with the Soviet Union.

Such comparative data make it difficult to conceive of the Soviet Union ever "winning" the historical competition by peaceful means. It could do so only if it detached Western Europe and Japan from the United States and was able to commandeer Western Europe's or Japan's economic resources. But such a massive turnaround in global arrangements could hardly be achieved by Moscow without heavy reliance on its military power. Otherwise, the Soviet Union is simply not a sufficiently attractive economic partner to entice either Western Europe or Japan into political subordination, nor is its social system sufficiently magnetic to gain the loyalty of the youth, the restlessly creative, or even the poor of Western Europe or Japan.

In essence, the unique character of the one-dimensional Soviet global challenge is that the Soviet Union is manifestly unequipped to provide constructive and sustained leadership if somehow it should by military leverage succeed in unseating the United States as the number-one world power. The Soviet Union could not provide global financial leadership. Its economy could not act as the locomotive for global development and technological innovation. Its mass culture has no wider appeal; its leading intellectuals and artists have been steadily fleeing the Soviet Union. American global displacement could not be followed by a Soviet global replacement.

Domination and Disruption

This condition has several consequences for Soviet grand strategy. It magnifies the traditional Russian and doctrinaire Communist suspicions of the outside world. The world is perceived as bent on dismantling Moscow's empire and on promoting an anti-Communist counterrevolution. Though the Soviets take great pride in their military prowess, and have used it to claim coequal status with the United States, in the Soviet perception of the world the United States looms as a giant, with its finances, communications, and mass media enveloping the world with many tentacles. American technology (currently, for instance, microelectronics) keeps on providing the U.S. military establishment with new capabilities that the Soviets regard gravely. In the Far East, there looms the potential for a Chinese-Japanese constellation, while in the West there is always the magnetic pull on Eastern Europe of a Europe that has not fully resigned itself to an indefinite post-Yalta division.

All this enhances Soviet paranoia. It also generates an erratic pattern of accommodation and competition with the United States. On the one hand, the Soviets seek to attain a transitional condominium with Washington. On the other hand, they fear becoming locked in the role of the junior partner, in effect committed to the maintenance of the global status quo. Moscow rejects this, for it not only would perpetuate American preponderance but — in Soviet eyes — it would also serve as the point of departure for policies designed to promote "peaceful evolution" of a contained Soviet Union — that is, its political subversion.

The rejection of the status quo enhances the importance of military power; it is all that Moscow has to protect what it has and hopes to acquire. It hopes that steady military pressure may over time wear down some of America's principal allies and cause a progressive shift in their orientation. Eventually, Moscow calculates, this could cause a more basic realignment in the global balance of power, detaching from the United States the countries that so decisively enhance America's socioeconomic superiority. At the same time, Moscow's military might ensures that no outside power will be able to undermine Soviet domination over the countries that became Soviet dependencies in the aftermath of World War II.

The promotion of regional conflicts, the inhibition of supranational cooperation, and opposition to what is called "world order" are all strategies that the Kremlin finds compatible with its own one-dimensional military power. That power permits Moscow to play a wide role in keeping with the Soviet imperial consciousness. It reduces the fear that regional conflicts could precipitate a head-on collision with the United States. It enables the Soviet Union to undermine American preeminence in areas hitherto considered to be U.S. safe havens. Particularly important and effective in this respect is Moscow's superior capacity to satisfy clients by prompt delivery from its large inventories of huge amounts of military equipment.

Yet military supplies aside, the Soviet capacity to influence developments in the third world is quite limited. For example, when the self-proclaimed Marxist-Leninist and highly pro-Soviet regime of Ethiopia was faced with a massive famine in 1985, the Soviet Union could provide only 7,500 tons of cereal food aid. The United States provided 3,075,000 tons, the EEC 1,780,000 tons. Even China sent 155,000. The meager Soviet aid was in keeping with the scandalously low levels of economic assistance provided by the Soviet Union to third-world countries. In 1982, the Organization for Economic Cooperation and Development (OECD) members extended $27,900 million in net aid disbursements to the developing countries. The Soviet contribution was only $2,400 million. Almost all of it went to pro-Communist developing states.

Moscow is thus discovering that global military reach is not the same as global political grasp. The Soviet Union has not yet been able to translate its increased military capabilities into enduring political benefits. The Soviet Union has become the major military supplier of the third world, but that world has shifted away from its earlier fascination with rapid industrialization (for which the Soviet Union might have served as a model). It has a growing interest in the scientific-technological revolution, in terms of both agriculture and high technology. In neither case is the Soviet experience relevant or helpful. Countries such as India and Algeria are turning to the United States for assistance and closer economic cooperation.

The Soviet leaders doubtless derive satisfaction that their global military power has politically outflanked the U.S. policy of geographic containment in Eurasia. Yet this has been achieved only at a cost and with risk. By expanding its military reach at a time when its own capacities are still very one-dimensional, the Soviet Union is exposing itself to the possibility of overextension and potentially to disaster in some premature military-political misadventure. In that respect Moscow's strategy of deliberate exploitation of global turbulence could turn out to be a case of playing with fire.

It certainly is a striking paradox that the world's domestically most reactionary power is actively promoting global revolutionary upheavals, while the world's domestically most dynamic power is basically striving to prop up the global status quo. Moscow may feel that it has no alternative. It can disrupt but not dominate. The desire to upset those conditions that reinforce American paramountcy is in part the inevitable product of frustration at its inability to compete with the United States on a broad front. Military leverage is an inadequate compensation. Domination through military means, and expansion by military means, is a policy that requires an inordinate commitment of resources. It also calls for prudence and patience. With Soviet ideological and economic appeal declining steadily since its high-water mark in the late 1950s, the Soviet Union has had to find some additional means for waging the global competition in a manner that imposes severe costs on its principal rival. Gradually, in the course of the 1960s, that alternative strategy emerged, and it has involved the embrace by the Soviet Union of international terrorism.

One must assume that such a development did not occur all at once and that it was grounded in deep analysis. From Soviet writings and speeches on international affairs, one derives the impression that in the 1950s Soviet leaders expected that developments in the third world would prompt new nations to adopt the political forms and the socioeconomic system derived largely from the Soviet experience. History was seen as tipping in the Soviet Union's favor; ''the world revolution'' was indeed to be achieved by massive global transformation. This was the era of high Soviet optimism, expressed eventually in Khrushchev's misguided challenge to the United States.

The years have disappointed these hopes and prompted a more basic reassessment. In the course of the 1960s, Moscow shifted its analysis away from its ideological hopes toward the grim conclusion that much of that world is faced by massive upheavals, and huge populations mired in poverty. Violent disintegration rather than successful imitation of the Soviet path came to be seen as the more likely prospect for the future. The population explosion in the developing world created the need for at least 700 million new jobs between the years 1980 and 2000. Some 300 million people in these countries were already underemployed or unemployed (about 40 percent of the total work force). The scenario was for violent disintegration and political radicalization. Ethnic conflicts, religious fanaticism, and social passions all augured attrition of world order.

It was in this larger context of felt opportunity and gnawing awareness of their own inadequacy that Soviet leaders came to adopt international terrorism as a useful tactic for disrupting an international system still dominated largely by the United States.

Though the Soviet Union occasionally did rely on individual acts of terrorism to promote its interests — for example, the assassination of Leon Trotsky in 1940 — it was not until the mid-1960s that it developed a more extensive role in international terrorist organizations and activities. Soviet spending in support of such activities shot up, while in January 1966 Fidel Castro convened, with enthusiastic Soviet support, the so-called Tricontinental Congress, embracing more than eighty groups from the third world, some of which were actively involved in international terrorism. The congress endorsed the principle of close cohesion between "the socialist countries" and all the various radical movements working actively to disrupt the status quo.

Shortly thereafter, a chain of training camps for terrorists was opened in the Soviet Union as well as in several East European countries controlled by Moscow, notably East Germany, Bulgaria, and Czechoslovakia, as well as in Cuba. Defectors from terrorist groups have identified the location of the main training camps in the Soviet Union as Batum, Baku, Simferopol, Tashkent, and Odessa, and these camps are typically run by KGB personnel. In 1968, the alumni of some of these camps engaged in a wave of terrorist attacks throughout the Middle East, South America, and Western Europe. By 1971, Soviet leaders had begun to articulate more openly their support of terrorist activities. Boris Ponomarev, the senior Soviet official responsible for international Communist affairs, developed the proposition that even though such activities are often undertaken by "various types of adventuristic elements, including Maoists and Trotskyites," they do represent objectively an effort to undermine Western capitalism, and therefore to neglect them would be "to weaken the anti-imperialist struggle. . . ."

Soviet-backed terrorist activity has been targeted against several vulnerable countries closely allied with the United States. Turkey, Italy, and West Germany became the objects of disruptive terrorist activity, in each case with strong circumstantial evidence suggesting support from a Soviet-dominated East European country. A major effort to destabilize Turkey — which at one point involved, according to official Turkish estimates, as many as 60,000–70,000 subversives — was apparently backed by funds and arms from Bulgaria. A corresponding, though more modest, effort to destabilize Italy in the mid-1970s enjoyed support from Czechoslovakia. Funds and arms flowed from there and so did broadcasts from an ostensibly underground red radio station. East Germany became active in training terrorist groups in advanced security and countersecurity techniques. It provided an emergency safe house for the Baader-Meinhoff Gang. It has established an elaborate system for getting fugitives in and out of West Germany. Finally, Cuba has provided support for the Sandinista revolution in Nicaragua and subsequently for at least some of the radical elements in El Salvador.

Outside of the Soviet bloc itself, Libya, Syria, and Southern Yemen, in each case with professional Soviet or East European support, have provided refuge and training for terrorists from a variety of groups, such as the West German Red Army Faction, the Italian Red Brigades, the Japanese Red Army, the Basque separatists, the Turkish Liberation Army, the Argentinian Monteneros, the Brazilian Vangarda, the Popular Front of the Arabian Peninsula, the South Saharan Polisario Front, Egyptian and Tunisian extremists, the IRA Provisionals, and so forth.

The Soviet objective in all this is the attrition of global order — which is a target because it is seen as reinforcing American primacy. It is essentially a long-term diversionary strategy, not geared to immediate gains but rather designed to promote erosion on the flanks, while Soviet military-political pressure is applied on the central front. But it is also a strategy derived from a sense of weakness. It implicitly acknowledges an incapacity to provide an effective substitute for American preponderance. It thereby unmasks the historical significance of the contest. A Soviet triumph over the United States as a result of some strategic breakthrough on the Eurasian continent would be less likely to create enduring Soviet hegemony and more likely to promote global chaos.

U.S.–Soviet Scenarios: The Next Ten Years

This threat assessment is not meant to be a catalog of Soviet strengths and weaknesses. Its data are designed to provide a base for gauging the dynamics of the great historical rivalry with America. It has focused on those elements most critical for Soviet conduct, and it has set the stage for an outline of the needed geopolitical and strategic response from the United States. That response has to be designed to meet the thrust of Soviet policy but it also has to take into account a number of crises or changes that could occur in the U.S.–Soviet relationship.

The twelve scenarios below look to the next decade. They are not predictions but possibilities. More than one could transpire within the same time frame. They are enumerated in order of their discontinuity from the existing situation: the first is the one that involves the greatest departure from the present. Yet all of them are possibilities inherent in the U.S.–Soviet global rivalry.

(1) A central nuclear war. Given the suicidal character of a massive nuclear exchange, such a central strategic war is likely to take place only in the event that an American escalation of a conventional conflict and a Soviet counterescalation spiral out of control, or in the event that the Kremlin decides it has obtained the military capability to disarm through a first strike the U.S. strategic retaliatory response.

(2) A large-scale decentralization of the Soviet Union that produces a more creative and productive society, ideologically more pluralistic, with China and Eastern Europe (including

Yugoslavia) forming a closer and basically voluntary relationship with Moscow, which consequently would make the Soviet Union a more formidable and less one-dimensional global rival. Such a development would require a fundamental change in the way the Soviet Union is governed, including the eventual fading away of the ruling Communist party and the emergence of alternative sources of decision making and of societal innovation. It would be a change amounting to nothing short of a political revolution or transformation. And even then, it is far from certain that such a Soviet Union could attract into a close relationship its nationally suspicious and sensitive Communist neighbors.

(3) A broad U.S.–Soviet détente and enduring reconciliation on the basis of the global status quo. An accommodation of this sort would require, not only a truly basic change in the way America and Russia perceive each other, but also a far greater quiescence on the global scene and within their respective imperial domains. It would require restraint in the face of tempting openings for political expansion, a wide-ranging and fully verifiable termination of the arms race, and a fading of imperial national impulses.

(4) A conventional war on the first central strategic front, with the United States accommodating itself to a conventional defeat in Western Europe. The Soviet Union could undertake such a military operation only if truly confident that two basic preconditions had been attained: (1) conventional superiority to a degree that predetermines the outcome of a conflict, and (2) massive nuclear superiority to a degree that totally inhibits any U.S. nuclear response, including one with nuclear weapons already deployed in Europe and integrated into NATO operational doctrine.

(5) An explosion in one of the globe's two incendiary regions (the Middle East or southern Africa), including a local U.S.–Soviet collision, with the United States prevailing mili-

tarily. The Soviet Union might be tempted to intervene militarily in either conflict, though more likely in the Middle East, but it would risk defeat at the hands of the U.S. RDF — unless Soviet nuclear superiority were to inhibit American determination to deny the Soviet Union a free military hand in such sensitive regions.

(6) An emergence of a fourth central strategic front on the Rio Grande. Such a prospect depends less on Soviet actions and more on the degree to which Mexico's internal problems are mismanaged by the Mexicans and then worsened by clumsy U.S. reactions. The transformation of such internal upheaval into a fourth U.S.–Soviet front would probably also require some established Soviet logistical and military presence in Central America as a springboard.

(7) A gradual socioeconomic decay in the Soviet Union and progressive emancipation of Eastern Europe from Soviet control in the context of larger all-European cooperation. Such emancipation would also be dependent on the emergence in Western Europe of a greater sense of shared political purpose, one that would encourage the West Europeans to take advantage of Soviet decay to forge more binding ties with their East European brethren.

(8) A conventional war on the third central strategic front, with the United States accommodating itself to conventional defeat in the Persian Gulf. The Soviet Union may replicate here the Afghan experience. First it would destabilize its southern neighbors politically and then move militarily on the presumption that the U.S. response required by the Carter Doctrine would not lead to nuclear escalation.

(9) An explosion in one of the globe's two incendiary regions (the Middle East or southern Africa), with no U.S.–Soviet military collision but extensive regional expansion of Soviet political influence. Any regional conflict in the Middle East or southern Africa inevitably increases political openings for

the Soviet Union — though Soviet incapacity to provide militarily decisive aid might work against the effective Soviet exploitation of such political opportunities.

(10) A fragmentation of either Iran or Pakistan, with Soviet political influence established on the Persian Gulf. Such influence could be attained primarily as a consequence of political fragmentation, in part purposely encouraged by the Soviets, and then as a result of gradual intrusion of Soviet military forces.

(11) A transformation of much of Western Europe into states that are neutralist in substance but not in form, with U.S. influence declining and Soviet rising. The emergence of such de facto neutralism would most likely be a piecemeal process, with gradual separation of the European nations from the United States on non-European issues and with West Germany increasingly accommodating itself to Soviet foreign policy requirements as a price for obtaining greater all-German social intercourse.

(12) A continuation of present trends: the Soviet Union decays economically, remains frozen politically but powerful militarily, jealously protecting its decaying empire in Eastern Europe, without any major change in the relationship with the United States and with continued competition on the three central strategic fronts. This involves a continuing national rivalry that remains essentially unchanged — a prospect most easy to assimilate intellectually, though history teaches us to expect sudden discontinuities.

The threat assessment, as well as this list of possible scenarios, provides an appropriate point of departure for the definition of what U.S. policy should be. The task for such policy must be to avoid the most dangerous scenarios and to promote the most desirable ones — all the while bearing in mind that the Soviet Union is like a giant with steel hands but rotten innards. It can crush in its grip weaker opponents but a spreading corrosion is eating away at its system.

V

U.S. Strategic Imperatives

A SINGLE central consequence stems from the nature of the Soviet challenge: once its military power is checked, the Soviet Union ceases to be a historically threatening rival. Accordingly, American strategy's first task is to prevent the Soviet Union from using military force to advance its offensive objectives. Once the United States has done that, it will be in the position to pursue more constructive goals designed to temper the more hostile manifestations of the U.S.–Soviet rivalry and even to prompt a contraction of the bloated Soviet empire.

To neutralize Soviet military power, the United States must maintain a military capability sufficient (1) to negate any Soviet effort to intimidate countries in which the United States has a security stake; (2) to block Soviet attempts to use its own forces or those of its proxies to expand the scope of its political control; (3) to deprive the Kremlin leaders of the certainty of a quick conventional victory on any one of the three central Eurasian strategic fronts and to increase their uncertainty regarding possible U.S. nuclear escalation in the event of such a war; (4) to counter at all levels of nuclear escalation the Soviet Union's strategic war-fighting capability; (5) to maintain a secure nuclear retaliatory force capable of inflicting massive devastation on Soviet society even after a Soviet first strike directed at U.S. strategic forces.

Each of these five strategic imperatives is essential to preserve peace between the United States and the Soviet Union and to prevent a decisive shift of the world balance of power in Moscow's favor. This, in turn, requires that U.S. military power satisfy several criteria. It must have political credibility to reassure allies and friends. That means it must be physically adequate to protect them if they are threatened or attacked and politically sufficient to demonstrate American will. It must be flexible enough for use in varying geopolitical, climatic, and logistical settings, often in areas remote from the United States. Its conventional forces must be strong enough to deny the Soviets a rapid victory in an intense nonnuclear engagement. Its tactical nuclear weaponry must be integrated into U.S. operational plans to such a degree that Soviet military strategists cannot confidently expect to be able to disaggregate on Soviet terms conventional and nuclear warfare. But to make the threat of escalation credible, the United States must have nuclear forces that can survive a Soviet first strike. It must be able to employ them at levels ranging from the tactical to the strategic, selectively at a large variety of targets, and over protracted periods of time.

In effect, the United States must maintain an integrated military capability for surface, sea, and space combat as the prerequisite for an enduring and consuming *political* contest for earth control. In the globally decisive struggle for Eurasia, America and the Soviet Union have been aware of three fundamental geostrategic facts. First, only through oceanic domination has the United States been able to deny the vital peripheries of the central Eurasian landmass to its dominant state, the Soviet Union. Second, if the Soviet Union were to control the entire central Eurasian landmass, it could effectively contest U.S. control of the Atlantic and the Pacific. Third, if the Soviet Union were to achieve oceanic domination, it would turn the United States into an isolated and increasingly vulnerable fortress America. Moscow would then be able to exploit anti-American national sentiments even in the Western Hemisphere itself, on the very peripheries of the United States.

Over the last thirty years, however, the American-Soviet contest has acquired a further, potentially decisive dimension. Surface and sea control have become dependent on control of space. Indeed, to the foregoing three key geostrategic propositions, a fourth must now be added: the power that dominates space can thereby dominate both the earth's surface and its seas. The struggle for space is the successor to the earlier struggles for the sea. In previous national rivalries, the power that ruled the seas controlled access to the continents, which led to mastery over the littoral and eventually even to domination of the continents themselves. In our age, military control over space is similarly becoming a potential source of decisive leverage for exacting geopolitical compliance on earth. Indeed, given the massive destructive power than can be leveled against earth targets with nuclear weapons, ultimate preponderance in space is likely to be far more critical than naval supremacy ever was. And domination of space can be rapidly translated into fundamental geopolitical gains on earth. Not to acquiesce in political demands from the power that exercises preponderance in space would be to invite destruction without the means for retaliation. In essence, unlike land wars but like naval combat, the contest in space is not so much for spoils as for decisive strategic leverage.

The United States must make certain that the Soviet Union does not win it. Conceivably, ironclad U.S.–Soviet arrangements might preclude the deployment in space of both offensive and defensive systems; such agreements would have to be integrally linked to an equally binding and mutually stabilizing limit on the deployment of earth-based but space-traversing offensive weaponry. Without this the United States will have to take two actions. First, it should acquire the capability to wage a conflict confined purely to space (on the analogy with sea battles of the past) so as to be able to assert decisive control—when need be—of outer space. Second, it should deploy at least defensive weapons in space to provide protection in depth against Soviet strategic systems targeted against the United States and its allies.

These highly generalized strategic imperatives have specific policy implications for U.S. goals in arms control negotiations with the Soviet Union; for the modernization of U.S. strategic doctrine and forces with or without arms control agreements; for the deployment and distribution of U.S. global conventional forces; and for the role of technology in the attainment of the centrally important objective of neutralizing Soviet military power.

Strategic Impotence: The Threat of Arms Control

For many well-meaning Americans, arms control is the shortcut to peace and security. For Soviet leaders, it is a tool for seeking strategic preponderance. The uses and limits of arms control must be properly understood lest its more extremist manifestations should someday render the United States strategically impotent.

The contamination of strategy by pacifism is the key danger for the United States inherent in crusading arms control. Strategy in international affairs involves doctrine and techniques backed by the forces required to prevail — either politically or by combat. The ability to stop the opponent from winning militarily is the precondition for competing politically. Strategy and force are thus organically linked. But pacifism, a natural corollary of the democratic condition, reflects the understandable and morally righteous popular rejection of violence as the means of settling disputes. Its most simplistic manifestation is represented by the willingness to disarm unilaterally in the proclaimed belief ''better red than dead.'' Its more sophisticated, and strategically relevant, variant places a premium on arms control as the central facet of the U.S.–Soviet relationship — elevating these negotiations almost to a fetish and seeing in them the key to ending the nightmare created by the appearance of nuclear weapons.

The problem with this approach, more a matter of mood than doctrine, is, first, that it thrives only in the pluralistic and democratic nations: an independent arms control lobby is not tolerated in the Soviet Union. Second, it focuses on the symptoms and not the causes of U.S.–Soviet tensions and their threat to peace. It disregards the fact that the nuclear arms race is the product of a deeper, historically rooted political conflict. Many arms control enthusiasts ignore the central historical lesson of the forty-year-old U.S.–Soviet contest: without the fearful restraint generated by the destructive capacity of nuclear weapons, the two superpowers in all probability would have gone to war against each other on more than one occasion.

Moreover, arms control zealotry hurts constructive arms control. It places enormous political pressure on U.S. decision makers to make concessions to Moscow for the sake of agreements but without putting corresponding pressures on Soviet decision makers. Additionally, many of the more outspoken proponents of arms control have opposed since the mid-1970s the acquisition by the United States of new strategic weapons systems. Kremlin leaders have therefore had an incentive to stall in negotiations. They wait patiently for political pressures to induce unilateral concessions. They watch happily as the U.S. strategic modernization program is steadily eroded. In the meantime, the negotiation of a truly stabilizing arms control agreement with the Soviet Union has been rendered more difficult.

It is not happenstance that Soviet officials and propagandists are frequent participants in American arms control gatherings and institutes. With no Soviet counterpart to such organizations permitted to interfere with Moscow's strategic decision making, the American arms control constituency offers the Kremlin a unique opportunity for mobilizing domestic public opinion against U.S. defense programs, for attempting to influence U.S. strategic thought, and even for gaining access to internal U.S. discussions of strategy and of military technological innovation. In this manner, the Soviets have become in effect indirect participants in the American strategic dialogue, thereby gaining both influence and military intelligence.

This corruption of the domestic American discussion on the centrally important issue of survival in the nuclear age is one of the more damaging consequences of arms control pacifism. To formulate sound policy in the setting of the mutual potential for mass destruction requires political prudence, technical sophistication, and some instinct for the strategic doctrines of the opponent. In other democratic countries with nuclear weapons, like France or Britain, the issue of strategic survival and of the need for an independent nuclear force has been debated in a much more reasoned fashion, even though these countries are far more vulnerable than the United States to destruction by the Soviet Union. Yet in recent years the American discussion of strategic matters has been reduced on the public level to a series of deceptive slogans and political hoaxes that have heightened emotions while detracting from a reasoned debate.

Two recent examples — the debate over the "no first use" issue and over a nuclear freeze — illustrate the point. In the early 1980s, arms control enthusiasts pressed the United States to pledge not to be the first to use nuclear weapons, even in the event of a conventional Soviet attack on Western Europe. The assumption, based on faith — that if both superpowers adopt a no-first-use position a nuclear war cannot begin — was their answer to the vital and complex question of the relationship between effective conventional defense and nuclear deterrence in the protection of Europe. The arms controllers qualified their argument somewhat by suggesting that, of course, NATO should build up its conventional forces. But the fact remains that it is highly unlikely that NATO would do so to a level matching the Soviet conventional capabilities. Thus, once stripped to its true strategic significance for the Kremlin leaders, the proposition advanced by some of the most prominent spokesmen for the arms control constituency amounted to nothing less than a blanket American guarantee to the Soviet Union that Moscow could seek to win a conventional war in Europe without the complicating fear of a nuclear escalation.

Similarly, during the 1984 presidential election, the Democratic party campaigned in favor of a freeze on the production and deployment of nuclear weapons. Indeed, the ''nuclear freeze'' became the centerpiece of the Democratic party's contribution to what should have been a national debate on how well the administration had handled the strategic issue. The Republican administration had come to power in 1981 committed to enhancing U.S. strategic capabilities, but had totally mishandled the MX missile issue. First, political expediency led it to abandon its Democratic predecessor's congressionally approved decision to deploy in western states two hundred survivably based launchers with two thousand missiles. Then, simple strategic incompetence led the administration to advocate such vulnerable MX basing modes that Congress was provoked to reduce the number of missiles to fewer than fifty. There was therefore ample room for a critical appraisal.

Yet instead of engaging in the needed public debate, the Democratic party was diverted into advocacy of a nuclear ''freeze.'' This was largely in response to pressures generated during the presidential primaries by arms control adherents. And the freeze issue was a hoax. It provided a seemingly simple and easy solution to the uncertainties inherent in the continued arms race. Yet even its most prominent adherents could not indicate precisely what was to be ''frozen'' and how. A convincing answer would have required a precise indication of which weapons systems would be affected; what had to be done to make certain that ''a freeze'' could not be evaded under the guise of peaceful nuclear energy applications; what verification techniques would be used and at what stages of weapons production compliance would be monitored; what would be the strategic consequences both of an effective "freeze" and also of its one-sided evasion. In brief, the issue was posed as a slogan and not as a serious strategic option.

Similar emotions and irrelevancies had been sparked by President Ronald Reagan's initiative, announced in March 1983, to explore the desirability of strategic defense. Launched without adequate preparation and formulated in vague and even utopian terms, the president's Strategic Defense Initiative (SDI) invited criticism. But given the centrality of the issue of nuclear deterrence, it deserved a serious examination. It did not get it. The lead was taken by many of the most active opponents of the MX missile and the most devoted supporters of the "nuclear freeze" or the "no first use" proposal. What needed scrutiny was whether ongoing deployments of offensive weapons might over time render increasingly precarious the existing deterrent to war — the threat of mutual assured destruction (MAD) — and whether the alternative of strategic defense could be implemented either unilaterally or through bilateral agreement with the Soviet Union in a manner that would actually increase mutual security. Instead, it was immediately postulated that the initiative amounted to "star wars," that another escalation of the arms race would be its immediate consequence, and that arms control would be its immediate victim. Not surprisingly, the Soviets have been most supportive of the arguments made in the United States for the nuclear freeze and against the Strategic Defense Initiative. While this consideration alone should not determine the American position, it surely is appropriate to note that such Soviet attitudes must indicate what outcome Moscow views as most beneficial to its interests.

Arguments launched against the SDI, notably those of scientists actively engaged in the political efforts of the arms control community, were a flurry of self-contradictory propositions. They argued that a strategic defense would be technologically impossible to build, that it would be prohibitively expensive, that it could easily be overwhelmed by Soviet countermeasures, that it would be highly destabilizing, and that it would force the Soviets to follow the U.S. lead, thereby producing an arms race in space. Of course, if the initiative is technically unfeasible, economically ruinous, and militarily easy to counter, it is unclear why the SDI would still be destabilizing and why the Soviets should object to America's embarking on such a self-defeating enterprise, and even less clear why the Soviets would then follow suit in reproducing such an undesirable thing for themselves. But what these arguments reflected more basically was a deep-seated unwillingness to face an unpleasant reality: that strategic stability may have to be sought through unilateral initiatives based on technological innovation rather than through contrived arms control arrangements — unless and until the American-Soviet political relationship significantly improves.

That proposition is especially unpalatable to those who view arms control as the centerpiece of U.S.–Soviet relations and who argue that these negotiations should somehow be isolated from the geopolitical conflicts that have fueled and continue to dominate American-Soviet tensions. Such an attempt to isolate arms control from the political context is both dangerous and counterproductive, even to arms control itself. It encourages the Soviets to pursue assertive policies even while negotiating arms control, as they did in Angola after the SALT I agreement of 1972 and the Vladivostok talks in 1974 and in Ethiopia and Afghanistan during the negotiation of and the ratification debate over the SALT II accord. Eventually, the indifference to Soviet actions on the part of arms controllers prompted an understandable public reaction against all arms control agreements — even when these were in the interest of the United States.

Quite understandably, the Soviets do favor separating arms control from geopolitics. It permits them to wage the political struggle while benefiting from the political impression that the rivalry has waned. Soviet leaders are aware that the American people, as well as the media, are inclined to generalize the state of the U.S.–Soviet relationship either as positive (especially in the wake of arms control agreements) or hostile (particularly during a regional crisis). Euphoria generated by arms control treaties tends to inhibit American defense programs — particularly in the area of strategic weapons — or geopolitical responses to Soviet challenges. SALT agreements, which have not formally limited either American or Soviet strategic weapons innovation, have nonetheless had the effect of uniquely obstructing the modernization of U.S. forces. Within the American body politic the impression grew that such programs were no longer needed and indeed were counter to the spirit or even to the letter of arms accords. Arms control has thereby become a political weapon for the Soviets in their effort to achieve the one-sided disarmament of their opponent, rather than a means of enhancing mutual security.

The history of both the SALT I and the SALT II negotiations is painfully instructive. Throughout both these negotiations the Soviets strove to create the impression of a more generalized accommodation. Thus, Soviet leaders placed special emphasis on the Nixon-Brezhnev declaration of joint principles and spoke grandly of the era of détente — while simultaneously pressing assertive geopolitical initiatives and striving to limit U.S. advances in strategic weaponry. The Soviet focus has been less on the shaping of genuine and reciprocal strategic security and more on stopping the introduction of new U.S. strategic systems.

This Soviet approach doubtless in part stemmed from Moscow's healthy respect for American technology; it realizes that it cannot catch up in an unconstrained competition in weapons development. In part it was motivated by the Soviet desire to protect the strategic edge it acquired during the 1970s in prompt counterforce systems, which have been deployed in numbers sufficient to place U.S. ICBMs in jeopardy. Given the central role of the Soviet military in Moscow's arms control positions, it can be assumed that the determination not to trade away that strategic edge was directly connected with Soviet war planning.

But arms control has consequences beyond the military balance — and the Soviets have shown themselves to be sensitive to its political-perceptual dimensions. Although adding up the numbers of strategic systems can produce a misleading analysis of power militarily, the numbers do matter politically. During the 1974 summit in Moscow, a senior U.S. official exclaimed at a press conference, "What in the name of God is strategic superiority?" In previous back-channel negotiations, the United States had agreed to a formula allowing a larger number of SLBMs for the Soviet Union than for the United States and 308 Soviet heavy missiles to none for the United States. Soviet leaders derived evident satisfaction from the resulting public perception of Soviet strategic superiority. They were well aware that power and status in international affairs are inseparable.

This does not mean that we should abandon arms control. But it does mean that it must be pursued with the clear awareness, publicly articulated and frequently reiterated, of one key fact: arms control is part of our national defense policy, not a substitute for it. Arms control agreements imply neither political accommodation nor an end to strategic competition. Indeed, innovation in weapons technology will be a necessary concomitant of any arms control arrangements — barring the unlikely event of a comprehensive and verifiable agreement that is associated also with a substantive, political accommodation.

Short of such a historical transformation of the American-Soviet relationship, the more promising route for arms control is to seek narrowly focused, highly specific — perhaps "interim" — arrangements. These must be subject to verification, including on-site inspection of mobile missile launchers. Furthermore, they must concentrate on the central issues: those existing weapons systems, or ones soon to be deployed, that represent the most acute security threat for each side. It cannot be emphasized too strongly that numerical reductions per se are not arms control. Genuine arms control should increase the security *of both sides*. It requires much more refined trade-offs than the quest for numerical symmetry. Neither the United States nor the Soviet Union can in the near future avoid societal devastation in the event of nuclear war, so arms control has to deal with the longer-range danger that a preemptive attack could disarm one side's strategic forces, thereby foreclosing effective retaliation. That means concentrating on agreeing to limit and reduce strategic systems that have the capacity or have been designed primarily for strategic attack and not for societal retaliation.

In other words, fewer is not necessarily better. An arms control agreement that cuts strategic nuclear arsenals by 50 percent would simply produce greater instability if it left both sides with proportionately more first-strike systems — for, unless otherwise specified, each side is likely to dismantle first its older, less accurate systems. The emphasis in future comprehensive arms control agreements must shift from quantitative reductions to qualitative prohibitions. The number of systems capable of undertaking a precise first-strike attack must be driven below the number required to make such an attack militarily effective.

This would require a significant reduction in the deployment of the principal existing Soviet counterforce weapon, the SS-18 missile, to about the levels proposed by the United States in 1977 — no more than 150 launchers with 1,500 warheads. There would have to a corresponding limit on the deployment of counterforce-capable Soviet SLBM warheads, and of the new SS-24 and SS-25 ICBMs. On the American side, corresponding limits would have to apply to the MX, the proposed mobile Midgetman, and the Trident-based D-5 missiles, in amounts equal to the Soviet levels. Moreover, such limitations would have to be accompanied by a binding prohibition on the introduction of any new highly accurate ballistic missiles or the further modernization of existing ones. All such reductions and prohibitions would have to be subject to foolproof verification.

Reaching agreement on verification, already made difficult by the Soviet penchant for secrecy, is likely to be further complicated by developments in new weapons technology. How does one verify confidently the number of mobile launchers? How does one differentiate nuclear-armed cruise missiles from conventionally armed cruise missiles? On-site verification is likely to be necessary, and the United States should not accept any limitations it cannot confidently confirm. The alternative to on-site verification may have to be a total ban on such systems as mobile ICBM launchers, and perhaps at some point even on ballistic missile flight testing, since a total ban is much easier to monitor. Anything less than this would simply give the Soviets an incentive to cheat.

Since verification is the key to compliance and thus confidence, the American side should make Soviet military secrecy more of a political issue because of its negative effects on arms control. Soviet strategic secrecy is, in fact, a major threat to U.S.–Soviet stability. Few realize that even the U.S.–Soviet arms control negotiations are based entirely on data concerning *both* the American and the Soviet systems provided by the American side alone. The Soviet side then negotiates on the basis of these numbers but otherwise is silent about its arsenal. There are no Soviet data about the numbers and performance of the Soviet weapons. The official Soviet defense budget is a patent fraud, and Soviet strategic offensive and defensive weapons are being developed and deployed in total secrecy.

Surreptitious military planning, development, and deployment by the Kremlin stimulates anxiety and the suspicion that arms control may be seen by some Soviet leaders primarily as a breathing spell, designed to lull the United States into a false sense of security. Soviet strategic secrecy has another hazard: it could prompt American overestimates of Soviet deployment, thereby precipitating American responses that in their turn could cause the Soviets to escalate. Hence, Soviet strategic secrecy is simply incompatible with genuine and confidence-building arms control. The gradual termination of Soviet secrecy, complementing American openness about strategic intentions, should be an element of any comprehensive arms control accommodation. The United States must insist on this.

Arms control agreements should also be accompanied and reinforced by parallel arrangements for the security of space-based early warning and reconnaissance satellites. Imaginative proposals were advanced by Albert Wohlstetter and Brian Chow in the *Wall Street Journal* in July 1985 for designating zones in space for exclusive U.S. or Soviet satellite deployment. Entry into each zone of a space vehicle originating from the other side would be prohibited. Each side would have the right to destroy without notice any object entering its zone whether by design or accident. Both sides would benefit from such an arrangement because it would secure satellite deployments from sudden intrusive attack.

The basic obstacle to reaching such genuine arms control agreements is that the United States has no bargaining assets. The deployment of the MX missile, which has the power and accuracy to make the Soviet leadership consider the potential vulnerability of its land-based ICBMs and of its command and shelter centers, has been constrained both by congressional opposition and by programmatic mishandling by the Reagan administration. The D-5 missile is not scheduled for large-scale deployment until the mid-1990s and even then in numbers not sufficient to exert pressure on existing Soviet strategic forces. The future of the Midgetman missile, and even its strategic rationale, is in doubt. Congressionally mandated restrictions on its size may impair its penetrability, while its deployment in a mobile mode is likely to be costly and politically unpalatable.

In these circumstances, the quest for strategic security through arms control becomes more difficult, and the threat becomes more real that arms control agreements reached because of domestic political pressures may stifle U.S. strategic innovation. U.S. strategic impotence could thereby become the dangerous end result.

Mutual Strategic Security

Mutual strategic security should be a common American and Soviet objective. MSS means that each side is *strategically* secure — that it knows that a disarming first strike against its opponent would be militarily futile and that it is confident that a first strike by its opponent would be suicidal. In effect, the goal of MSS incorporates the essentials of the doctrine of MAD — for the ultimate sanction remains the same. It differs in its emphasis by placing the highest priority on the survivability of one's own strategic forces and on the maintenance of a flexible strategic counterforce capability for selective war-fighting and thus for deterrence at all levels of a potential nuclear conflict.

MSS can be sought in two ways. An arms control agreement along the lines sketched above would be the least costly. But if reaching doctrinal understanding on strategic convergence is impossible, MSS can and must be sought unilaterally. Indeed, a unilateral American effort may over time convince Soviet leaders that a genuine arms control accommodation is preferable to continued competition. Real arms control offers greater mutual predictability and stability and can enhance mutual security at lower costs than a full-blown race in weapons technology. But Moscow will not be convinced of this as long as it can assume that arms control can be used as a tool for halting U.S. strategic innovation while protecting and even enhancing the Soviet edge in strategic first-strike systems.

A unilateral effort by the United States to enhance mutual security will require an adjustment in its strategic doctrine and deployments. It is far from clear that the United States currently possesses a coherent strategic doctrine for meshing its military power with its foreign policy, or a unified geostrategic doctrine for the conduct of war. Yet both are needed if U.S. military power is to back U.S. foreign policy and provide a credible deterrent to the initiation of a nuclear war. Some movement in the direction of formulating a guiding framework started in the mid-1970s when under the initiative of then Secretary of Defense James Schlesinger the NSC issued National Security Directive Memorandum 242. It gave the president greater flexibility in responding to a nuclear attack. More ambitious initiatives followed during the Carter administration, with the president approving a series of proposals submitted by the National Security Council staff to modernize and refine the U.S. strategic posture.

Most public attention has focused on Presidential Directive 59, issued in June 1980. It marked an important new step in the evolution of American strategic thought. It gave the president flexibility beyond preplanned options. It placed greater targeting emphasis on military targets; on war-supporting Soviet industries; and on communication, command and control, and intelligence facilities (the so-called C^3I). It treated the survivability of the U.S. C^3I as a broader requirement, important for control of not only strategic but also general-purpose forces in a protracted conflict. It called for the development of a "look-shoot-look" capability for identifying new and moving targets during wartime. It increased the secure strategic Reserve Force so that it could be used for influencing military campaigns and not simply for psychological coercion. And, finally, for the first time it tied U.S. weapons acquisition policy to weapons employment policy.

Less noticed, yet also important, were two earlier presidential directives issued in 1978. The first, PD-41, stated flatly that the United States must seek to "enhance deterrence and stability in conjunction with our strategic offensive and other *strategic defensive forces*" (emphasis added) in order to "reduce the possibility that the U.S. could be coerced in time of crisis.'' The other, PD-53, mandated certain security precautions necessary "even during a protracted nuclear conflict." These directives reflected an emerging strategic perspective, advocated primarily by this author as the National Security Adviser and his military assistant, General William Odom. This view stated that a nuclear war might not be simply a short, spasmodic apocalypse that could best be deterred by a posture based on the doctrine of MAD, but that it might entail engagements at varying levels of intensity and over an extended period of time. It followed that to wage such a conflict effectively and, more important, to deter it, the United States needed a mix of offensive and *defensive* capabilities.

Such a mix would give the United States basic strategic confidence. Not the social invulnerability of a perfect defense against nuclear weapons but the needed margin of strategic safety in an essentially defensive posture. Not the capability for the United States to mount a disarming first strike but the ability to deny that to the potential enemy. Equally important, with this basic strategic confidence, the United States would have the flexibility for continued reliance on a nuclear deterrent against conventional Soviet attack — which is not possible in a setting of either U.S. strategic inferiority or strategic vulnerability.

A U.S. strategic posture that mixes offensive and defensive systems would thus negate Moscow's offensive posture. Soviet strategic deployments have concentrated heavily on first-strike systems and have been reinforced by the surreptitious development of a strategic defense capability. But to exploit this posture either politically or militarily the Soviet side needs to have absolute certainty that it possesses effective superiority as the point of departure for any major action. This precondition would be far more difficult for the Soviets to calculate and achieve against a U.S. posture that combined offensive and defensive strategic deployments. Furthermore, it would be easier for the United States to complicate Moscow's offensive war planning than it would be for the Soviet Union to achieve meaningful nuclear superiority by deploying more offensive systems.

The bipartisan gestation of new approaches to strategic security culminated in President Reagan's March 1983 announcement of the launching of the SDI. Though his own public remarks tended to focus on the more ambitious and more remote objective of a total population defense, the SDI did have the effect of setting in motion an intensive review of the desirability of a limited strategic defense. This has been overdue, given the changes over the last forty years in the way nuclear weapons potentially could be used. Originally, nuclear forces were messy weapons of mass destruction to be employed against an enemy who did not possess them. But the U.S. monopoly on the ability to deliver nuclear weapons lasted only from 1945 until the early 1950s. By the 1960s and 1970s, nuclear weapons had become for both sides essentially retaliatory deterrents, as conceptualized in the doctrine of MAD. By the 1980s they were becoming more precise tools that could be used for a preemptive and disarming attack designed to preclude effective retaliation.

In these new circumstances, a decisive shift was necessary in the nature of U.S. strategic doctrine and deployments. Arms control alone had failed to assure stability. The risk had developed of only the United States remaining vulnerable to assured destruction, with the Soviet Union free to move more decisively on the conventional level.

The United States needs to maintain into the twenty-first century a prudent mix of offensive and defensive strategic forces to prevent Soviet political intimidation, to preclude an outright Soviet military victory, and to preserve a credible and flexible nuclear deterrent against Soviet conventional aggression in areas vital to American national security. But the strategic offensive

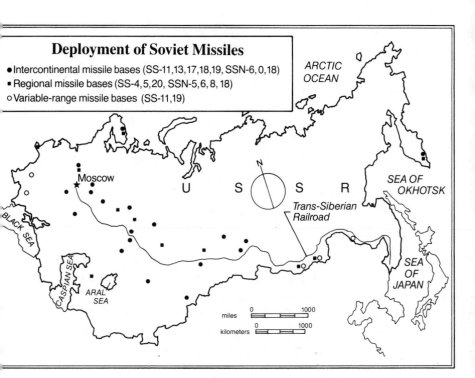

Deployment of Soviet Missiles

- Intercontinental missile bases (SS-11,13,17,18,19, SSN-6, 0,18)
- Regional missile bases (SS-4,5,20, SSN-5,6, 8, 18)
- Variable-range missile bases (SS-11,19)

forces should be deployed in numbers deliberately contrived *not to pose* a threat of a disarming first strike. U.S. deployments of first-strike systems, such as the MX missile and the Trident D-5 missile, or even more sophisticated future weapons, should be calibrated carefully to target only a portion of the most vital Soviet war-fighting capabilities (see map). They should not deprive the Soviet side of the assurance that in all circumstances it would still retain a broad retaliatory capability against U.S. society. Accordingly, further modernization of U.S. strategic forces should be constrained by the requirement that it not place in jeopardy the entirety of the Soviet nuclear arsenal, and hence at least one-half of U.S. strategic forces should be composed of essentially second-strike systems (such as cruise missiles).

An important coincidental aspect of U.S. targeting is the fact that the most significant Soviet offensive strategic systems are deployed along the major Soviet railroad trunk lines, including the Trans-Siberian Railroad. This map should be superimposed on the one in chapter one showing the territorial disposition of the various Soviet peoples. In the event of a conflict in which the primary targets were the war-fighting capabilities of the two powers and not their entire societies, the Great Russian population, whose distribution strikingly matches the geographical deployment of Soviet ICBMs, would be especially vulnerable — a consideration that would not be lost on the Kremlin leaders of the Great Russian empire.

The United States would jeopardize its own security if its self-restraint in the deployment of counterforce systems were unilateral and if its strategic efforts were confined to the selective and limited upgrading of offensive systems. A corresponding deployment of a limited strategic defense is therefore more than desirable — it is imperative. Such a strategic defense should not seek to create a population-wide screen, but to deny the Soviet side any possibility of destroying U.S. strategic forces. This would both enhance strategic deterrence and inhibit a Soviet conventional attack, because it would provide the United States with the confidence needed for responding firmly on various levels of any possible conflict.

A limited strategic defense — by definition — need not be perfect. There is much to be said for even a porous two-tier defense — a space-based screen to destroy missiles in the boost phase and a land-based terminal defense to intercept incoming warheads. It would have the key effect of introducing a high degree of randomness into any calculation of the consequences of a nuclear attack. The feasibility of such a limited strategic defense is generally conceded by the scientific community, in contrast to a much more ambitious and necessarily almost foolproof total population defense. The trade-offs between enhanced limited defense and increased offensive capabilities tend to favor defense. Moreover, deploying such a limited strategic defense system is possible within this century, and therefore the issue is relevant to policy today.

A limited defense against ballistic missiles would be a giant step toward achieving mutual strategic security. Even if it were unilaterally implemented by the United States, the American-Soviet strategic relationship would become more stable. It would deny to the Soviet Union the ability to make a threat to which it has no right — to launch a preemptive or disarming strategic attack on the United States while partially screening itself from possible retaliation with its own covertly deployed defenses. But Moscow, too, needs reassurance that American leaders are not seeking a first-strike capability. There has to be clearly defined and carefully calibrated U.S. restraint in deploying offensive and defensive systems. The U.S. defensive shield should be confined to the protection of strategic forces, the national command authority, and C^3I. This would provide a further reassurance that the United States is not trying to deprive the Soviet Union of its retaliatory capability.

If the United States does anything less than this, it will be left with two equally poor options. One is to hope against hope that arms control will somehow by itself stabilize the U.S.–Soviet strategic relationship, even though the United States has currently little with which to bargain. The other is to undertake a massive buildup of its own offensive systems by deploying many more MX and Trident D-5 missiles than currently planned and by proceeding with a major deployment of the single-warhead mobile Midgetman missile, on the scale of perhaps fifteen hundred or more launchers, despite its potential operational shortcomings. Not only would this second option be extremely costly — probably more so than that of a limited strategic defense — but it is difficult to see how such a desperate effort to preserve MAD through the accumulation of more offensive systems would offer greater stability for either side.

Critics of even limited strategic defense deployment have argued that it would simply pile up more weapons. For example, a *New York Times* editorial stated that strategic defense would be "highly provocative" to the Soviets, who would then be compelled to respond with "a destabilizing new buildup of Soviet offensive weapons." This argument fails to take into account two salient points. First, the Soviets themselves have been taking steps to enhance their strategic defenses, to a degree considerably greater than the United States has done or is planning to do, without evoking the charge from such editorial writers that these Soviet actions are "highly provocative." Second, a new Soviet offensive strategic buildup would not be remotely justified in response to a manifestly restrained deployment of U.S. offensive systems and merely a limited U.S. strategic defense. Such a Soviet response would be menacing. It would both signal and confirm a Soviet determination to acquire a first-strike attack capability. There could be no other credible motive. The exposure of such a Soviet strategic intent would be a further argument for a U.S. limited defense, not an argument against it.

It might be objected that the Soviets could misread an American deployment of a limited number of accurate offensive systems and a limited defense. They might interpret it as a preliminary step toward the acquisition of a full-blown first-strike capability that would be reinforced with a gradually expanding defensive screen. That argument is simply not credible. With lead times in strategic deployments measured in years and with Congress publicly reviewing U.S. strategic plans and usually limiting their funding, it is impossible for the United States to acquire such a one-sided capability without early and full warning to the Soviets. Moreover, there is no public support in the United States for such a massive effort to regain one-sided strategic superiority.

The best outcome for both the United States and the Soviet

Union would be to move jointly to relatively similar mixed but limited offensive-defensive postures. It is more likely that such movement will be undertaken tacitly than through formally contrived agreements because of the overwhelming difficulties of verification and of formulating complicated trade-offs. Thus, a gradual reduction in Soviet first-strike deployments and some expansion in present Soviet ABM capabilities should be paralleled by an American deployment of a limited strategic defense against Soviet first-strike systems. This could give both sides greater strategic security than they enjoy today. Even unilateral movement in this direction by the United States will make it more likely that Soviet leaders will decide that the further acquisition of first-strike systems is economically wasteful and neither strategically nor politically justifiable. That decision, in turn, might lead the Kremlin to see that some reciprocal accommodation is preferable.

Indeed, a strong case can be made for a unilateral U.S. rejection of the limitations on strategic defense of the 1972 Anti-Ballistic Missile Treaty, based on the now anachronistic strategic assumptions of the era of MAD. A forceful act of this kind, conveying U.S. determination to move away from MAD, might precipitate a more conclusive, comprehensive, and stabilizing arms control accommodation dedicated to mutual strategic security. Should such a step become the catalyst for a more forthcoming Soviet attitude on arms control, the United States could in return pledge to defer for the life of any new agreement the actual deployment of the otherwise needed counter-first-strike SDI system. To move events in that direction the United States should propose to the Soviet Union a renegotiation of the ABM treaty to permit some limited deployment of space-based defenses. Subsequently, in response to the likely negative Soviet reaction, the United States should announce that it is initiating a careful reassessment of the continued strategic and political value of the ABM treaty, including the possibility of terminating the U.S. adherence to it. The United States should also indicate its intention to proceed with the deployment of a two-tier, limited, counter-first-strike strategic defense, unless in the meantime the Soviets agree to a truly stabilizing arms control agreement.

In summation, the United States is currently sliding into the worst possible strategic posture. While premature top-level talk of population-wide strategic defense has probably made Soviet leaders accelerate their own strategic defense efforts, the United States is not moving decisively either to augment its own strategic offensive forces or to deploy a strategic defense for its retaliatory forces. Meanwhile, the Soviet Union is doing both. To overcome this danger, the United States must make a determined choice among three basic options: (1) to rely on arms control — which only makes sense if it results in a comprehensive and verifiable agreement that massively reduces the Soviet first-strike systems; (2) to maintain the precarious state of mutual assured destruction by proliferating at very high cost its own survivable strategic forces so as to counter the projected enormous expansion in Soviet first-strike systems and the Soviet covert enhancements in strategic defense; or (3) to move toward a relationship of mutual strategic security through a moderate expansion and modernization of U.S. strategic attack forces and the deployment within the decade of a two-tier strategic defense to counter Soviet first-strike weapons.

Option three is the best. It provides greater security. It also constitutes the one course of action most likely to persuade the Soviet Union seriously to consider a truly comprehensive, mutually stabilizing, and fully verifiable arms control agreement.

Global Conventional Flexibility

The maintenance both of nuclear stability and of a credible strategic deterrent is the point of departure for coping with the threat of a conventional attack by the Soviet Union. But that threat also has special dimensions. At the outset of this analysis, I registered three imperatives pertaining to conventional conflict: the United States must be able to negate any Soviet military intimidation of countries in which the United States has a special stake, to block Soviet conventional military expansion, and to deprive the Soviets of a quick conventional victory on any one of the three central Eurasian strategic fronts. Neither the current U.S. doctrine nor the composition and deployment of U.S. conventional forces provides the confidence that these tasks could be executed.

U.S. doctrine is vague, overgeneralized, and poses — if taken seriously — the real risk of military overextension. In recent years, top U.S. defense officials have articulated a defense doctrine intended to convey American determination to fight on several fronts at the same time, almost in a politically and strategically indiscriminate fashion. Secretary of Defense Caspar Weinberger in his 1983 annual report to Congress warned that the Soviets have the "capability to launch simultaneous attacks" on all three key fronts and that therefore the United States must "be capable of defending all theaters simultaneously." This assertion is open to challenge. Notwithstanding the Soviet Union's large conventional forces, it is highly doubtful that Moscow could launch truly major operations on all three fronts *simultaneously*. Moreover, the military rationale of such a huge conventional operation, which would disperse Soviet conventional superiority rather than concentrate it, is even more open to doubt. It is unclear why Moscow would choose to wage a massive and consequently more prolonged three-front conventional war that would be more likely to escalate into a nuclear conflict than a concentrated and quick conventional assault on one of the three fronts. It is therefore very unlikely that the Soviets would mindlessly disperse their forces and maximize the number of their enemies.

Even more skepticism is justified regarding the administration's strategic prescription for the United States. Is it seriously recommended that the United States engage in a large-scale, three-front conventional conflict? This would require massive advance deployments and pre-positioning of equipment in order to anticipate the eventual Soviet onslaught. Existing or even planned forces are simply inadequate for that purpose. In brief, both the strategic assumptions about the potential enemy and the strategic prescription for the appropriate response are unsatisfactory.

The actual disposition of U.S. conventional forces compounds the problem. These relatively modest forces are neither deployed nor prepared to fight on the three fronts simultaneously. At the same time, they are not structured for a prompt response to a serious security threat outside of Eurasia's three principal theaters. The bulk of American conventional ground forces is stationed in the United States. The second largest ground deployment — including the best-equipped and best-trained units — is in Western Europe, and a more modest army presence is in South Korea. The U.S. Navy is divided into two major components, one heavily committed to NATO and the other representing the principal American force in the Pacific, with smaller naval and amphibious units positioned in the Persian Gulf / Indian Ocean region. U.S. tactical air power deployments largely match the distribution of the ground forces (see appendix, ''Where Major U.S. Defense Forces Stand'').

Overall U.S. overseas deployments come to about 540,000 troops. Approximately 340,000 are positioned in Europe, 150,000 in the Far East (of whom 39,000 are in South Korea), 16,000 in the Middle East and Persian Gulf area, and 30,000 in Central America. In the summer 1985 issue of *Foreign Affairs,* Earl Ravenal calculated from the annual Defense Department posture statement

that, for fiscal year 1986, the Reagan administration intends the following regional attribution of our total of 21 active ground divisions: NATO/Europe, eleven and two-thirds divisions; east Asia, three and two-thirds divisions; other regions and the strategic reserve, five and two-thirds divisions. By applying these fractions to the total cost of our general purpose forces, $241 billion, we can calculate the rough cost of our regional commitments. By my estimate, Europe accounts for $134 billion (Asia absorbs $42 billion, and the strategic reserve, including an expanded requirement for rapid deployment forces, mostly for CENTCOM — that is, the Persian Gulf and southwest Asia — takes $65 billion).

It is clear that the allocations for the defense of Western Europe represent a massively disproportionate share of the overall U.S. military budget. This was even more strikingly confirmed when the secretary of defense testified to Congress in June 1984 that the Defense Department calculated that in the event of a prolonged European conflict, approximately $177 billion would be required to support American forces in Europe as well as their reinforcements from the United States.

These unbalanced global deployments have more to do with history than with strategy. They reflect neither the actual estimate of the Soviet military threat nor a measure of each area's relative geopolitical importance. They are a vestige of earlier preoccupations, both political and military. The U.S. defense commitment in Europe was initially brought about because of a massive intelligence underestimation of the Soviet Union's postwar demobilization. It was premised on the notion that there was a huge Red Army in a state of high readiness poised to sweep across the Rhine and beyond. Soviet use of force to impose the Berlin blockade of 1948 and the Soviet sponsorship of the North Korean attack in 1950 gave these concerns added impetus. Many American officials did not exclude the possibility of an attack on Europe. In fact, many both feared and expected it. Within the government, a widespread expectation of the outbreak of World War III developed, prompting not only a significant U.S. military buildup but also even an attempt to plan for postwar political arrangements.

As a result, the U.S. engagement in Europe has had from the beginning a strongly military focus, and was reinforced in the early days by explicit threats of nuclear retaliation in the event of a Soviet transgression. The commitment was formally institutionalized at European insistence. West Europeans feared that America might at some point grow weary of its involvement, and were therefore eager to commit the United States in a binding fashion.

The enduring outcome of these impulses and institutional commitments has been a heavy and direct U.S. commitment to the defense of Europe. It is by far the single largest and most costly fixed deployment of U.S. forces outside the United States, with about 250,000 troops concentrated in West Germany alone. Although NATO's European members have now recovered economically, the percentage of GNP allocated to defense by the United States continues to be appreciably higher than that by its NATO allies (see accompanying table). Moreover, even in Europe itself our NATO allies have been shirking their defense obligations. Most notably, they have not fulfilled their pledges regarding enhanced sustainability for conventional combat. A most glaring example is their failure to stockpile ammunition for their NATO forces, with the result that U.S. troops would be left to fight alone after the initial phase of combat. U.S. allies also now consider the scope of the alliance to be confined to the European theater and therefore do not feel any obligation to share the burdens of competing with the Soviet Union elsewhere.

In the Far East after 1945, the United States waged two prolonged wars, requiring massive expenditures and a large-scale commitment of forces. Peak U.S. deployments in the Korean and Vietnam wars involved 473,000 and 543,000 servicemen, respectively. These two wars aside, however, the American engagement on the second central strategic front has placed less emphasis than on the first on a direct and large-

MILITARY EXPENDITURES OF NATO COUNTRIES

Country	GNP Percentage Spent on Defense (1983)	Defense Spending per Capita (1983)*
NATO, All	5.2	$527
NATO, Europe	3.9	$293
Belgium	3.3	282
Denmark	2.5	278
France	4.2	417
Great Britain	5.4	470
Greece	6.2	244
Iceland	0.0	0
Italy	2.7	162
Luxembourg	1.0	106
Netherlands	3.2	311
Norway	3.2	413
Portugal	3.5	78
Spain	2.1	102
Turkey	4.9	55
West Germany	3.4	367
NATO, North America		
Canada	2.2	$248
United States	6.6	888

*Constant 1982 U.S. dollars
(SOURCE: Arms Control and Disarmament Agency)

scale U.S. military presence. Instead, it has emphasized political relationships and defense treaty obligations with Japan and South Korea, buttressed by offshore air and naval power. U.S. military power has been dispersed throughout the Pacific and the Far East, with air and naval deployments in Japan, Okinawa, the Philippines, and Guam. At the same time, America's principal Far Eastern ally, Japan, has confined its defense budget to about 1 percent of its GNP. Japan is gradually building up its armed forces, particularly its navy and air force, to provide for the defense of the Japanese islands and of a maritime perimeter to the south. But Japanese forces still have only a limited capability. Among U.S. allies in the Far East, only South Korea has made a major effort, keeping more than 600,000 men under arms and spending 7.5 percent of its GNP on defense.

The disproportion between the U.S. military involvement in Western Europe and in the Far East has been mitigated by a corresponding imbalance in the disposition of Soviet forces. The bulk of the more modern Soviet units are deployed in the European Soviet Union and in central Europe. Moreover, the geopolitical realities of the Far East have been transformed by the Sino-Soviet split, which sharply reduced the direct Soviet security threat to the region. Most of Moscow's ground forces in the Far East, which had grown from approximately twelve divisions in 1960 to fifty-two divisions by 1985, have been deployed against China. This means the United States and its allies face only the Soviet naval and air force units stationed in the Soviet Far East and Vietnam, though these are growing.

The U.S. engagement on the third Eurasian strategic front has been undertaken in the face of even more formidable difficulties. The Soviet southward push has been met by a largely improvised military-political response. In 1978, on the initiative of the National Security Council, President Carter approved the creation of the Rapid Deployment Force. Its purpose was to enable the United States to project its power into areas where no U.S. forces are permanently stationed. During 1979 and 1980, the Defense Department fleshed out the initiative, and it was implemented and expanded further by the Reagan administration. Also, President Carter approved an NSC proposal late in 1979 to approach Somalia, Oman, and Kenya for access to local air and naval facilities for emergency support for any RDF deployment in the region. These initiatives proved their timeliness when the Soviets invaded Afghanistan in December 1979. The U.S. military presence in the region has remained meager, however, largely because the countries concerned, notably those on the Arabian Peninsula, prefer not to be overtly and directly linked with Washington.

An American military response to a Soviet move in this area therefore has had to be of a contingent nature. The air- and sea-lift capability for the RDF has been expanded, and the forward logistical facilities that could be used temporarily in the event of hostilities have been upgraded. The United States has built up and dedicated four relatively light army divisions for quick deployment to the region. By 1985, "planning strengths" for a conflict in south Asia included also the Marine Corps, the four light army divisions, one Air Cavalry brigade, supported by tactical air units, and three aircraft-carrier naval battle groups.

Nonetheless, a perilous paradox has developed. Today, the United States is weakest where it is most vulnerable — along the strategic front that poses the greatest risk of either a major Soviet geopolitical thrust or an American-Soviet collision. And it is strongest where its allies have the greatest capacity for doing more on their own behalf. While American power is tenuous along the third strategic front in southwest Asia, the United States still allocates more than half its total military spending for the defense of the first front in Europe. Given Western Europe's economic potential and America's other strategic responsibilities, a military posture so skewed in favor of Europe clearly needs to be adjusted.

A gradual — and certainly only partial — reduction in the level of the American forces in Europe is necessary to increase U.S. flexibility for meeting security threats elsewhere. America needs to be able and ready to deal with challenges, not only on the other two Eurasian fronts, but also in Central America, perhaps even southern Africa, certainly in the Middle East, with its ever-present danger of a major explosion; and in the Persian Gulf, where a U.S.–Soviet collision would have huge stakes. In terms of planning for such contingencies, the fixed deployment of heavy ground divisions in Europe represents the single greatest limitation on effective U.S. responsiveness.

This conclusion represents neither a novel judgment nor a reflection of isolationism. It is a little-known fact that President Eisenhower, a former NATO commander whose entire career made his especially sensitive to the importance of the defense of Europe, strongly advocated such a reduction shortly after taking office in 1953. In a memorandum he personally dictated to his special assistant for national security affairs, Robert Cutler, in August 1953, Eisenhower stated:

> From the beginning, people who really studied foreign and military problems have considered that the stationing of American troops abroad was a temporary expedient.

It was a stopgap operation to bring confidence and security to our friends overseas, who were desperately exposed to Communist aggression.

Any thinking individual, in the services or out, always understood that the basic purpose of so stationing American troops was to produce among our friends morale, confidence, economic and military strength, in order that they would be able to hold vital areas with indigenous troops until American help could arrive.

This idea from the beginning placed a premium on
1. safety of the U.S. from surprise and destructive attack,
2. existence of highly mobile forces,
3. comprehensive mobilization plans quickly to marshal our entire strength in support of our national security (ourselves and our friends).

In a National Security Council discussion in November 1953, President Eisenhower also said "that properly speaking the stationing of U.S. divisions in Europe had been at the outset an emergency measure not intended to last indefinitely. Unhappily, however, the European nations have been slow in building up their military forces and have now come to expect our forces to remain in Europe indefinitely." The president was supported by the Joint Chiefs of Staff, whose comments reflected the view that U.S. military dispositions were excessively and too rigidly concentrated in Europe. Eisenhower refrained from acting on his predisposition only because of a concern that premature U.S. troop reductions might derail the ongoing European efforts to revitalize their own defense capabilities.

Since then, the European contribution to NATO has increased substantially, though not in keeping with Western Europe's economic capacity to sustain an even larger effort. One very major improvement has been the buildup of the West German army. It is now the single largest military force on Western Europe's central front. In recent years, France, which continues to station three divisions in West Germany, has been quietly coordinating its military plans with NATO, despite the fact that it formally withdrew from the alliance's unified military command in 1965. This not only assures NATO of greater defense in depth but further complicates Soviet planning by raising the possibility that French nuclear forces could act as a catalyst to escalate a conventional conflict into a broader nuclear one. The cumulative effect of these efforts has been to reduce Soviet superiority on Europe's central front from approximately three to one in the early 1950s to about one and a half to one today.

Moreover, NATO's intention to exploit advanced technology in conventional combat, capitalizing on the West's superiority in scientific innovation, has enabled its planners to consider politically desirable adjustments in strategic concepts. In the early 1950s, NATO's weakness in conventional power forced it to have a strategy of falling back to the Rhine, which meant that West Germany would in effect be abandoned. In the mid-1960s, NATO strategy shifted to creating a "trip wire," which, if breached, would touch off a tactical nuclear war, thereby extending any potential conflict into Eastern bloc territory. In the mid-1970s, NATO adopted a strategy of "active defense," placing the forward line of defense virtually on the boundary

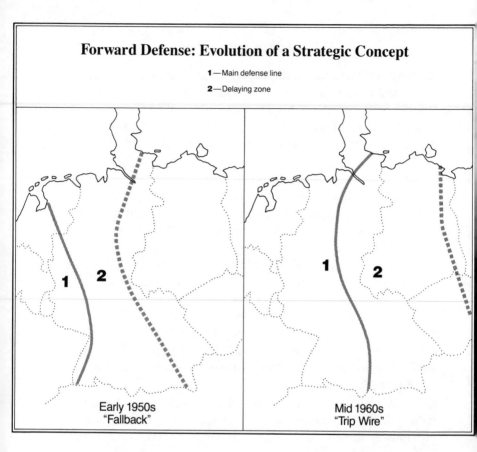

Forward Defense: Evolution of a Strategic Concept

1—Main defense line

2—Delaying zone

Early 1950s
"Fallback"

Mid 1960s
"Trip Wire"

between the two blocs, while keeping all tactical nuclear weapons in reserve until a Soviet conventional breakthrough. For the late 1980s, NATO strategy is considering an "air/land battle," which will keep the forward line of defense on the East-West frontier but which, through the use of high-technology conventional weapons, will focus on interdicting second-echelon enemy forces on their own territory before they reach the front.

Nonetheless, the buildup and modernization of Soviet and Warsaw Pact forces in central Europe still assures Moscow of a conventional advantage. This highlights the importance of further increasing the West European contribution to Europe's defense and the continuing relevance — indeed, the centrality

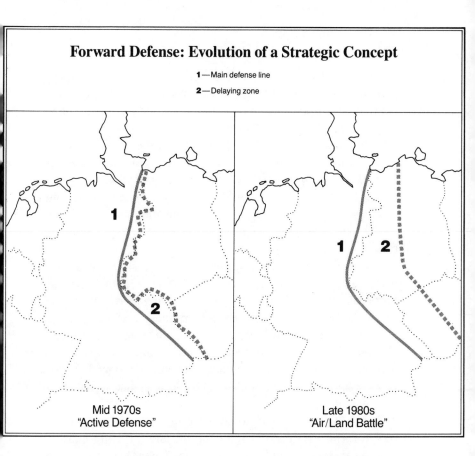

Forward Defense: Evolution of a Strategic Concept

1 —Main defense line

2 —Delaying zone

Mid 1970s
"Active Defense"

Late 1980s
"Air/Land Battle"

— of a credible U.S. nuclear deterrent. It is ultimately those U.S. strategic nuclear forces — which could potentially be triggered by an attack on U.S. combat forces in forward defense positions in West Germany or by a unilateral nuclear escalation by the French — that deprive Soviet military planners of the reassuring expectation that a war in Europe could be won on the conventional level. Until and unless the European members of NATO are prepared to raise and maintain enough conventional forces to fight those of the Soviet Union to a standstill, the U.S. strategic deterrent and the U.S. frontline forces that would become immediately engaged in combat remain a vital component of the overall Western effort to deter war in Europe.

Undoubtedly, some Europeans will claim that any redeployment of any U.S. troops will weaken Western Europe's defenses. An obvious response is that in such a case the Europeans should do more for their own defense. But there are other measures that the alliance can also take to offset any U.S. withdrawals. New technological opportunities are emerging for enhancing U.S.–European cooperation in conventional defense. These potential breakthroughs could not only compensate for any anxiety generated by the proposed reduction in U.S. ground forces but also hold the promise of even strengthening Europe's security.

The SDI, for example, provides two possible steps along these lines. First, NATO could undertake a joint American-European effort to develop an antitactical missile defense (ATM) to protect those key West European military assets most likely to be targeted by the Soviets. Current SDI research suggests that an ATM system is feasible, and a joint initiative would involve Western Europe's industry in an important high-tech venture as well. It would also calm the fear that an American SDI would decouple Europe's security from America's. Second, NATO could apply to conventional warfare some of the new tracking, acquisition, computing, and targeting capabilities and innovative and exotic weapons technologies generated by the SDI. These are likely to involve a quantum leap in the ability to pinpoint and destroy, without the use of nuclear weapons, offensive conventional forces and their rear echelons. In brief, a technological revolution in conventional warfare is in the offing. If it coincides with a strategically and geopolitically needed reallocation of U.S. conventional ground forces, this revolution could mitigate the psychological and political shock waves caused by any redeployments.

The fullest exploitation of the emerging revolution in strategic and conventional defense capabilities is clearly in America's and NATO's interest. It would permit long-overdue innovation in an area where America leads from strength. It would not pose a greater threat to the Soviets but would offset the greatest Soviet threat — the military one — to the West. It would permit geopolitical adjustments in our global strategy, making possible more defense where it is needed most and creating political flexibility where it is potentially most promising.

A gradual reduction of approximately 100,000 troops would also free U.S. budgetary and manpower resources for the flexibility needed to respond to other geostrategic threats. Because an increase in permanently stationed U.S. forces in the Far East is not necessary and because positioning more forces in the Persian Gulf is not likely to be feasible politically, these resources should be channeled primarily in two directions: budgetary savings should be allocated to a significant expansion of U.S. airlift capability, and newly available ground combat manpower should be absorbed into an enlarged RDF through the creation of additional light divisions for use in military contingencies not involving heavy Soviet armor.

Airlift capability is very costly. But the need for a strategically effective airlift is obvious. Without it, the United States will be at a great disadvantage in the crises most likely to develop in the foreseeable future. Despite its efforts over the last decade, the United States still lacks true strategic mobility. It cannot rapidly deploy a truly substantial military force to any likely trouble spot in which significant U.S. security interests become engaged. Current programs to enhance strategic mobility through the acquisition of fifty additional giant C-5 transports would not meet the likely needs and the smaller, more versatile, though more expensive C-17 is not slated for production until the early 1990s. Moreover, the air force prefers to spend funds on increasing its combat role, and therefore its commanders are less than enthusiastic over expenditures designed to provide transport for another service, the army. But if funding for additional airlift capability were diverted from ongoing expenditures for maintaining, largely for reasons of history and of European convenience, combat forces in Europe, the prospects of attaining true strategic mobility would be greatly increased.

Strategic mobility would be enhanced by a corresponding increase in the number of light divisions. Encumbered with less heavy equipment, these units of about ten thousand troops are much smaller than existing heavy divisions, which range from fourteen to eighteen thousand troops. As a result, a light division requires only about 40 percent of the airlift of a heavy division. Designed and trained for use in areas where U.S. forces cannot be permanently stationed, these light divisions would give the United States the ability to respond rapidly and without overkill. The performance by the British light infantry in the Falklands campaign, which included long marches and combat in arduous terrain, provided a good example of what such a force could do. Expanding the present plan for the RDF to include five light divisions would give the United States the possibility of a speedy answer in the event of a major Soviet push into such areas as the mountainous terrain of central Iran or Pakistan.

A more powerful RDF would incorporate these light army divisions and airborne forces but also the Marine Corps. With them the United States could back its interests with credible power even where its forces cannot be deployed on a permanent basis. This would represent a strategically, as well as politically, effective response to changed geopolitical circumstances. The U.S.–Soviet competition has been diverted from its early focus on Europe, and critical engagements could soon occur in regions where the United States is weak and where friendly regimes are unstable. For Moscow, this enhanced U.S. capability would create a major deterrent to any contemplated projection of power into areas remote from the Soviet Union (such as the Middle East, southern Africa, or even Central America). It would also establish a situation on the third central strategic front analogous to that in central Europe. Any

Soviet conventional military move would be likely to result in a militarily significant collision with rapidly arriving U.S. forces — with the attendant risks of nuclear escalation.

Inherent in such a strategic readjustment is the need for a more precise definition of the role of the U.S. Navy. First of all, its capacity for nuclear attack should be separated from its geostrategic mission of controlling the seas. A separate strategic forces command might be created to direct all U.S. strategic nuclear forces, including the navy's SLBMs, capable of executing a massive nuclear attack on the Soviet Union. Achieving sea control should be the navy's central preoccupation. Without effective sea control, the overall geopolitical structure of America's global engagement collapses, for the United States would simply be unable to sustain its efforts on any one of the three Eurasian central fronts. This highlights the imperative of designing the navy for its crucial role. That role is not to carry strategic warfare to Soviet home ports through the use of aircraft carriers, which are largely a vestige of World War II. Nor is it to conduct strategic nuclear warfare. The pivotal task is to maintain sea control and to project American power into distant local conflicts. That means the navy should rely more heavily on attack submarines, deploy only those aircraft carriers necessary for power projection in conventional warfare, and focus above all on developing the forces necessary to prevent Soviet disruption of its mission to support and sustain U.S. deployments abroad.

To achieve effective sea control, the U.S. Navy must be able to do three things simultaneously: (1) sustain U.S. trans-oceanic conventional forces; (2) cork up Soviet fleets in their respective "sea-bottles"; and (3) destroy Soviet foreign bases that might sustain Soviet long-range naval operations. These goals require a different configuration of U.S. naval forces. Less emphasis should be placed on accumulating more aircraft-carrier and battleship naval battle groups. These forces are most effective in assisting through air support and bombardment the infusion of U.S. ground forces into coastal areas, or in intimidating a potential opponent from interfering with U.S. access to maritime routes, such as the Strait of Hormuz. But available funds should be concentrated on enhancing the navy's central mission of sea control — a mission absolutely crucial to U.S. global conventional flexibility.

By combining global conventional flexibility with a posture of mutual strategic security, the United States would be taking a significant step toward an overall strategy more in keeping with the likely geopolitical and military requirements of the rest of this century. It would represent a timely break with the inflexible strategic commitments that have been shaped largely by history, that have overemphasized a massive conventional commitment to a single front, and that have made national survival dependent on the increasingly antiquated doctrine of mutual assured destruction.

The Centrality of Technological Superiority

To maintain both mutual strategic security and conventional global flexibility, the United States must exploit and protect its major asset: technological superiority. This is what has so far denied the Soviet Union the fruits of its massive military expenditures and of coerced domestic sacrifices. Without American technological superiority, the Soviet Union would probably already today enjoy a decisive strategic and conventional advantage, with all the far-reaching geopolitical consequences that implies.

American technological superiority stems from the decentralized and highly creative character of its research and development, spurred by competition and institutional pluralism. Competition generates innovation and experimentation. These cannot be formally planned in a highly centralized fashion. The very nature of the bureaucratic process is inimical to risk taking, a necessary attribute of any significant breakthrough.

This is why, for example, the Soviet Union tends to improve its weapons incrementally, providing safe upgrading for existing systems and adopting altogether novel systems only after they have proven their worth elsewhere, such as the V-rockets of Germany or the SLBMs of the United States.

The systemic diversity of the American economy and the underlying affinity for technological tinkering are incalculable assets. But their strategic application must still be channeled by a powerful stimulus. Today, it is the SDI — for it focuses attention on the strategically critical question of space control. Ultimately, the SDI's importance lies not in whether it may provide a population-wide defense or a more limited shield against Soviet first-strike systems that can be deployed or traded for massive reductions in those Soviet forces. Its importance turns on whether or not it generates new U.S. capabilities for denying space control to its adversary and, if necessary, for asserting U.S. preponderance in space.

The SDI has become the new catalyst for innovation in a strategic area that could prove critical. In so doing, it is also generating spin-offs in a variety of fields — in lasers, particle beams, kinetic energy, and computers. These will have a variety of other military applications. The SDI could lead to revolutionary changes in the nature of weaponry even on the conventional level.

Moscow's efforts to halt the SDI program are rooted in the realization that at this stage the Soviet Union cannot win a qualitative competition. The Kremlin has not forgotten that, despite Sputnik, it was unable to compete with the U.S. program to put a man on the moon. The SDI is reminiscent of the lunar program in its potential for spin-offs for military and civilian technology. And SDI is not the only project with potentially far-reaching strategic consequences. The highly sensitive — and too much talked about — "stealth" program for making planes invisible to radar must alarm the Soviets because it could render the multi-hundred-billion-ruble air defense system ineffective against undetectable U.S. bombers and swarms of cruise missiles.

On the conventional military level, microelectronics has been playing the role of a force-multiplier, a factor of enormous significance given Soviet quantitative superiority in conventional weaponry. The Israelis' exploitation of microelectronics gave them air superiority during the Israeli-Syrian air clashes in 1983. Other innovations in conventional munitions and delivery systems, such as the planned "assault breaker/skeet" weapons technology, hold the potential for massive nonnuclear attrition of concentrated tank formations, for surgical elimination of command bunkers, for instant destruction of airfields and other military assets. These developments are lethally effective in terms of both kill-ratios and depth of reach — so much so that NATO strategists have been encouraged to plan for defense based in part on a "deep/counter/attack" designed to disrupt a massed Soviet conventional offensive and to destroy follow-on echelons even before they enter into battle.

Some analysts forecast even that nonnuclear weapons might soon be able to accomplish the military missions for which strategic nuclear weapons are required today. Over the last ten years, accuracies of intercontinental missiles have improved by an order of ten. Similar advances are likely to occur in coming years. With incremental improvements in other technology, such as cruise missiles with terrain-matching guidance systems or warheads with terminal homing, it may soon become possible to deliver a shaped-charge explosive on the door of an ICBM silo half a world away. This is not to say that a revolution in strategic weapons is imminent, or that nuclear weapons will become obsolete or cost-ineffective. But it does underline the fallacy of basing policy on the idea that technological development of strategic forces has already run its course. These prospective applications of new military technology vastly complicate Soviet operational planning and pose for the Soviets the danger that their massive outlays for conventional weaponry could prove militarily pointless. At the very least, innovation introduces major uncertainty into Soviet military planning.

There is already a measure of dissension among Soviet strategists. In May 1984, the chief of the Soviet General Staff, Marshal Nikolai Ogarkov, said in an interview that a further buildup of nuclear weapons was becoming "senseless" and that "rapid changes" in conventional weapons, such as drone aircraft, cruise missiles with conventional warheads, and new electronic control systems, had enhanced "the destructive potential of conventional weapons, bringing them closer, so to speak, to weapons of mass destruction in terms of their effectiveness." With the United States actively pursuing these developments, Ogarkov said the Soviet Union could not afford to ignore them. His outspoken stance led to his demotion four months later. But it is significant that he returned to prominence after Gorbachev took power.

Marshal Ogarkov's fear that American innovations might enable Washington to leapfrog Soviet doctrines for conventional war serves to point out the critical importance of U.S. technological superiority in the overall military balance. It is therefore vital for the United States to maintain its current lead. According to recent studies, the American advantage is dwindling not only at the level of research and development but also in deployed systems. A Defense Department report stated that in 1984 the United States led in the development of fifteen out of twenty selected foundation technologies, while the Soviet Union held an advantage in none. Of these, however, the American edge was eroding in seven. American technological superiority was smaller when measured in terms of deployed weapons systems. Among thirty-one key weapons systems, American technology was superior to that of the Soviet Union in seventeen, equal in ten, and inferior in four. But if current trends continue into the near future, those figures will become nine, sixteen, and six, respectively. Both the Pentagon bureaucracy and the congressional authorization process obstruct the rapid incorporation of incremental technological improvements, favoring instead the production of new weapons only after a "breakthrough" is achieved. As a result, long lead times for developing U.S. weapons are inevitable. It is a trend to reverse.

Still, the United States maintains a distinct lead in military technology. In computers — today's single most important technology — the American edge is large and growing. Computers are revolutionizing weaponry and military systems in all areas, including command, control, intelligence, space systems, cruise missiles, and electronic warfare. With the development of ever-smaller and ever-faster integrated circuits, the sophistication and intelligence of weapons is making quantum leaps. As one analyst remarked, the "smart" bombs of today will be "brilliant" tomorrow.

To protect is qualitative military advantage, the United States must streamline its procurement system, as well as take steps to prevent the Soviet Union from acquiring key technologies either on the open market or through espionage. Moscow has developed a sophisticated system for obtaining foreign technology. It steals designs and concepts and evades Western export restrictions.

According to a Western intelligence report based on Soviet documentation, the Soviet Union has two programs to acquire Western technology. First, the Military Industrial Commission seeks military and dual-use hardware, as well as blueprints or test equipment, to upgrade Soviet weapons systems and manufacturing processes. Second, the Ministry of Foreign Trade and the Soviet intelligence agencies obtain dual-use equipment through trade diversion for direct use in Soviet military industries. The KGB's Directorate T, which specializes in gathering scientific and technological data, has about 300 agents on foreign assignment. The GRU, the Soviet military intelligence apparatus, has 1,500 officers serving abroad. Their proficiency now enables military planners to target acquisition of specific Western hardware or documents. In the early 1980s, more than 3,500 items were targeted annually, and about one-third were obtained each year. Of the 5 to 10 percent regarded most significant to military research projects, about 90 percent were acquired each year, and about 60 percent of those were obtained from U.S. sources.

It is a systematic effort. Of the ten largest U.S. defense contractors, six ranked among the top ten firms in terms of the frequency with which Moscow targeted their technologies for acquisition. It is no accident that the U.S. universities most often identified as sources of needed technologies — the Massachusetts Institute of Technology, Carnegie-Mellon University, Harvard University, the University of Michigan, the California Institute of Technology, and Princeton University — were the ones most frequently visited by Soviet-bloc scientists.

Such espionage saves the Soviet Union hundreds of millions of rubles in defense expenditures every year. Virtually all of the Soviet Union's long- and short-term research projects for military systems benefit from knowledge or technology acquired in the West. Each year, foreign data help redirect Soviet approaches in about one hundred research projects, initiate hundreds of others, shorten research in about a thousand more, and improve the technical level of still more thousands. This is particularly critical since the Soviets have been most active in strategic missiles, air defense, general-purpose naval and antisubmarine warfare, space and antisatellite weapons, and tactical forces. In some cases, these efforts have enabled the Soviet Union to speed up its weapons acquisition cycle by two years. In a few cases — such as the look-down/shoot-down radars in the latest Soviet fighters — the CIA reports that Soviet documents estimate their savings at five years in development time.

The hemorrhage of Western technology poses a serious threat. Qualitatively superior American weapons have served to offset

Ruble Savings from Only a Part of Soviet Western Technology Acquisitions

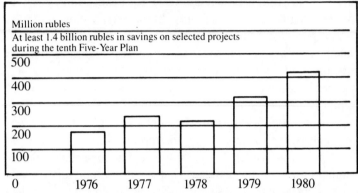

Million rubles

At least 1.4 billion rubles in savings on selected projects during the tenth Five-Year Plan

500

400

300

200

100

0   1976   1977   1978   1979   1980

The above savings generally are conservative estimates by the Soviets resulting from the elimination of stages of military research and design projects, the reduction in time to carry them out, and the adoption of new technical approaches. The savings are not cumulative; that is, a 20-million-ruble annual saving from the acquisition of U.S. and other Western fiberglass plastics production technology used in manufacturing high-pressure air tanks for submarines was counted for one year only, the year of acquisition.

Roughly 400 million rubles ($640 million) were saved in 1980 for only a portion of the Western technology acquired. Most of these savings were in long-term military research projects for weapons of the late 1980s and early 1990s. They therefore were most likely given in terms of manpower savings. By this measure several tens of thousands of Soviet man-years of scientific research effort were saved in 1980.

Source: CIA, *Soviet Acquisition of Militarily Significant Western Technology: An Update*

quantitatively superior Soviet forces. In Europe, it is highly unlikely that the United States and its allies will ever match the levels of Warsaw Pact deployments, for these would include increasing defense spending radically. Western democracies will not be able to beat the Eastern dictatorships in a competition to see which can impose harsher sacrifices on their peoples. As a result, it is imperative that the United States maintain the military balance of power by focusing on the qualitative dimension of the arms rivalry.

At the very least, the United States must hold a technological edge sufficient to make the value of Moscow's numerical advantage ambiguous. As long as Kremlin leaders are unsure whether their quantitative lead would survive a test of arms, they are less likely to engage in the test. But if our lead were to erode to the point that such a strategic calculus held out a certainty of success, Moscow would enjoy the single condition for the exploitation of its military power through assertive pressures or direct aggression.

An Integrated Strategic Framework

The United States does not have an up-to-date, integrated, overall strategic doctrine. Its nuclear strategy does not match nuclear realities. Its conventional ground posture is in a mismatch with geopolitical dangers, and its naval forces are preoccupied by their strategic mission. On the strategic nuclear level, despite the doctrinal initiatives of recent years, the United States is still largely poised for a spasmodic, apocalyptic counterattack, while its strategic forces are gradually becoming more vulnerable to a disarming attack, with the enemy seeking to develop a reserve strategic force to checkmate any possible U.S. societal retaliation. On the conventional level, U.S. combat-ready ground forces are highly concentrated on the first central strategic front — the one front most likely to escalate into a nuclear collision in the event of major hostilities. And they are thinly deployed or unavailable for a conventional defense on the other fronts — where protracted conventional warfare is more likely. In naval strategy, the emphasis has lately been on enhancing the U.S. capacity both to carry conflict to Soviet home ports and to project U.S. power through close-up heavy naval/air bombardment of the enemy. As a result, the United States suffers from a series of handicaps: *rigidity* at the highest strategic level that undermines the credibility of its nuclear deterrent at less than total war; a *lack* of mobility and geopolitical balance in terms of conventional combat capability; and a degree of *uncertainty,* even about whether the U.S. can control the oceans in a prolonged conventional engagement.

An integrated strategy, combining mutual strategic security with conventional global flexibility, should seek to combine capacities we need for a wide variety of nuclear responses to enhance extended deterrence with ground and naval strength to deny the Soviets a quick conventional victory in any Eurasian theater, and ground and naval strength to defeat the Soviets in any non-Eurasian clash. Accordingly, survivable U.S. strategic forces necessary for deterrence must be able both to destroy selectively high-value Soviet military targets and to retaliate comprehensively against Soviet society. In other words, to keep its deterrent credible, the United States must have not only secure nuclear forces but also communications, command and control, and intelligence systems designed for actual war fighting. Offensively, that means U.S. strategic systems capable of attacking a significant portion of the Soviet command and control facilities, leadership shelters, and hardened Soviet first-strike strategic weapons — but with such U.S. forces not deployed in numbers that could pose a first-strike threat to the Soviet side — as well as a survivable U.S. second-strike force capable of inflicting prohibitive damage on the Soviet society as a whole, notably on its imperial Great Russian component. Defensively, it means a U.S. counter-first-strike strategic defense capable of protecting most valued U.S. command and control facilities and at least a significant portion of the U.S. second-strike retaliatory strategic force.

In conventional warfare, U.S. ground forces must reinforce — but not assume the major burden of — the regional defense of the far western and the far eastern extremities of the Eurasian continent. They must also be capable of deploying rapidly to the southwestern Eurasian front, and of inflicting a clear-cut defeat on any Soviet forces that threaten U.S. interests beyond Eurasia. U.S. naval forces must maintain, above all, effective sea control in support of conventional ground missions, including blockading Soviet naval choke points if necessary.

Arms control must be seen as an integral part of an effort to deny the Soviets a politically decisive military edge. Accordingly, the United States should seek a comprehensive arms control agreement that genuinely promotes strategic security by reducing the number of systems with a first-strike capability below the number of likely targets; by instituting ironclad assurances against future deployment of such systems; and by setting the overall number of the nuclear arsenals at equal levels on both sides for political, psychological, and strategic reasons. If that proves to be impossible, highly specialized, narrower arms control arrangements designed to enhance stability in a specific weapons category are preferable to a numerically comprehensive but strategically unrefined and politically misleading arms control accord. Moreover, if comprehensive arms control is unattainable, the United States should unilaterally pursue mutual strategic security by combining limited offensive strategic forces with the deployment of a counter-first-strike strategic defense. That is clearly preferable to a continued reliance on the doctrine of MAD, with its endless multiplication of offensive strategic systems.

To assure American political success, U.S. forces need not be designed to crush the Soviet Union militarily. But they must be designed to ensure that in no circumstances can the Kremlin leaders calculate that their military power has become history's decisive tool.

VI

U.S. Geopolitical Priorities

"**D**EMOCRACY,**"** wrote Sir Halford Mackinder in the light of Europe's painful wartime experiences, "refuses to think strategically unless and until compelled to do so for purposes of defense." Yet today democracy must think, not only stategically for the purpose of defense, but also geopolitically for the purpose of offense. To prevail in the American-Soviet historical conflict, the United States must shape international arrangements that are congenial to democratic values and promote simultaneously both peace and greater opportunity for national and individual self-expression. Not to do so would be tantamount to losing by default.

Americans are not accustomed to thinking in either strategic or geopolitical terms. Though plunged by historical circumstances into a protracted contest with a state that has a tradition of political craftsmanship, American political culture continues to be marked by the absence of a strategic or geopolitical consciousness. American political leaders — in part because of electoral necessity — think mostly in terms of the immediate moment, often subordinating longer-term geostrategic concerns to their more proximate political priorities. American schools go at best through the motions of teaching history, geography, or civics, all of which are essential prerequisites for strategic thinking. American mass media tend to focus public attention on the role of personality, drawing exaggerated conclusions from personal encounters between American and Soviet leaders or from superficial assessments of the personal qualities of the top Soviet leaders. In recent times, for example, the elevation to power of both Yuri Andropov and Mikhail Gorbachev was greeted in the American press with predictions of a fresh start in the U.S.–Soviet relationship.

Yet such a fresh start — which would require a significant change in the Great Russian geopolitical goals — can come only if the United States both neutralizes Soviet military power and reshapes the geopolitical context within which the American-Soviet rivalry is waged. This means the United States must, over a long period, promote several key geopolitical objectives to temper and maybe even to metamorphose the relationship into one of lessened antagonism. Favorable conditions for such a strategy do exist, for during the last two decades the Soviet Union has been defeated in ideological and in economic competition with the United States. Consequently, the remaining task for America is not to lose in the military competition and then to prevail in the geopolitical one.

The ideological defeat of the Soviet Union coincided with the economic one. On both levels, the Soviet Union has lost global credibility during the last two decades. Its experience is no longer perceived either as an attractive social experiment or as the key to rapid economic modernization. Moscow is left with only two options. The first is to enhance its standing through military intimidation and aggression — which America can check — or, second, to capitalize on regional political unrest to undermine America's position. As noted earlier, the policy of stimulating regional unrest and local anti-American sentiments is a weak substitute for the loss of Soviet appeal, but it is the best that the Soviet Union can do for now.

If America seizes its opportunity, Soviet leaders will have

to accept a greater degree of global political pluralism or they will be faced with maximized domestic problems. In both cases the Soviet effort to gain a preponderant position in Eurasia will lose intensity. Thus America must promote four broad geopolitical priorities: (1) accelerate the emergence of a more self-reliant Western Europe and, eventually, a Europe restored from its postwar division; (2) promote an informal strategic triangle in the Far East through wider economic and political cooperation among the United States, Japan, and China; (3) shore up the soft underbelly of southwest Asia by strengthening politically and reinforcing militarily the Soviet Union's southern neighbors; and (4) support the internal pressures in the Soviet-dominated East European states and even within the Soviet Union itself for greater political diversity and tolerance.

A long-term effort designed to shape a more stable geopolitical context for the American-Soviet relationship is the only policy likely to temper and maybe even eventually to transform that conflict into a less threatening relationship. But to avoid overextension the United States will have to be discriminating in the use of its leverage. In Europe, America should mostly pursue a political effort, reducing somewhat the centrality of its military involvement. In the Far East, America should use economics as the principal tool for cementing relationships that also have a strategic significance. In southwest Asia, America should upgrade its effort and recognize that the military dimension is critical defensively and the political one is the key offensively. Within the Soviet bloc, America should energetically exploit advanced communications technology as the principal means for encouraging positive change.

A More Self-Reliant Europe

Forty years after World War II and thirty years after Western Europe's economic recovery, the far western tip of the

Eurasian continent still remains an American military protectorate. Though Western Europe has reemerged as a major trading, financial, and economic power in world affairs, it remains politically fragmented and militarily unable, and also largely unwilling, to provide fully for its own defense. And in a larger sense the cultural-geographical entity known as Europe continues to be the victim of a partition into American and Soviet zones of political preponderance.

This condition is unhealthy for the American-European relationship, while also intensifying the American-Soviet rivalry. It breeds tensions and resentments in the transatlantic partnership, while any change in the political orientations of either Western or Eastern Europe automatically becomes a major geopolitical concern for both America and Russia. Though the current partition of Europe appears on the surface to be stable, it is in fact a case of "metastability" — a physically rigid condition that, if shaken, can suddenly crack massively. Its collapse would have drastic consequences for the East-West relationship.

In these circumstances, what are the basic options for Europe's future and which one would best serve U.S. geopolitical interests? The simplest and the easiest answer, of course, is to continue with the present arrangements, including the maintenance of a very large U.S. military ground presence in Europe in the context of the existing Atlantic alliance linking the United States with half of Europe. But that assumes no change in the political and psychological underpinnings of a relationship that not only protects Western Europe's security but also indirectly perpetuates Europe's division.

That is a doubtful premise, given the fact that the partition of Germany within the partition of Europe makes both divisions a live issue. This guarantees a continuing political struggle for the future of Germany and, consequently, for the future of Europe. It locks America and Russia into a strategically central conflict, but with stakes so high that neither can countenance a direct defeat. With divided Germany serving as the permanent catalyst for change, the future of Europe remains a live issue, despite the stalemate of the last forty years.

The situation might have been altogether different if the division of Europe had not entailed simultaneously the division of Germany. If the geopolitical American-Soviet frontier had been fixed on the Rhine or on the Oder-Neisse line instead of the Elbe, the division of Europe into two spheres of influence would have been neater and politically easier to maintain. With the Rhine as the dividing line, the West European rump would have felt so threatened by the Soviet presence, backed by a Sovietized Germany, that henceforth its enduring preoccupation would have been to ensure the closest possible ties with America, forgetting altogether about the fate of Soviet-dominated central and Eastern Europe. If, on the other hand, Soviet control had been extended only to the Oder-Neisse line, the Poles and the Czechs would have been so fearful that an American-backed Germany might resume its traditional *Drang nach Osten* that the partition of Europe would have been of very secondary concern.

As it happens, the existing stalemate is increasingly resented by all Europeans. West Germans — no longer dominated by feelings of war guilt, less mesmerized by the American ideal, and distressed by the failure of Europe to become an alternative to divisive nationalisms — are naturally drawn to a growing preoccupation with the fate of their brethren living under an alien system. The notion that the destiny of a united Germany depends on a close relationship with Russia is not a new one in German political tradition. Frustration with the nation's division is giving it a new lease on life.

As a consequence, West Germany is already pursuing a distinctive policy of its own toward the East. It carefully avoids provoking Moscow on such neuralgic issues as Poland — the geopolitical linchpin state of Eastern Europe — and cultivates a special economic relationship with East Germany. East Germany is perhaps Moscow's most effective partner in gathering intelligence in the West. It is an active supporter of some international terrorist activities. It is the provider of secret police training and security personnel for some pro-Moscow third-world radical regimes. It is the very determined opponent of any political liberalization in Eastern Europe. Yet this reactionary and dangerous regime has been the beneficiary of significant West German economic assistance — and this has very directly contributed to East Germany's emergence as Moscow's most important junior partner. West Germany's interest-free credit, direct annual payments, and other financial transfers provide East Germany with approximately 2.5 billion deutsche marks each year. In addition, Bonn has sponsored arrangements that give East German goods free access to the West European Common Market. It has been estimated that this provides an additional $2-billion annual subsidy to the East German economy. In effect, nothing short of massive economic aid is being provided to a key member of the Warsaw Pact, with the Soviet Union being the indirect beneficiary.

These special economic links are reinforced by growing political ties that are subtly transforming the West German political orientation to a greater extent than they are affecting the more tightly controlled East Germany. The evolution in the foreign policy outlook of the SPD, the West German Socialist party, has already taken it a long way toward neutralism. In 1985, the SPD joined the ruling Communist party of East Germany, the SED, in advocating an essentially unverifiable ban on chemical warfare and a joint consideration of a nuclear-free zone in central Europe — both of which are long-standing Soviet propaganda proposals. When the Solidarity movement was crushed in Poland, such leading West German Socialist spokesmen as former chancellor Helmut Schmidt and editor Theo Sommer publicly endorsed the action, in marked contrast to the condemnation with which it was received by other West European Socialists.

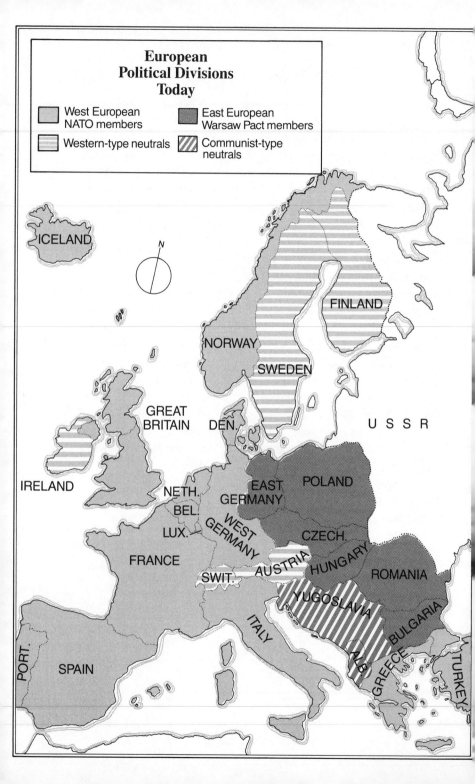

European Political Divisions Today

- West European NATO members
- East European Warsaw Pact members
- Western-type neutrals
- Communist-type neutrals

N

ICELAND

FINLAND

NORWAY

SWEDEN

GREAT BRITAIN

DEN.

U S S R

IRELAND

NETH.

BEL.

LUX.

EAST GERMANY

POLAND

WEST GERMANY

CZECH.

FRANCE

SWIT.

AUSTRIA

HUNGARY

ROMANIA

YUGOSLAVIA

ITALY

ALB.

BULGARIA

PORT.

SPAIN

GREECE

TURKEY

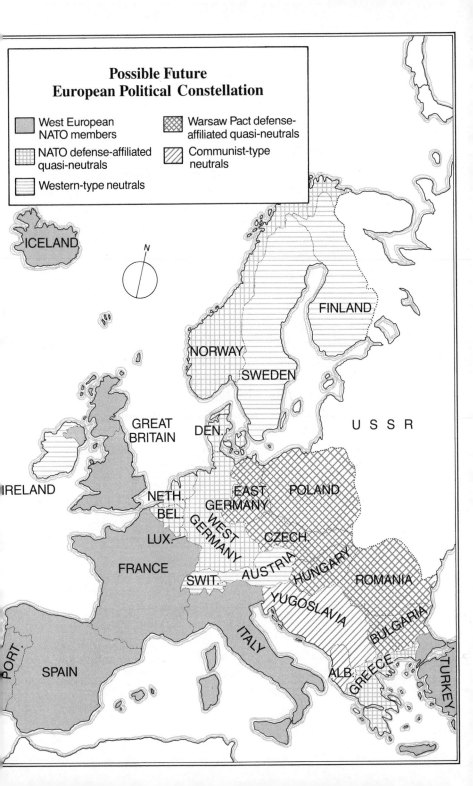

Possible Future European Political Constellation

- West European NATO members
- NATO defense-affiliated quasi-neutrals
- Western-type neutrals
- Warsaw Pact defense-affiliated quasi-neutrals
- Communist-type neutrals

N

ICELAND

IRELAND

GREAT BRITAIN

DEN.

NORWAY

SWEDEN

FINLAND

U S S R

NETH.

BEL.

LUX.

FRANCE

SWIT.

WEST GERMANY

EAST GERMANY

POLAND

CZECH.

AUSTRIA

HUNGARY

ROMANIA

YUGOSLAVIA

BULGARIA

ALB.

GREECE

ITALY

PORT.

SPAIN

TURKEY

Moreover, for Germany in particular but also for Western Europe in general, the East holds a special economic attraction. It has been the traditional market for West European industrial goods. As Western Europe discovers that in its fragmented condition it is becoming less competitive with the high-tech economies of America and Japan, the notion of a special economic relationship with Eastern Europe becomes particularly appealing. The fear that America may be turning from the Atlantic to the Pacific has in this connection a self-fulfilling and a self-validating function: it justifies a wider economic, and potentially even a political, accommodation between a technologically lagging Western Europe and the even more backward Soviet bloc, a logical consumer for what Western Europe can produce.

To register all this is not to say that Europe will simply drift into a separate accommodation with the Soviet Union, fulfilling long-standing Soviet ambitions. It is to note, however, the potential and growing West European susceptibility to a Soviet policy based more on seduction than on intimidation. A Soviet policy designed to exploit more subtly the continued absence of a united Europe, the mounting American frustration with the low level of the European defense effort, and the inevitable appeal of such escapist notions as nuclear freezes could have a polarizing impact on both American and European public opinion.

In Europe itself, a subtle Soviet policy would aim not at dismantling NATO as such but at depriving it of any political or military substance. Exploiting the duality of German feelings and the growing ties between Bonn and East Berlin, it would seek to transform Germany into a politically quasi-neutral member of NATO, thereby alarming and further fragmenting Western Europe. Instead of concentrating on trying to inflict on America a visible and direct political defeat in Europe, it would play on European unwillingness to associate itself with America in the wider global and ideological rivalry with Russia so as to achieve gradual European acquiescence to a subordinate relationship with Moscow.

It is not self-fulfilling pessimism to note that a Europe dependent militarily, fragmented politically, and anachronistic economically remains a Europe more vulnerable to such blandishments. An Atlantic relationship in which Europe has neither a vision nor a policy and America has a policy but no vision may prove to be historically inadequate in meeting the Soviet challenge. In brief, a sustained Soviet peace offensive poses the greater danger that Moscow finally might succeed in splitting Europe from America and thus, taking advantage of Europe's continued historical fatigue, attain finally what Stalin had vainly sought at Yalta.

But is there any alternative to a deteriorating status quo? Five alternatives may be envisaged to the present situation, in which the western half of Europe is tied to the United States through NATO and in which the eastern half continues to be dominated by the Soviet Union and formally linked to it by membership in the Warsaw Pact: (1) the emergence of a Soviet-dominated Europe, more through political acquiescence than through military conquest; (2) a neutralized Western Europe, autonomous internally but deferential to Soviet foreign policy concerns; (3) a politically and militarily more integrated Western Europe, less dependent on the United States but still tied to it by a strategic alliance; (4) a politically and militarily more integrated Western Europe that also promotes closer links with Eastern Europe, as both America and Russia gradually disengage or are pressed to disengage from their present confrontation on the banks of the Elbe in the heart of Europe; and (5) the expansion of NATO Europe to all of Europe, up to the western frontiers of the Soviet Union.

Of the above five, the first and the last can be dismissed as quite improbable — since each would constitute a massive defeat for either America or Russia, a development that both superpowers would resist at high cost. The first variant, moreover, would be opposed by most West Europeans as well, and there is little reason to expect that a self-reliant France and a generally prosperous Western Europe would acquiesce in overt Soviet domination. In this respect, the economic and cultural gulf between Western Europe and Russia also creates a political barrier. The fifth variant would be possible only if there were massive internal turbulence within the Soviet Union itself, to the point of prompting both a unilateral Soviet military withdrawal from central Europe and the collapse in the Kremlin of the political will to preserve the empire.

The real danger, which U.S. policy must anticipate, is posed by the second variant. It could gradually emerge in the malign mix of an economic crisis in the West, political frustration in Western Europe, and transatlantic tensions. As noted, Germany is the geopolitical linchpin state that could serve as the catalyst. To avoid such a prospect, the United States should promote the third variant — which contains within it the potential for evolution into the fourth variant.

The emergence of a politically and militarily more integrated Western Europe, less dependent on the United States for its defense but still tied to it by a strategic alliance, would require more political will than Europe has been able to demonstrate in recent years. The painful fact is that Europe continues to suffer from historical fatigue, induced by the shattering effects of two colossally destructive wars. The initial positive impetus to create an integrated Europe tied to America quietly waned, once the immediate post–World War II economic misery had been relieved and once the seeming urgency of the Soviet military threat had been offset by America's enduring commitment to Europe's security. It became more convenient to disengage from America's global competition with Russia while continuing to benefit from America's regional protection.

It is unlikely that in the foreseeable future a more self-reliant Europe will emerge on the initiative of the Europeans themselves. The French and Germans would have to cooperate in defense, perhaps even replacing the American supreme commander of NATO with a European (preferably a Frenchman). And the Europeans would have to fund more of their common defense. All of this requires a political leadership in Western Europe able to articulate a common purpose for a Europe desirous of playing a more autonomous role in world affairs. A few European leaders have advocated it. Some French and German statesmen have advanced proposals for Franco-German military cooperation in the context of a revitalized Western European Union (WEU). But the status quo conveys no sense of urgency to the public. The voices for a greater Europe have not so far been heeded.

America can help these efforts. The political need is matched by the military case for some U.S. redeployment of ground forces from Europe. A progressive redeployment of some American forces would inevitably focus European attention on Europe's long-term collective security. It would compel European leaders to address the issue more directly. The fact is that the Europeans, now economically fully recovered, are doing much less for their defense than is the American public, and some adjustment in respective efforts is long overdue. A nonbelligerent and nonpunitive American redeployment, justified strategically by U.S. global requirements, would confront the Europeans with the necessity of addressing a basic question: Do they feel that the Soviet Union poses a military threat to Western Europe? If not, then some removal of U.S. forces should not be damaging to their sense of security; if they do, then a greater European defense effort is surely in order.

Until such a question is posed, the majority of Europeans obviously find it more convenient for the United States to commit major forces, and to undertake disproportionate financial burdens. It is sometimes argued that a gradual withdrawal of some U.S. ground forces would prompt a stampede in Western Europe toward neutralism, precipitating in effect the second and otherwise most probable variant. It is difficult to give this credence. On the contrary, a gradual reduction is more likely to stimulate among the Europeans the realization that the time has come to assume direct responsibility for a more autonomous and also a more authentic Europe. After all, most Europeans know that subordination to Moscow would have nasty socioeconomic consequences for them, consequences that it is in their power to avoid.

One should not underestimate Western Europe's capacity to provide more substantially for its defense. In 1983, its population was larger than that of the Soviet Union (332 million versus 275 million), its GNP much more substantial ($2,597 billion versus $1,769 billion), and its per capita income greater ($7,500 versus $6,490). Moreover, by the mid-1990s, Franco-British nuclear forces will have the capacity to cover more than 1,500 Soviet targets, while greater integration into common European defense of French forces and the badly needed improvements in readiness and sustainability of existing German forces could compensate for the proposed reductions in the U.S. ground presence in Western Europe.

Besides, there is no special magic to any particular number of U.S. troops in Europe. The total is not the consequence of a purely military calculus. The current figure represents an increase since 1970, preceded by a steady drop between 1955 and 1970, even though in 1960 the Berlin crisis might have warranted an increase. Moreover, the increase since 1970 does not reflect the improvement in East-West relations in Europe, including the Helsinki agreements, the much reduced European expectation of Soviet military aggression, or the increased capacity of Western Europe to provide for its defense.

A militarily justified and politically beneficial partial U.S. redeployment from Europe — below the 1970 levels — could be undertaken unilaterally because of U.S. global military needs. Or, at least initially, it could be part of some limited joint U.S.–Soviet reductions. To promote such Soviet reductions,

U.S. TROOP LEVELS IN EUROPE
(in thousands)

1950	1955	1960	1965	1970	1975	1980	1985
122	418	375	330	263	301	331	323

(SOURCE: Department of Defense Directorate of Information, Operations, and Reports, Manpower and Management Information Division)

the United States could adopt a more flexible position in the Mutual Balanced Force Reduction (MBFR) negotiations. As early as September 1953, President Eisenhower in a private memorandum to his secretary of state noted that he favored "mutual withdrawals of Red Army forces and of United States Forces." Reductions that initially would involve both U.S. and Soviet forces under the MBFR umbrella would generate less immediate West European concern and help to avoid the undesirable impression that the United States is disengaging from Europe. But if this is not possible it should not delay an American withdrawal program. It would be mild shock therapy for the more lethargic and complacent Europeans.

There is bipartisan political support in America for such reductions. In recent years several prominent Americans have advocated downward adjustments in U.S. ground troop levels in Europe so as to make NATO into a more vital regional defense alliance. Far from reflecting an isolationist impulse, alternative plans for gradual reductions and for the enhancement of the European role in NATO have been advanced by such long-standing and respected advocates of close U.S.–European ties as, on the Republican side, Professors Richard Pipes and Henry Kissinger, and, on the Democratic, Senators John Glenn and Sam Nunn.

For the United States, the gradual emergence of a more self-reliant Europe would be a geopolitical boon. It would be a giant step toward the creation of a more pluralistic globe, less polarized by the U.S.–Soviet conflict. It would enable Western Europe to attract Eastern Europe — without that attraction becoming automatically an American success at Russia's expense. A closer relationship between the two halves of Europe could evolve by stages, leading from all-European economic cooperation eventually to some special security arrangements for central Europe, modeled perhaps on the Austrian Peace Treaty of 1955. In any case, as Western Europe recovers its sense of historical destiny, it is also more likely to heed the admonition of the noted British historian, the late Hugh Seton-Watson, in his last published work in 1985:

Let us stop thinking of the Soviet colonial empire as permanent, and stop speaking of the EEC's neo-Carolingian empire as Europe. There is nothing warmongering or sacrilegious about these small changes in vocabulary.

The European cultural community includes the peoples living beyond Germany and Italy; and this is something which we should never forget, something in no way annulled by the fact that they cannot today belong to an all-European economic or political community. This is all the more reason for promoting, and for making the best possible use of, every sort of cultural contact with them that offers itself, and to show constantly that we recognise them as fellow-Europeans.

Some will dismiss as an impractical vision this idea of a more self-reliant Europe, eventually restored to a more central role in world affairs and more capable of attracting Eastern Europe. But nothing is more dangerous than presuming things will remain as they are. Either Europe will change on its own, in ways that could be dangerous, or it can be refashioned as part of a deliberate strategy. Indeed, just a cursory review of the changes that took place in Europe in a mere quarter of a century reminds one that in a historically brief period even basic changes are possible.

1950	*1975*
1. Wartime allies feud over the future of Europe	A global rivalry, beyond partitioned Europe, is waged by the United States and the USSR
2. Germany is divided and its future uncertain	A reconstituted West German state is a leading member of NATO
3. France expresses preference for a Germany permanently divided	France and West Germany enhance their military cooperation
4. The United Kingdom, still an imperial power, seeks a special global relationship with the United States	The United Kingdom increasingly integrates itself into Europe as a regional power
5. Europe is fragmented and economically ruined	The EEC increasingly becomes a world economic force
6. Europe is defenseless	U.K. and French nuclear forces become increasingly significant while West Germany provides the bulk of NATO forces on the central front
7. Eastern Europe is submerged by the Soviet Union	Yugoslavia and Romania pursue independent foreign policies and Hungary an autonomous economic policy; in Poland a quasi-autonomous society begins to assert itself

In the next twenty-five years, changes just as momentous could take place. It is therefore timely and geopolitically desirable to pursue as the next goal of the Atlantic alliance — an alliance that still represents one of America's two central global relationships — the emergence of a more self-reliant Europe at the western extremity of the Eurasian landmass.

The Pacific Triangle

The model for Europe is emerging in the far eastern extremity of Eurasia: the major regional players grow more self-reliant, reinforced in South Korea and Japan by a limited U.S. military presence and clear-cut security commitments, and backed by a larger U.S. military force in the Pacific.

Four basic questions need to be resolved before this can evolve into an effective regional arrangement capable of ensuring geopolitical stability: (1) What is the perimeter of U.S. national security in the Far East? (2) How can the U.S. encourage Japan to play a more active security role without precipitating regional anxieties and without intensifying Japanese domestic discord? (3) How can the United States expand cooperation with China without stimulating Chinese suspicions that Washington is pursuing the relationship primarily as a tactic to put pressure on the Soviet Union, especially if Moscow and Beijing take further steps in normalization of their relations? (4) What should the United States do to contribute to the stability and security of the Far East's two linchpin states, South Korea and the Philippines?

Where to draw the American security line is an important matter. Ambiguity on this issue contributed to the outbreak of the Korean War, and it is essential not to repeat that mistake, even though American treaty obligations in the Far East are not as wide-ranging as those in the Atlantic relationship. South Korea and Japan clearly fall within the range of U.S. vital interests, with the United States treaty-bound to respond to an attack on them. The U.S. military presence in the Philippines also carries a clear mandate, reinforced by the geopolitical importance of the islands themselves. The United States also has a vital interest in Thailand — especially because of its proximity to the Strait of Malacca — and would have to react to the threat of a pro-Soviet or Vietnamese takeover of the country, though at first possibly at a level short of direct military intervention. Thus, the perimeter defining critical U.S. national security interests begins with the Japanese islands, includes South Korea and the Philippines, and runs all the way down to Thailand.

It becomes a more complicated and sensitive question with regard to the People's Republic of China. There is no formal security arrangement between the United States and China, even though some joint undertakings in this area have developed in recent years. At the same time, Beijing shares Washington's deep concern about the Vietnamese occupation of Kampuchea (Cambodia) and the growing Soviet military presence in Vietnam. America and China have also collaborated in responding to the Soviet invasion of Afghanistan. Both countries are highly critical of the continuing Soviet occupation, and both sustain the Afghan resistance. So, common strategic interests do exist.

Moreover, as the United States has repeatedly declared, a strong and secure China is in the interest of the United States. Only such a China can pursue an independent foreign policy, critical of the United States on some issues while opposing the Soviet Union on others. Although the American-Chinese relationship is important in its own right, China is a critical factor in the American-Soviet rivalry. Even more relevant than China's opposition to specific Soviet actions is the fact that China itself is a major obstacle to Soviet regional hegemony. A strong and secure China pursuing its own national interest is a major impediment to Soviet preponderance in the Far East, even if Sino-Soviet relations become less hostile. Therefore, in a political sense, the perimeter of U.S. vital interests includes China. The United States could be neither indifferent nor passive in the face of a forceful Soviet attempt either to alter China's leadership or to threaten China's independence.

This means the United States cannot protect its vital interests in the Far East through a purely offshore strategy. It must concern itself with security on the mainland of the far eastern periphery of Eurasia, especially including China and Thailand. An independent and secure China reduces the probability of renewed conflict on the Korean peninsula, and it enhances the security of Japan. Similarly, a secure Thailand increases the security of all the nations linked together in the Association of Southeast Asian Nations, whose political and economic vitality clearly benefits international stability. American security policy must therefore convey to all concerned that the United States would see its own interests as threatened by any hostile actions that jeopardize the security of these two mainland Asian states.

But to accomplish that objective the United States must continue, above all, to maintain and enhance its strategic cooperation with Japan. This relationship must be the cornerstone of U.S. security policy in the Far East. If economic protectionism and other related issues were to weaken or poison American-Japanese relations, the entire structure of U.S. security policy in the Far East would be at risk. Cultivating and expanding the security dimensions of that relationship require American sensitivity. The United States has to be acutely aware of reservations in Japan about increasing defense spending and of regional anxieties about Japan's assuming a central military role. There are still many memories of World War II.

The United States, quite understandably, has pressed Japan to increase its defense effort. While the proportion of GNP the United States spends on defense is about 6.6 percent and that of the major powers of Western Europe ranges from 2.8 to 5.3 percent, Japan has kept its defense budget at approximately 1 percent of GNP. South Korea, from whose security Japan certainly benefits, spends 7.5 percent of its GNP on defense. While it costs the average American about $890 each year for defense and the average Briton, Frenchman, and West German about $470, $420, and $370, respectively, it costs the Japanese only about $100. Given the robust vitality of Japan's economy, its defense is disproportionately small, and this in turn creates political resentments in the United States.

Yet, Americans must respect the sincerity and depth of Japanese antimilitarism. These feelings derive from painful historical experience; they are not merely a cynical mask for selfishness. It was at American insistence that antimilitarist principles were inserted into the Japanese constitution, and it is a credit to the Japanese people that they take these principles seriously. Moreover, overt and heavy-handed American pressure on Japan to build up its military could split the existing Japanese consensus on the desirability of the American-Japanese alliance and sharpen cleavages within Japanese politics. In recent years, an overwhelming majority of the Japanese electorate has favored close American-Japanese political and security cooperation. It would be foolish to risk that orientation.

Japan is, in any event, adjusting its posture. At the Williamsburg summit meeting in May 1983, the Japanese joined the heads of the other advanced industrial democracies in issuing a declaration that stated: "the security of our countries is indivisible and must be approached on a global basis." Tokyo's current five-year defense program increases military spending significantly and will improve Japan's security position, particularly its air and sea patrol and air defense capabilities. In addition, the new program adopted by the Japanese cabinet in 1985 no longer holds defense spending below the arbitrary ceiling of 1 percent of the GNP. That decision represents an important psychological breakthrough and should not be belittled. It is noteworthy that this program was approved with relatively little political opposition.

Nonetheless, the fact remains that for the foreseeable future, Japan will contribute less to collective security than will the United States and its other principal allies. A corrective needs to be found. And there is an option that is in keeping with both the spirit of the Williamsburg resolution and Japanese antimilitarism and yet redresses the imbalance. Japan should be encouraged to make an indirect, but still vital, contribution to common security by increasing its *strategic* economic aid to those developing countries in which the Western democracies have a vital interest. These include Egypt, Thailand, the Philippines, and Pakistan. They already receive relatively modest sums of Japanese economic aid, a total of $803 million in economic assistance in 1983. Another $290 million went to South Korea. In 1984, Japan allocated over $1 billion of aid to the Philippines. These amounts should be considered as part of the Japanese defense contribution, for they enhance the security of countries in which not only the United States or Western Europe but Japan as well has a special interest.

Current plans to increase the level of overall Japanese economic aid to foreign countries from $4 billion in 1986 to $8 billion in 1992 are a step forward. But given the strength of the Japanese economy, the total proportion of the GNP committed to defense and strategic economic aid should at some point reach the level of approximately 4 percent — roughly equal to the current West European effort devoted to defense alone. This aid should be targeted at states in which both Japan and the United States have a high strategic stake. It should be channeled not only to the present recipients in Asia but also to other geopolitically key countries in other regions. For instance, Central America qualifies, especially given the importance of the Panama Canal to Japan's foreign trade.

Such an increase in Japanese economic assistance and defense spending combined would push the overall Japanese contribution to collective security to a level above $50 billion — in contrast to current defense expenditures in the range of $10 billion to $15 billion. This would be a substantial contribution, and it would be up to the Japanese to determine how it should be split between defense and strategic economic aid. Western collective security would be thus enhanced. Japan's role in shaping those security arrangements would be elevated. Japanese influence would be brought to a level commensurate with its economic importance.

Japan's enhanced status should facilitate the transformation of the annual economic summit of the leaders of the advanced industrial democracies into a strategic summit. There is a need for an informal coordinating organ through which leaders of America, Europe, and Japan can discuss the longer-term strategic implications of their shared interest in preventing Eurasia's domination by one power. An annual strategic summit that focuses both on global economics and on global security would fill this gap.

At the core of Tokyo's growing strategic role must be Japanese participation in the emerging relationship among the United States, Japan, and China — what might be called the Pacific triangle. Cooperative relations between the United States and China and between Japan and China are a relatively new element in the Far East, and both relationships are still evolving. How they evolve will in large measure determine the degree of security that Japan and the United States will enjoy in the Pacific Basin.

China has a longer common border with the Soviet Union than any other country, and across that boundary stand overwhelmingly superior Soviet forces. This central reality impresses upon the minds of the Chinese leaders a basic geostrategic conclusion, well described by Jonathan Pollack in a 1984 Rand study:

Leaders in Peking understand that the Sino-Soviet relationship represents a far more intractable problem than their disagreements and difficulties with the United States. Unlike the Soviet Union, the United States no longer poses a frontal military challenge to the PRC. The USSR maintains large, sophisticated, well-equipped military forces along a still partially contested Sino-Soviet border. A strengthening across the entire spectrum of Soviet military capabilities — ground forces, air forces, naval power, as well as strategic nuclear weaponry — has now been sustained for more than a decade. East Asia no longer represents a peripheral military front for the Soviet military leadership, a fact formalized by the establishment of an independent theater command in the region in late 1978. A long-term Soviet goal has been achieved at enormous expense: The Soviet Union has become a credible two-front power, with the capacity to pressure, coerce, and encircle China from the north, east or south.

Without Japan and the United States, China cannot cope with the Soviet military threat. Alone, it could become vulnerable to intimidation. It could neither modernize its economy nor effectively upgrade its military capability. Here is the basis for an enduring, though informal, security relationship within the Pacific triangle.

It would be a mistake, however, to assume that the Soviet threat by itself will keep the United States and China together. The threat certainly brought them together in the first place in 1972, and it figured prominently among the considerations of both sides when normalization of relations was agreed upon in 1979. Indeed, at that time Chinese leaders even spoke of a de facto alliance with the United States against the Soviet Union. Since then China has preferred to adopt a more neutral course. While China bases its long-term modernization drive on an economic opening to the West, it is now clear that Beijing no longer wishes to couple this with an overt and binding military-political alliance.

Assiduous cultivation of economic ties within the Pacific triangle is therefore necessary to cement the informal strategic relationship. Trade expanded rapidly in the wake of normalization and proved a useful buffer to the political frictions of the early years of the Reagan administration. In the fourteen years since the American-Chinese rapprochement, total trade has grown from $96 million to well over $7 billion a year. During the same period, total trade between Japan and China increased from $823 million to over $13 billion a year. These expanding trade relations reflect the Chinese commitment to modernize through closer ties with Japan and the United States. Japan shares the American interest in seeing the emergence of a strong and more modern China. During Prime Minister Yasuhiro Nakasone's visit to Beijing in March 1984, Japan extended $2 billion in credits to China, while both governments declared their intention to intensify their economic and technological cooperation "throughout the twenty-first century and beyond." Soloviev's nightmare of a China modernized by Japanese know-how (see page 70) could be coming to pass!

Two regions of China are particularly in need of economic modernization. One is Manchuria, the country's traditional center of industrial activity, whose equipment is largely outdated. Both American and Japanese investment is necessary. The Japanese particularly should have a stake in offering preferential assistance to Chinese Manchuria over Soviet Siberia. The other region is the northwest, including Xinjiang province. Chinese leaders have recently announced plans to develop this most retarded area. Like Manchuria, it is geopolitically sensitive. It borders on the Soviet Union and is vulnerable to Soviet intrusion. Indeed, both Manchuria and Xinjiang have in the past been objects of Soviet territorial expansionism. An important aspect of the Chinese effort is to build up a communications network, not only to link Xinjiang more tightly with the rest of China, but also to improve direct access to Pakistan. The latter goal has clearly important and desirable military-political implications for closer cooperation between China and Pakistan. Chinese leaders refer to the proposed transportation network as "rebuilding the Silk Road and going out to the world," and European industrial delegations have already shown interest in assisting China in reestablishing the route once taken by Marco Polo. American and Japanese help here would have an obvious geopolitical significance.

As long as Chinese economic expansion continues, the United States can take a relatively relaxed attitude toward the normalization of Sino-Soviet relations. China's three conditions for a genuine improvement in those relations — a Soviet withdrawal from Afghanistan, a Vietnamese withdrawal from Kampuchea, and a thinning out of Soviet forces on the Sino-Soviet frontier and in Mongolia — are more than acceptable from the American perspective. Therefore, it is unlikely that normalization of relations between Beijing and Moscow would obstruct the enhancement of the triangular relationship among China, Japan, and the United States.

A greater danger — and the opportunity for which the Soviets are probably waiting — is the possibility that Deng Xiaoping's policies may be reversed after his departure. Some turmoil and some political retrenchment by conservative Communist bureaucrats is then likely. But the political reforms and the changes in the Chinese leadership that Deng has recently imposed make a complete reversal less probable. There appears to be little sentiment in China either for restoring complete control of the economy by the political center or for returning to the days of heavy economic dependence on the Soviet Union. The expansion of economic relations with the United States and Japan is seen by most of the Chinese elite as the necessary precondition for China's successful and rapid modernization. The Chinese know that a strong and secure China is in the American interest. But they also know that it might not be in the Russian interest, and that puts a premium on long-term economic cooperation with the United States and Japan.

In this cooperative context, the United States and Japan must quietly seek to define the scope of shared security concerns with China. Discreet consultations on defense matters already occasionally take place among these three countries, and there is a clear security dimension to the help that the United States and Japan give to Chinese economic efforts. The scope of overt transfers of military technology to China will probably expand, and this in turn may lead to more liaison on regional security.

It is therefore likely that the triangle of economic, political, and informal strategic cooperation in east Asia will further develop. The Japan-U.S. axis is the strongest but because both are working with the Chinese, a more binding regional relationship is clearly emerging. As with Western Europe, the Soviet Union will intensify its efforts to incite cleavage between the United States and Japan and between the United States and China. Unlike Western Europe, however, Japan and China are both in a sense still irredentist countries as far as the Soviet Union is concerned. Territorial-historical animosities inhibit Soviet prospects and contribute a strong psychological underpinning for the vital Pacific triangle.

For similar reasons South Korea looks secure. North Korea is unlikely to mount a major attack unless assured of support from at least one of the two major Communist powers and of the benevolent neutrality of the other. And the presence of U.S. ground forces provides the important assurance that any attack would engage America. South Korea does have political problems that raise a question mark regarding its stability and could create tension with the United States. But as its economy grows, it should be able to make political reforms — and the United States should quietly encourage it to do so. At the same time, American public opinion and mass media should be sensitive to South Korea's special security problem, and therefore overt external pressure should be avoided.

A more immediate problem is posed by political instability, even an emerging systemic crisis, in the Philippines. Japan can help to reduce some of the economic causes for social unrest by increasing aid as part of its enhanced strategic aid program, but American intervention may be needed to avert political collapse. American contacts with the Philippine business community and with the military leadership are so extensive that unambiguous encouragement should suffice to precipitate the needed social reforms. Given the lessons of the fall of Somoza in Nicaragua and the Shah in Iran, however, it is essential that any such initiative be accompanied by arrangements for a stable and efficient government, capable of undertaking a long-term program of economic renewal and development. This will require both U.S. economic assistance and intrusive political backing.

Overall trends in the Pacific region are favorable to stability and compatible with basic American interests. Japan is emerging as a true world power and is assuming the corresponding political and even military responsibilities. China, far from being "lost" to Moscow, has emerged as a major and effective opponent of Soviet regional hegemonic aspirations. South Korea has performed extremely well economically, outstripping North Korea by far. With growing American economic involvement in the Pacific Basin as a whole and with American military power reinforcing the sense of political security in the region, the emerging Pacific triangle represents the most promising development for the United States in the global American-Soviet rivalry.

The Soft Underbelly

The most urgent and difficult geopolitical priority for the United States is to the southwest of the Soviet Union, where the linchpin states are Iran or the combination of Afghanistan and Pakistan. Long the object of Great Russian imperial designs, the region is vulnerable to Soviet political and military pressure. A dominant Moscow would sever the direct links between the far western and the far eastern Eurasian allies of the United States. It would be able to control access to oil from the Persian Gulf. And it would gain a direct warm-water oceanic window to the world.

Southwest Asia poses a geostrategic challenge of daunting magnitude. In Western Europe, the United States can in a sense accomplish more by doing less. In the Far East, it can succeed by staying on its present course, though acting on the basis of a more deliberate strategic design. But in the soft underbelly of the Eurasian continent, a major effort is required if the Soviet Union is to be denied over the next decade its major breakthrough to the south. That goal is coming ever closer to being within Soviet grasp.

It needs to be reiterated that the Soviet expansion in the region is sought by protracted, prolonged, and patient exploitation of internal weaknesses, sociopolitical fragmentation, and ethnic conflicts. It is not so much a sudden leap forward that threatens the interests of the West. If opportunities beckon, occasional sudden spurts do occur — as in Afghanistan in late 1979 — but the enduring pattern is one of seepage, gradual attrition, steady pressure, all designed to promote incremental but eventually decisive change.

Left to their own resources, the countries in this region cannot in the long run stand up to the Soviet Union. Iran is fatigued by its long war with Iraq. Its internal condition is made fragile by the fundamentalist reaction to the Shah's policy of rapid modernization. The Soviets might well calculate that prospects for political and ethnic violence are high. And Iran's international isolation — with its simultaneous hostility to the United States, the Soviet Union, and the adjoining Arab countries except for Syria — increases its vulnerability.

Pakistan faces similar, though less acute, problems. India's continuing hostility imposes a heavy military burden. Pakistan has to defend two fronts. It has to protect its major cities from nearby Indian forces, and it has to reinforce the volatile Pakistan-Afghan frontier. The gradual shift toward civilian rule will surface currently suppressed doubts about the desirability of helping to sustain Afghan resistance against Soviet occupation. This ambivalence is already widespread not only within the intelligentsia but also within some business circles. Yet the desire to appease Moscow is tempered by the knowledge that the abandonment of the Afghans could, in turn, hurt Pakistan's relations with the United States and even with China.

In the final analysis, the strongest barrier to Soviet expansion is the political and religious desire of these countries not to be dominated by the powerful neighbor from the north. No policy undertaken by the United States can substitute for this will. But this will must be sustained by the certainty of America's long-term security commitment. Local determination will not suffice.

To cope with this regional problem there has to be a comprehensive five-point effort building on the Carter Doctrine, reaffirmed subsequently by President Reagan: (1) to reinforce the anti-Soviet resilience of the region's key countries, notably Pakistan and Iran, and to cooperate with China to improve Pakistan's security; (2) to increase the U.S. capacity to mount a prompt military response should the Soviets attack; (3) to keep the Afghan issue alive by sustaining the resistance, while simultaneously probing for Soviet willingness to restore genuine neutrality and internal self-determination to Afghanistan; (4) to engage India in at least the diplomatic efforts for the resolution of the Afghan problem and to promote a less tense Pakistani-Indian relationship; and (5) to help stimulate a more distinctive political consciousness among the Soviet Muslims as a deterrent to the further Soviet absorption of Islamic peoples.

These components of a long-term geostrategy will require collectively a major political, military, and economic undertaking. Such an effort is justified by the huge stakes and is facilitated to some extent by the relatively favorable trends on the other two central strategic fronts. Accordingly, for the United States to concentrate its initiative and resources on this region is both justified and feasible.

To reinforce the resilience of Pakistan against Soviet pressure the United States will have to provide substantial military and economic aid. Pakistan has indicated that from 1988 to 1993 it will need approximately $6.5 billion, of which 55 percent would be economic development assistance and 45 percent would be military aid. As large as this sum is, it is considerably less than the United States commits to either Israel or Egypt. With the savings that would result from lower U.S. expenditures for the defense of Europe, the United States should be able to go a long way toward meeting Pakistan's needs; and Pakistan should also receive funds from an enlarged Japanese strategic economic assistance program.

The United States should certainly support China's plan to revive the ancient "Silk Road," which would link China and Pakistan more tightly. This physical link would have obvious strategic consequences. It would improve China's access to the West and enhance the cooperation between the two Asian countries most directly interested in containing Soviet hegemony. The route would reinforce China's control of exposed and strategically important Xinjiang province and would fortify Pakistan's hold on the territory to the south of the Soviet Union across the Wakhan Corridor, the small strip of Afghanistan separating the Soviet Union from Pakistan. As the earlier plans for Russian railroad construction in this underdeveloped region implied, the expansion of communications automatically entails political and military consequences, and by-products of the Pakistani-Chinese link would be a contribution to regional stability.

A more difficult, but no less important, task is to restore some degree of American-Iranian cooperation. Despite the officially cultivated hostility of Iran toward the United States, the fact remains that in the long run Iran needs at least indirect American support to sustain its independence and territorial integrity. After Khomeini's death and the inevitable political turmoil, a gradual normalization will probably take place. The United States should clearly signal a willingness to improve American-Iranian relations, because its interest in an independent Iran transcends even the current Iranian hostility. That American interest stems from a larger geopolitical concern for a key linchpin state in the U.S.–Soviet contest, and should not be compromised by transitory emotions.

America's Western European and Japanese allies should

maintain their indirect ties with Iran. These help to prevent the collapse of Iran's economy. They keep the prospects alive for a turn eventually toward moderation in Iran. If these links are preserved in the near term, Iran's anti-Russian nationalism and anti-Communist religious feelings, as well as its desire for economic development, will sooner or later push Tehran into a more cooperative relationship with the West.

These efforts on behalf of regional stability must be reinforced with a credible American deterrent against Soviet invasion. Credibility is crucial. Ambiguity about U.S. intentions contributed to the North Korean decision to attack South Korea in 1950 and perhaps even to the Soviet decision to invade Afghanistan in 1979. Soviet uncertainty about how the United States would react to a military move in southwest Asia could be just as dangerous. With the further development and enlargement of the Rapid Deployment Force, the United States is gradually acquiring the capability to react strongly to a Soviet invasion of Iran or Pakistan, especially if local forces also oppose the intruders. As extensive Defense Department studies suggest, the difficult terrain and the poor lines of communication ensure that the Soviets would encounter major logistical difficulties on a move southward. In these circumstances, the RDF could even today play a significant role in reinforcing local resistance. In any case, it is essential that Kremlin leaders should not be able to conclude that they can act unilaterally against either Pakistan or Iran, as they did against Afghanistan.

While it improves its capability to project its conventional forces into southwest Asia, the United States must continue to keep alive the issue of the Soviet occupation of Afghanistan. This requires a three-pronged strategy. First, the fighting: the United States must keep supplying the Afghan resistance with money, weapons, and ammunition. It must upgrade the equipment provided to the *mujahideen,* including delivering more advance weaponry such as heat-seeking antiaircraft missiles.

Second, world opinion: the United States should assist more direct mass media coverage of the war itself by improving arrangements for television and radio coverage. This will help to intensify international condemnation of Moscow — the highest cost the Soviet Union is paying for its aggression. Soviet standing has already declined significantly in the third world, particularly among Muslim countries. India, too, should be encouraged to change its attitude of benign acceptance of Soviet aggression and brutality. If New Delhi were to become more critical of Moscow, the Soviet calculus of costs and benefits might shift toward finding a way out. The United States should emphasize to the Indians that India can promote better U.S. – Soviet relations only by contributing to a peaceful solution of the Soviet-Afghan war — and that this will become possible only when Moscow concludes that the political costs of the venture are prohibitively high.

Third, diplomacy: the United States must prepare a diplomatic formula for the disengagement of Soviet forces. As well as the *mujahideen* have fought, they can never expect to defeat the Soviet Union militarily. At the same time, the Soviets will not disengage voluntarily unless a way can be found to ensure that a Soviet withdrawal does not make Afghanistan an anti-Soviet outpost. To reassure Moscow, the United States should make clear that it would be prepared to participate along with the Soviet Union, China, Pakistan, and India in a five-power agreement to guarantee the genuine neutrality of Afghanistan. This might be modeled on the Austrian Peace Treaty of 1955. In addition, the United States could propose that the prompt removal of Soviet forces from Afghanistan be accompanied by the temporary introduction of peacekeeping forces from Islamic countries with foreign policies not unfriendly to the Soviet Union, such as Algeria or Syria. This might reassure Moscow that the departure of the Soviet troops would not be followed by the massacre of all pro-Soviet Afghans.

In short, the goal for a political solution should be external neutralization and internal self-determination. Over time, the combination of mounting international condemnation and increasingly effective *mujahideen* resistance might persuade the Kremlin to accept this formula. The Kremlin might calculate that its longer-range hopes regarding internal unrest in Iran and Pakistan are better served by a breathing spell that helps to cool anti-Soviet passions among the Muslims.

Perhaps the best deterrent to a continued Soviet push southward exists within the Soviet Union itself — and it represents an opportunity that the United States has so far failed to exploit. Muslims in the Soviet Union now number approximately 55 million people, and they have been subdued — or "Sovietized" — on the surface. It should be recalled, however, that local resistance to Soviet — or, in reality, Great Russian — domination took more than a decade of fighting to suppress, ending only in the early 1930s. Today, there is considerable evidence of persistent local resentment of Moscow's policy of Russification. Moreover, since Islam has not been extirpated, Soviet Muslims have doubtless been affected by the worldwide resurgence of Islamic culture and religion. There is here the potential for a serious religious-ethnic challenge over Moscow's control of Soviet central Asia.

The "holy war" against the Soviets in Afghanistan, the fundamentalist revolution in Iran, the strong support for the Afghan *mujahideen,* and the institution of Islamic law in Pakistan, all reflect a similar phenomenon — a widespread awakening of a more self-assertive orientation based on ethnicity and Islamic faith. This new outlook has now collided with Soviet expansionism. At first, Soviet Muslims reacted to the collision with ambivalence, but resentment is developing. The United States can accelerate this alliance of hostility with greatly intensified radio broadcasts beamed at Soviet central Asia. Washington already plans to set up one new broadcasting facility, Radio Free Afghanistan. It should be used to this end, with special programs targeting Soviet Muslims and stressing the anti-Islamic character of Soviet policies in Afghanistan. In addition, the United States should offer technical support for similar efforts from other Islamic countries. The Kremlin leaders are more likely to exercise restraint if they become convinced that regional unrest will inevitably spill over into the Soviet Union itself.

The U.S. ability to constrain Soviet ambitions on this third front could be undermined, however, if Moscow takes advantage of the Arab-Israeli conflict to leapfrog into the Middle East, thereby outflanking the Persian Gulf. The Middle East problem is not of Soviet making, and it does not involve a head-on U.S.–Soviet collision. Instead, it is an indirect U.S.–Soviet conflict, with the Soviet Union seeking to exploit regional tensions to enhance its influence among radical Arab states and hoping ultimately to reap the benefits of an American failure to promote an Israeli-Arab peace settlement. In brief, the Kremlin calculates that the Middle East will play the same role for the third front that Imperial Germany's social collapse in 1918 did for the German western front: the disintegrating rear.

This represents more than simply a threat that the United States will be isolated among the Arab states in the Middle East. A potential result is the creation of Soviet bases or the deployment of Soviet forces — in Libya, for example — that would jeopardize American freedom of action in the region. An even more ominous opening for the Soviet Union could be created by growing political instability within the Persian Gulf states, with contentious domestic factions, restless Palestinian immigrants, and Islamic fundamentalism combining to bring anti-American governments to power. These threats highlight the importance of U.S. actions to enhance regional stability, particularly through a renewed push to advance the Arab-Israeli peace process.

Although American and Soviet interests in the Middle East conflict and although the stakes are high, both countries recognize the necessity for caution and restraint. Both know that a collision would jeopardize vital American interests and would therefore require a strong American reaction. Moreover, occasional Soviet gains could easily be undercut by the fluidity of Arab politics and the unpredictability of the Arab leaders. As a result, a shared interest in avoiding a head-on collision has constrained the conduct of the United States and the Soviet Union in the Middle East.

On the American side, it has also led to sharp swings of policy regarding the Soviet Union's role in the region, particularly concerning Arab-Israeli peace negotiations. Broadly speaking, there are two U.S. approaches.

One seeks to exclude the Soviet Union from the Middle East peace process as much as possible. The Nixon administration's policies were based on this premise. The Soviet inclination to prevent or complicate any constructive resolution of the Middle East problem has reinforced this U.S. approach. Moscow knows that only by hindering peace efforts can the Soviet Union reduce U.S. influence in the region and enhance its own.

The other approach seeks to engage the Soviets in the peace process to the extent possible. This was the policy of the Carter administration during its first year. A deliberate effort was made to make Moscow a partner in the search for a resolution to regional conflicts on the grounds that a head-on collision would endanger both superpowers. This effort was frustrated for the simple reason that Moscow's ability to increase its regional influence depended on the absence of peace. The Kremlin knows that the resolution of the Middle East conflict would for a variety of ideological, religious, and economic reasons enhance the regional influence of the West, particularly that of the United States. Consequently, the option of actively engaging the USSR in the peace process collides with real Soviet interests, and a

Soviet Union included in the peace process is a Soviet Union with leverage to escalate maximalist Arab demands so as to inhibit progress toward peace.

The United States has therefore been driven back to the first option of seeking to exclude the Soviets. This worked in the negotiation of the Camp David agreements and the earlier Sinai disengagement accords that in some ways led to Camp David. It is important to realize, however, that for success this approach has depended in the past — and will depend in the future — on U.S. willingness to mount a major peace effort and to apply the necessary persuasion on Israel and the Arab states. In other words, only by being assertive and active in promoting peace can the United States exclude the Soviet Union from the region and force the parties to the conflict to appreciate the centrality of the U.S. role and the necessity of accommodating themselves to it.

Given the nature of the U.S. political system, a major diplomatic engagement demands more than a governmental initiative. It demands also a personal commitment on the part of the president and secretary of state. This means that they have to make the search for Middle East peace a priority of their foreign policy and, given the nature of the issue, even of their domestic policy. It also implies that they must be willing to run a political gauntlet and must be ready to undertake a long, arduous, and at times painful task with no guarantee of success. It is therefore not surprising that U.S. policymakers are wary of undertaking this task and generally tend to look for ways to shift the burden to others or to mark time until there is a uniquely opportune moment that could guarantee a successful outcome.

There is a stage, however, at which it might be unavoidable and even desirable to involve the Soviets. Once real progress has been achieved the Soviets should be invited to play a formal role as part of a reassuring ritual capping of negotiations dominated in the earlier and more critical stages by the United States alone. This might be the scenario if the initiatives of King Hussein of Jordan, President Hosni Mubarak of Egypt, and Prime Minister Shimon Peres of Israel succeed in removing the principal obstacles to an eventual confederation of Jordan and a demilitarized West Bank. Progress in that direction will require at some point a dialogue with Syria as well, because President Hafiz al-Assad has the capacity to disrupt the peace process. To feel secure, Syria in turn will require that its sponsor — the USSR — be engaged at least to a limited degree to balance Israel's sponsor — the United States. For this reason, a formula may have to be contrived for a formal Soviet role in the ratification stage. Soviet participation could await, for example, the final phase of a multilateral, perhaps UN-sponsored, ratification of the American-initiated peace process.

While reluctant, the Soviets might join such a peace process once they realized that the United States was serious about promoting peace and might even succeed without their participation. At that stage, the Kremlin might prefer even nominal participation to total exclusion. For the United States, granting Moscow such a role would be a small price to pay for the cumulative effect that a major U.S. peace effort could have in stabilizing the otherwise geopolitically dangerous rear of the third central strategic front.

Imperial Retraction

A repressive empire tends to be an expansive empire. Ultimately, a more stable U.S.–Soviet relationship demands a change in both the scope and character of Soviet power. That can take place peacefully; but promoting it is the needed offensive component of a U.S. strategy designed to mitigate American-Soviet hostility and eventually to bring about a more cooperative relationship. But until then, promoting change within the Soviet realm serves — to put it bluntly — as a means for peacefully seizing the geopolitical initiative in the protracted historical conflict.

The suppressed aspiration of East European nations and the internal national contradictions of the modern-day Great Russian empire provide the springboard for seeking two central and interdependent goals. The first is to weaken the Kremlin's offensive capacity by increasing its domestic preoccupations. The second is to promote the pluralization of the Soviet bloc and eventually of the Soviet Union itself by cautiously encouraging national self-assertiveness.

In an interview in 1983, Milovan Djilas made an apt comparison between the Soviet system of national domination and that of the late Ottoman Empire. He noted that both systems fused political and religious or ideological authority at the highest level of the state and that in both cases expansionism was inherent in the system of power itself. The Ottoman Empire, he continued, sought security and confidence through expansion and "even when it started to decay, [it] could not cease to expand . . . when that expansion was stopped, then the empire started to disintegrate slowly, as national and social rebellions erupted." Drawing a parallel with far-reaching consequences, Djilas concluded, "In the long run, the Soviet Union must disintegrate, and will disintegrate faster if [its] expansionism is stopped."

Stopping that expansionism — especially on the three central Eurasian fronts — can be facilitated by the promotion of internal change within the Soviet realm. A progressively more independent Eastern Europe would certainly reduce the Soviet military threat to Western Europe. A more assertive attitude on the part of the Soviet Muslims, as well as the Ukrainians, Balts, and other national minorities, would distract the Kremlin. It would increase the Soviet stake in a more accommodating relationship with its neighbors and with the United States.

Eastern Europe is the natural focus for a dilution of Moscow's imperial power. The basic policy formula, advanced a quarter of a century ago in *Foreign Affairs* by William Griffith and this writer, remains generally valid: ". . . the United States should adopt a policy of what might be called peaceful engagement in Eastern Europe. This policy should: (1) aim at stimulating further diversity in the Communist bloc; (2) thus increasing the likelihood that the East European states can achieve a greater measure of political independence from Soviet domination; (3) thereby ultimately leading to the creation of a neutral belt of states which . . . would enjoy genuine popular freedom of choice in internal policy while not being hostile to the Soviet Union and not belonging to Western military alliances . . ." It is important to stress that the goal should not be to transform Eastern Europe into an extension of NATO. The United States should build on the temper in Eastern Europe for self-emancipation. It should seek to create a situation that, in effect, would be the mirror image of the Soviet Union's ambitions in the West: to transform the essence of Eastern Europe's relationship with Moscow without necessarily disrupting its formal framework.

Conditions in Eastern Europe are ripe. Moscow's growing internal socioeconomic difficulties, the evident political restlessness in Poland, and the prospects for a significant political and economic crisis in Romania all pose a painful dilemma for the Kremlin. Controlling the Soviet empire means stabilizing Eastern Europe, but stabilizing Eastern Europe means sharing more Soviet economic resources and opening more political safety valves. Judging by Gorbachev's initial moves in Eastern Europe, Moscow is moving in the opposite direction. The Soviets have decreased economic aid and increased pressures for greater economic and political integration of Eastern Europe with the Soviet Union. Even the Communist elites of Eastern Europe do not find this policy congenial.

In these circumstances, the EEC, with U.S. backing, should offer Eastern Europe economic options that even the Communist regimes (not to speak of the peoples themselves) will find attractive. Enhancement of all-European economic cooperation would lead indirectly to closer political ties, but without the upheaval that would precipitate a direct Soviet response.

To promote the reemergence of a more genuinely autonomous Eastern Europe, the existence of an independent-minded and increasingly self-assertive East European public opinion is essential. The most important, and perhaps least recognized, service that America has rendered over the years to the preservation of a European identity in Eastern Europe has been its sponsorship since 1950 of Radio Free Europe. These broadcasts, beamed in national languages to the peoples of Eastern Europe, have focused their programming specifically on these countries' internal dilemmas. Though fiercely denounced by the Communist regimes, and though its broadcasts have been frequently jammed, RFE has almost single-handedly prevented Moscow from accomplishing a central objective: the isolation of Eastern Europe from the rest of Europe and the ideological indoctrination of its peoples. Today, according to the systematic polling undertaken among East European travelers to Western Europe (which because of selective passport policies tends to bias the sample toward those least opposed to the Communist regimes), RFE audiences in Eastern Europe include 66 percent of the adult population in Poland, 63 percent in Romania, 59 percent in Hungary, 40 percent in Bulgaria, and 38 percent in Czechoslovakia. In addition, the fact that the East European publics have this alternative source of news forces the Communist mass media not only to be more informative but to respond to criticisms raised in the RFE broadcasts.

With the onset of new communications techniques, such as videocassettes, miniaturized printers, and word processors, the opportunities have widened for a more massive intellectual and cultural offensive. Totalitarian control over mass communications is now easier to pierce, and the audiences will grow ever more receptive as East Europeans chafe at Moscow's cultural and economic backwardness, which is denying them the fruits of today's material and technological revolution. As that resentment intensifies, the attraction of a more cooperative relationship with Western Europe will grow. Even the Communist rulers of Eastern Europe — many of whom are more motivated by the desire to stay in power than by the goal of propagating communism — will be susceptible to this pull from the West.

It is worth reiterating that the appeal of freedom and plenty should be the principal focus of the West's peaceful engagement in Eastern Europe. Moscow will not accept political changes that reduce its power. But history teaches that Moscow will accommodate itself to gradual changes that it feels are too costly to prevent. Soviet economic and ideological sterility provide powerful impulses for a progressive process in Eastern Europe. The political realities can be transformed even without formal political changes.

As economic cooperation widens and as Communist ideology wanes, it should become possible for the West to negotiate the security issue in central Europe, capitalizing on the East European pressures for the eventual withdrawal of Soviet forces. For example, besides showing more flexibility in the MBFR talks in Vienna, the West should in general put more emphasis on the importance of mutual reductions in conventional forces. At a more distant stage, it might be appropriate to explore the possibility of some forms of denuclearization in specific regions of Europe, possibly in the Balkans, or in Scandinavia (including in such a case the Baltic republics and the Kola Peninsula). Also, NATO might declare that in the event of war those East European states that declare neutrality would be spared Western military retaliation. Although such a proposal would be attacked by the Communist regimes, it would certainly attract the East European publics.

Poland is bound to play a critical but sensitive role in this process. Since Poland is the linchpin state of Soviet control over Eastern Europe, change in Poland is bound to be of vital concern to Moscow. Kremlin leaders want a compliant, stable, and preferably weak Poland. A politically fragmented, economically laggard, socially demoralized Poland is less likely to challenge Russian control — and that is a formula that Moscow has applied to Poland since the partitions of the late eighteenth century. But today's Poland is nationally and religiously more homogeneous than ever before because of the loss or extinction of its national minorities. As a result, Moscow faces a dilemma: its efforts to dominate by the time-tested ploy of *divide et impera* might spark an uncontrollable rebellion born out of national frustration and desperation. That rebellion Moscow could certainly crush, but at a prohibitively high cost.

As a result, despite Moscow's apprehensions and martial law, Poland has succeeded in carving out for itself a margin of autonomy that preserves its distinctive national and religious character. That, in turn, tends to foster even more widespread social self-assertion. A quasi-independent society has developed, and pressures have grown for further change in the character of the regime and its relations with the Soviet Union. Most Poles, however, recognize that such a change must come gradually and must not aim for a rupture with the Soviet Union. Gradual and peaceful change could eventually shape a more equitable relationship between Poland and the Soviet Union. This would enhance East European autonomy and reassure Moscow that Poland and Eastern Europe are not being seduced into the camp of the adversary.

It follows from this that Polish membership in the International Monetary Fund and the eventual reinstatement of American Most Favored Nation trading status are geopolitically desirable. Also, U.S. economic sanctions against Poland should be matched by greater U.S. willingness to participate in a Western economic reconstruction package on the condition that the regime engages in genuine reconciliation with its people and the Solidarity leadership. Specific tactical considerations in the timing of a more constructive U.S. initiative — such as waiting for the termination of political repression against the leaders of Solidarity and the promotion of a more genuine dialogue between the regime and society — do not negate the longer-term desirability of fostering all-European economic cooperation. It should be kept in mind that the ultimate victim of such cooperation is bound to be the expansionist Soviet imperial impulse that seeks to isolate Eastern Europe. It would be a historic irony, indeed, if eventually, through such evolutionary change, the Warsaw Pact became less an instrument of Soviet control and more one of regional restraint on Soviet conduct.

But for such evolutionary change to be truly decisive in altering the intensity and even perhaps the nature of the U.S.–Soviet contest, it has to spill over into the Soviet Union itself. That spillover initially is bound to be quite limited, given the regimented political traditions of the Great Russian empire. But precisely because it is an empire, it cannot be hermetically sealed off through reliance on a self-contained and homogeneous culture, as was done in China. The multinational character of the Soviet Union creates fissures and openings, and the inescapable fact is that in the age of both nationalism and a reviving religious fervor the 55 million Soviet Muslims, the 50 million Ukrainians, the 10 million Balts, and the other non-Russian nations do not share totally the instinctive and deeply rooted political impulses of the Great Russians.

The United States should give sharper political definition to these trends through greatly intensified use of modern means of communication. The techniques that have proven so effective in breaking down Eastern Europe's isolation should be more actively applied to the Soviet Union itself. The object of the effort should not be to stoke national hatreds or even to foster the disintegration of the Soviet Union. The real opportunity is to mobilize the forces for genuine political participation, for greater national codetermination, for the dispersal of central power, and for the termination of heavy-handed central domination that breeds the expansionist impulse. By encouraging the non-Russians to demand greater respect for their national rights, the political process within the Soviet Union can gradually be refocused on a complicated and absorbing question that involves the very essence of a modern political system: the redistribution of political power. Surely from the standpoint of the West, it is more desirable that this issue should become the central concern of the Soviet leadership, and not one of the economic reforms that might enhance the Soviet capacity to compete with the United States.

Today, modern communication techniques make possible a campaign far more ambitious and diversified than the one launched when the United States began to broadcast to the East Europeans on Radio Free Europe and to address the Soviet peoples on Radio Liberty. In recent years, moreover, the Soviet Union has been placed on the ideological defensive. In Western Europe, Communist parties are on the decline. In the Far East, Soviet ideology is irrelevant. Even in Latin America, Moscow's appeal is declining. In the Middle East, the revival of Islamic faith has prevented the Soviets from capitalizing on increased anti-Americanism. Only in southern Africa do conditions favor increased Soviet ideological appeal. In these circumstances, the moment is ripe to take the initiative by an intensified program of multilanguage radio broadcasts, the inflow of audiovisual cassettes, and an effort to provide technical support for independent domestic political literature. U.S. funding of such programs should be at least tripled, for expenditures that change Soviet political attitudes are certainly more cost-effective than the arms race. This increase would only cost as much as a few B-1 bombers.

The Soviet Union's socioeconomic stagnation and its multinational makeup create fertile ground for encouraging a more critical political outlook among the Soviet peoples. Given decades of doctrinal conditioning and political isolation, the initial receptivity to this effort will be much lower than with the East Europeans. But the national and religious feelings of the non-Russians and the domestic failings of the Communist system do make the Soviet peoples potentially susceptible to aspirations already more widespread in Eastern Europe. When that potential begins to manifest itself, even Milovan Djilas's bold predictions might seem less than startling.

VII

Prevailing Historically

> . . . to win one hundred victories in one hundred bat-
> tles is not the acme of skill. To subdue the enemy with-
> out fighting is the acme of skill.
>
> Thus, what is of supreme importance in war is to attack
> the enemy's strategy.
>
> Sun Tzu (circa 400–320 B.C.)

FOR the United States, not losing in the American-Soviet rivalry means prevailing; for the Soviet Union, not pre-vailing means losing. That asymmetrical American advantage is inherent in the one-dimensional character of the Soviet chal-lenge. For Russia, no longer truly competitive ideologically and falling farther behind technologically, the proclaimed "in-evitable triumph of socialism" has been narrowed to the at-tainment of clear-cut and politically decisive military superi-ority. Failing to achieve that goal means lagging behind in every way.

But in this protracted rivalry, the Soviets have an edge and the United States has a liability: their persistence against our impatience and lack of constancy. The American public and even its foreign policy elite tend to alternate between utopian expectations of permanent peace and apocalyptic fears of a ter-minal war, between historically ignorant belief that politically

Americans and Russians are basically like-minded and the Manichaean obsession that no accommodation of any sort is possible with the "evil empire." In contrast, Moscow's policy toward the United States is geared to the long haul. It is patient, and persistent. Designed to exhaust its rival by attrition, Moscow's strategy counts on the cumulative consequences of Soviet military power and of regional turbulence to displace the United States as the world's principal power and prime stabilizer.

Accordingly, the United States is challenged on more than the three central strategic fronts. Even if America holds firm there, other regional crises not of Soviet making but susceptible to Soviet exploitation could also jeopardize America's global position. The dilemmas of peace in the Middle East, racial justice in South Africa, and political and economic democratization in Central America also confront the United States. None of these issues has been created by the Soviet Union, but intensified regional conflicts could revive Soviet geopolitical ambitions. There can be little doubt that the lack of progress on the Palestinian issue will continue to stimulate unrest in the Middle East. This will undercut U.S. efforts to create greater security in the area immediately to the southwest of the Soviet Union. American diplomacy must be active and imaginative in the Middle East as an essential extension of the geopolitical undertaking to stabilize the third central strategic front.

Similarly, in southern Africa and in Central America, the United States is faced by the danger that racial injustice and socioeconomic failures will inject new vitality into the appeal of Soviet ideology. In neither case is the Soviet Union the source of the basic problem, but in both Moscow can complicate the search for reform. It is very much in our geopolitical interest to accelerate a racial accommodation in South Africa, to advance regional economic development, and to create a more solid base for political democratization in Central America.

It is particularly important not to let Central America become a contested zone in the U.S.–Soviet rivalry. That would represent a defeat for the United States irrespective of the outcome, for it would signify the intrusion of Soviet power through Cuba onto the mainland of the Western Hemisphere. The United States must exert every effort — including the use of force if necessary — to obtain an outcome in Nicaragua along the lines of the one recommended earlier for Afghanistan: external neutralization and internal self-determination. The United States should be prepared to accept even a radical leftist regime in Nicaragua, if that should be the freely expressed will of the Nicaraguan people, provided that secure arrangements are established to assure the regime's external neutrality. But the United States should be equally prepared to apply force at any early sign of Soviet or Cuban military involvement in the suppression of opposition to the current Nicaraguan regime. The longer this issue festers, the more likely the prospect becomes of a fourth central strategic front emerging close to home.

American staying power is the essential precondition for not losing and eventually for prevailing. The United States must have constancy in purpose and continuity in geostrategy. Neither is easy to attain in a political system that puts a premium on novelty and in which each new president is associated with a new foreign policy "doctrine." An effective American policy toward the Soviets must be pursued steadily, over several decades. It must be immune alike to the utopian temptation and to the apocalyptic obsession.

Diversionary fads are a special American weakness. Since awareness of history, geopolitics, and strategy play a relatively unimportant role in shaping the American view of the world, Americans are prone to personalize international affairs, periodically seizing on this or that foreign dictator as the major threat to their security. For several years, Fidel Castro, the demagogic ruler of a small Caribbean island, was perceived by the public as posing an almost mortal danger to the world's premier superpower. More recently, national anxiety and hostility have focused on Muammar Qaddafi, the bizarre dictator of a distant and underpopulated North African country. The consequence in both cases has been to divert public attention from the larger Soviet geopolitical designs, in which Castro and Qaddafi were no more than useful bit players.

Faddist preoccupations also give birth to temporarily fashionable pseudostrategies. "Liberation" of Eastern Europe was an early example of a slogan substituting for substance, at great cost to those East Europeans who took it seriously. In the 1960s, "counterinsurgency" was the vogue, providing an alleged strategic response to Khrushchev's call for wars of national liberation but in fact justifying poor military tactics in the Vietnam War. Most recently, a new doctrine of anti-Communist liberation struggle has been evolving to create a rationale for American sponsorship of armed resistance against Soviet-backed Communist regimes in Afghanistan, Nicaragua, Angola, and Kampuchea. This new "strategy" links two conflicts that do directly involve the interests of the rival superpowers — namely, Afghanistan and Nicaragua — with peripheral conflicts that at most engage such interests only indirectly — as in Angola and Kampuchea. It is a policy that runs the risk of diverting public attention from the truly important and genuinely geostrategic foci of the long-term U.S.–Soviet confrontation.

One modest step toward greater constancy would be to improve consultations between the executive and legislative branches and long-term planning within the government departments that implement American foreign policy. Such moves might also stimulate more bipartisan consensus on the fundamentals of U.S. policy toward the Soviet Union. Pertinent congressional leaders should be invited to regular monthly sessions of an enlarged National Security Council. That could contribute to a more consistent and shared strategic outlook, and it could help keep policy on an even keel during the periodic upheavals in the composition of the executive branch.

Currently, such consultations are minimal and usually occur only during crises. These meetings should be routine. They should focus, however, not so much on specific issues as on the larger strategic and geopolitical design of U.S. policy.

Within the executive branch itself, there must be more emphasis on strategy. Occasionally, this has been provided by particularly insightful top policymakers. There have also been periods when all the top U.S. foreign policy decision makers have been quite unversed either in Soviet-American affairs or in matters of grand strategy. To compensate, the role of strategic planning should be enhanced. The Policy Planning Council in the State Department is not the right vehicle because all too often the State Department tends to confuse diplomacy with foreign policy. Only in the White House is it possible to generate the necessary broad, interagency approach to long-term planning. Hence, within the NSC, a top-level, civil-military geostrategic planning staff should be created to formulate and periodically revise the broad outlines of a long-term policy. U.S. policy is likely to become infused with the requisite longer-term geostrategic content only if the top decision makers or their immediate deputies are engaged in this undertaking, only if periodically the president himself is involved, and only if regular consultations are held with appropriate congressional leaders.

That policy can no longer seek a traditional victory. Today, as has been stressed repeatedly in these pages, the traditional concept of military victory has been outdated by the onset of the nuclear age — unless one side gains such strategic superiority that the other is deprived of any serious retaliatory capability. If that were to happen, the traditional concept of "winning" would again become relevant. But even if neither side attains such a terminally one-sided advantage, this still does not eliminate the danger that a significant, though not decisive, strategic edge could facilitate the political exploitation of regional turbulence to produce a basic shift in the global balance of power. That is why maintaining strategic stability is a much more complicated undertaking than simply deterring a nuclear war or even merely avoiding a one-sided strategic vulnerability.

The notion of "winning" must be substantially redefined in this context. Its pristine meaning, exemplified by the Allied insistence on "unconditional surrender" in World War II, has become anachronistic, provided there is no massive collapse of American will to compete with Russia strategically and geopolitically. But the term is still relevant in a more subtle and nonterminal sense. Today, "winning" is best described as "prevailing." It is a process, not a result. For the Soviet Union, prevailing primarily means the end of America's external primacy, followed perhaps by internal changes in the nature of the U.S. system. For the United States, prevailing means the transformation of Moscow's external conduct, which also implies some degree of internal evolution of the Soviet system into a less regimented one. In the first case, prevailing is defined largely in terms of a change in America's global status; in the second, it is primarily measured in terms of a change in Soviet behavior.

Thus, if the American-Soviet rivalry can be compared to an endless "game," it is one in which each side seeks to prevail by increasing its lead in points. Each may surge ahead or fall behind in some dimensions of the struggle, but it must stay even in one — namely, the military competition. A points loss here could become decisive and could suddenly terminate the game. While the game goes on, certain rudimentary rules of restraint have come to be shaped. They are, in effect, a code of reciprocal behavior guiding the competition, lessening the danger that it could become lethal.

It is the conclusion of the argument made in these pages that the United States can prevail — and that U.S. geostrategy can and must be designed to go beyond containing Soviet expansionism and offsetting Soviet military power. Prevailing politically is possible. Other options are unacceptable, impossible, or impractical. Pursuing victory in the traditional sense is anachronistic. The only alternatives left are those of acquiescing, accommodating, or prevailing.

Although acquiescing to the Soviet Union is not a policy option that anyone explicitly advocates, it could be the practical result of isolationism, or of unilateral disarmament, or even of excessive zeal in seeking arms control arrangements without sufficient regard for the need to maintain mutual strategic security. If the United States were to follow this course, it would lead to the emergence of Soviet military supremacy, which, in turn, would produce a global crisis of the greatest magnitude. It is unlikely, however, that a policy of yielding to Moscow will ever find much support among the American public, and the electoral fate of presidential candidates who have flirted with notions along these lines speaks eloquently for itself.

Accommodation with the Soviet Union is a more attractive concept. It comes in two versions, soft and hard, or "idealistic" versus "realistic." The first appeals both to American idealism and to the tradition of compromise. It strikes a responsive chord among those who prefer to believe that Soviet leaders and American presidents share the same aspirations. It seemingly provides an escape from the rigors and tensions of prolonged rivalry. It is, however, based on a profoundly ahistorical view of the nature of the American-Soviet struggle, seeing it as a temporary aberration that can be corrected by compromise, by some preemptive concessions, and by the display of consistent goodwill even in the face of hostile or aggressive Soviet actions. Those who believe in the idealistic form of accommodation interpret such Soviet actions largely as manifestations of an insecurity that can be cured by American patience and reassurances.

In its more "hard-nosed" variant, the quest for comprehensive accommodation takes the form of the search for a grand bargain, for a condominium arrangement between the two su-

perpowers that can then generate "a détente" and "a generation of peace" between them. This approach does not deny the
national hostility between the United States and the Soviet
Union, or ideological intensity of the rivalry. It is realistic in
its appraisal of the political gulf that separates the two powers.
Nonetheless, this school of thought is still based on the belief
that it is possible to reach a comprehensive accommodation on
the basis of the status quo.

Both the "idealistic" and "realistic" variants of the strategy are flawed because they underestimate the historical depth
of the American-Soviet antagonism, the degree of conflict
between the geopolitical interests of the two powers, and the
intensity of regional turbulence that by itself generates conflicting superpower responses. So they both fail to provide guide-
lines for managing the contest. Both tend to overemphasize
arms control as the central platform of détente. As a result, the
quest for a grand accommodation has produced disappointment, even when sought by realistic and skilled statesmen. The
fact that must be faced is that a grand accommodation — a
condominium — on the basis of the status quo is not possible
because the global status quo itself is too unstable and the two
rival states are still motivated by incompatible objectives.

Indeed, there are no good historical reasons to justify the
reassuring conclusion that bilateral imperial coexistence can
indefinitely endure. More likely, one side eventually will lose
momentum or weaken, and the other will gain the upper hand
because of superior organization, higher determination, and more
effective geostrategy. A U.S. policy designed to prevail must
therefore be based on the hardheaded acknowledgment that the
American-Soviet contest (1) is historically enduring and inherent in the internal systems and geopolitical situations of the
two powers; (2) is global in scope but focused primarily on a
contest for Eurasian supremacy and more specifically for control over several key geopolitical linchpin states; (3) requires a
long-term strategy responsive to geostrategic needs; and (4)
will in all probability be historical in duration and thus last far

beyond the end of this century, occasional fluctuations in its intensity notwithstanding.

The side that prevails in the American-Soviet contest is likely to become aware of this fact only in hindsight — historically, so to speak — and not at any specific single moment, as with traditional victory.

In that context, there are for the United States certain minimum requirements of survival. Geopolitically, it must seek to encourage the emergence of a more self-reliant Europe that can also attract the countries of Eastern Europe; to infuse also some informal political-strategic content into the economically growing Pacific triangle; and to preserve an independent, and possibly partially neutral, southwest Asia. Strategically, it must adapt its strategic and conventional military postures to changing circumstances so as to maintain at least a balance with the Soviet Union. Ideologically, it should carry the torch into the Soviet realm, reinforcing the internal pressures for greater national codetermination. These policies are needed to avoid the more dangerous scenarios in the U.S.–Soviet competition outlined at the end of chapter four and to prevent a shift over the next ten years in the strategic balance of power.

Persistently competing does not preclude occasionally agreeing. Indeed, conciliation can also be an effective tool of competition. The policies recommended here are required not only for the defensive purpose of "defanging" Soviet strategy but also, over time, for achieving the goal of more basically "pacifying" Soviet conduct. An important component must be the quest for agreements designed to reduce the scope for arbitrary Soviet actions. These efforts might include gradual expansion of arms control arrangements; the search for a resolution of specific regional problems, like the war in Afghanistan; and the negotiation of joint troop withdrawals, or neutrality belts, or perhaps even atom-free zones in some parts of Europe. But it is critically important that each initiative be carefully designed to promote the central American objective of checking the outward thrust of Soviet power and of gradually altering the manner in which the Soviet Union conducts the rivalry.

That central objective should also guide the U.S. conduct of meetings between the president of the United States and the general secretary of the Communist party of the Soviet Union. In 1977, the Carter administration proposed annual summits. The Soviet side was unwilling. The thought behind the proposal was that, whatever else they achieved, annual summits would "demystify" the occasional encounter between the top leaders. This would reduce fevers of public expectation. The Soviets are always ready to exploit these in hope of gaining American concessions for the sake of a "successful" summit. Regular, annual summits would permit the development of a more serious, ongoing dialogue. Perhaps, over time, they would even contribute to a genuine accommodation on some of the truly important strategic and geopolitical issues and thus to a more basic change in Soviet conduct itself.

In addition, through a more sustained dialogue, we might engage the Soviets in constructive responses to the acute global problems confronting humanity. As noted earlier, the Soviet record has not been encouraging. Soviet foreign aid amounts to only one-tenth of 1 percent of the Soviet GNP. The Soviet Union has taken on the whole a self-serving and expedient position on such matters as the future of the oceans or the need for a major global food reserve or the desirability of a global demographic policy. Nonetheless, with time and increasing sophistication, the Soviet Union might come to appreciate the need for global cooperation. Progress has already been made in some technical fields, and America should encourage more. After all, the ultimate purpose of the American-Soviet dialogue ought to be to effect change in the Soviet perception of its world role: instead of trying to recast the world in its own image, the Soviet Union should increasingly join in coping with the world as it actually is.

Such external pacification of Soviet behavior cannot be separated entirely from the internal character of the Soviet system. As far as changing the nature of that system is concerned, maximum U.S. objectives cannot be defined precisely. But it is certainly relevant to note that the long-run future of the Soviet Union is more of an open question than the future of much more organic states, such as France or Japan. The Soviet Union's political order, which is based on the dominance of the Great Russian people, rests primarily on enforced social compliance and on the political subordination of the non-Russian nations. Consequently, if Moscow's capacity to rule weakens, the political character and even the territorial integrity of the Soviet Union could come into question. This is particularly important because internal strains in the Soviet Union are likely to grow as the contradictions intensify between the political requirements of a dogmatic regime and the economic needs of a system that to compete with America must somehow enter into the age of information, high technology, and science. The central question likely to dominate Soviet realities during the next twenty years is whether the Soviet Union can truly modernize its society without having substantially to reduce the totalitarian character of its political system.

Since a regimented and doctrinaire Soviet Union is by definition a more hostile Soviet Union, the decentralization of the Soviet orbit internally and the pacification of Soviet behavior externally are the unavoidable long-term requirements of enduring peace. U.S. geostrategy should actively seek to promote both, for external pacification and internal decentralization of the Soviet Union are interrelated. Greater national codetermination within the Soviet Union would inevitably weaken both the external Great Russian imperial impulse and the internal concentration of power within the Kremlin. Even the dissolution of the Great Russian empire might eventually follow.

Progress toward these distant goals, patiently pursued over several decades, will provide the substance of what is meant by prevailing historically. A key point to bear in mind is that historically, external defeats have been the sources of the greatest stimuli for political change within the Russian system. Such external jolts as defeat in World War I, the earlier Japanese victory in the Russo-Japanese War of 1905, or even Stalin's fear of a German success in 1941–1942 all produced major domestic concessions, in each case at the cost of centralized and authoritarian power. Thus, the geostrategic goal of defeating the Soviet quest for domination over Eurasia is directly linked to the prospects for promoting significant change in the nature of the Soviet system itself.

But America can achieve its goals only if its long-term geostrategic game plan is infused with historical awareness and geopolitical consciousness. Historical amnesia is a costly malaise that even America — for all its wealth and power — can ill afford. The history of the American-Soviet contest is long, and the conflict itself has deep roots. The contest is real. It is enduring. But each generation of Americans does not have to improvise from scratch, to entertain illusory hopes, or to be guided by obsessive fears.

It was Sun Tzu's comment that in war, attacking the enemy's strategy is of supreme importance. That is also true for waging a protracted historical conflict. To paraphrase Sun Tzu, for the United States to prevail in the American-Soviet rivalry without war, it is of supreme importance to checkmate Soviet policy and to exploit Soviet weaknesses. Guided by a broad geostrategic perspective, America should be capable of doing both.

Executive Summary

KEY SUBSTANTIVE PROPOSITIONS

I. THE IMPERIAL COLLISION

A. A Historical Contest

- The American-Soviet relationship is a classic historical conflict between two major powers. It is not susceptible to a broad and quick resolution.
- Geopolitical and strategic considerations are critical in determining the focus, the substance, and eventually the outcome of the historical contest between the leading oceanic power and the dominant land power.
- Geopolitical factors laid the groundwork for a collision between the United States and the Soviet Union following World War II. The fact that America and Russia differed from each other to a greater extent than any previous historical rivals made conflict almost inevitable.
- By all previous historical standards, the United States and the Soviet Union should have gone to war against each other on some occasions, but the destructiveness of nuclear weapons has induced an unprecedented measure of restraint.

B. An Imperial Contest

- The American-Soviet rivalry is also a conflict between two imperial systems.
- Moscow's empire is predominantly territorially contiguous and is the product of a sustained and unrelenting historical drive by the Great Russian component of the USSR.
- Russia's imperial consciousness has in the modern era helped to generate and sustain a world outlook in which the drive to global preeminence has become the central energizing impulse.
- Although early U.S. imperial expansion was largely traditional in nature, the American empire emerged full-blown only after World War II by virtue of the fact that the United States came through the war unscathed.
- The American empire is in the main territorially noncontiguous, relatively porous, and held together through indirect ties.
- American foreign policy debates today center on how best to protect and manage the American imperial domain.

C. A Global Contest

- The American-Soviet rivalry is global in scope.
- Modern weaponry, in terms of both range and destructiveness, gives substance to the concept of a genuinely global war and reality to the threat of global devastation.
- Mass communications and mass literacy make the political-ideological contest geographically unlimited. No continent is unaffected by conflicting appeals and competing social models.

II. THE STRUGGLE FOR EURASIA

- Although the American-Soviet contest is global in scope, its central priority is Eurasia — the world's central landmass, containing the bulk of the world's people, territory, and wealth.
- The struggle for Eurasia is waged on three central strategic fronts: the far western, the far eastern, and the southwestern.

A. Russia and Eurasia

- Both tsarist and Soviet statesmen have sought with unrelenting vigor and strategic persistence certain key goals along Eurasia's three central strategic fronts designed to attain continental predominance.
- For the Soviet leaders, the exclusion of America from Eurasia has been a major political goal since their agreement to that effect with Hitler in 1940.

B. Three Central Strategic Fronts

- Europe, the first central strategic front, is geopolitically critical: it encompasses the most vital and industrialized section of Eurasia, and the one that controls the principal outlets to the Atlantic Ocean.
- The Far East, the second central strategic front, is geopolitically important because it controls the principal outlets to the Pacific Ocean. It emerged as an arena of American-Soviet competition with President Truman's decision to block Communist aggression in Korea.
- A Soviet breakthrough on the third central strategic front, in southwest Asia, would carry grave implications, for it would automatically give the Soviet Union enormous leverage in the competition with the United States on the other two fronts.

C. Geopolitical Linchpin States

- The outcome of the contests on each of the three central strategic fronts is likely to be determined largely by who gains or retains control over several key countries that have become geopolitical linchpins — states that are both geostrategically important and in some sense "up for grabs."
- The linchpin states are Poland and West Germany on the far western front, South Korea and the Philippines on the far eastern front, and Iran or the combination of Afghanistan and Pakistan on the southwestern front.

D. Soviet Geostrategy

- Moscow's greatest fear is a united Western Europe that is militarily and politically revitalized, that is allied with the United States, and that exercises a magnetic attraction on Eastern Europe. It also fears a close American-Japanese-Chinese connection, with China and Japan eventually capable of applying massive pressure on the relatively empty territories of Soviet Siberia.
- On the far western front, Moscow has pursued a strategy of political attrition designed to achieve progressive and piecemeal neutralization of Western Europe.
- On the far eastern front, the Soviets have relied on the tactics of diplomacy and propaganda, rather than either military pressure or subversion, to try to prevent the emergence of a strategic triangle of the United States, Japan, and China.
- On the southwestern front, military pressure, subversion, diplomacy, and propaganda — in that order — have been the instruments of Soviet policy, and the prospects for a Soviet breakthrough are far greater on this front than on the other two.

III. PERIPHERAL ZONES OF SPECIAL
VULNERABILITY

A. Unstable Imperial Domains

- The predominant character of the relations between
the United States and Central America and between
the Soviet Union and Eastern Europe is essentially
imperial.
- The United States faces in Central America both an
internal crisis of the region's antiquated social and
political structures and the entrance into the region
of an alien ideological power through the revolu-
tions in Cuba and Nicaragua.
- Despite forty years of enforced indoctrination, all
of the Communist regimes in Eastern Europe remain in power through heavy reliance on severe
police control, reinforced by the potential threat of
Soviet military intervention.
- This inherent instability is intensified by a condition that is unique in the history of imperial regimes — the absence of a social or cultural magnetism on the part of the dominant power, which
makes the region an even less secure imperial
domain.

B. Historical Enmity and Geopolitical Necessity

- The relationships between the Soviet Union and
Poland, and between the United States and Mexico, present particularly troublesome problems, with
both smaller powers motivated by intense historical
memories of inflicted injustice.
- In the long term, the Soviet Union faces the threat
that its insistence on continued ideological-political
subordination of Poland will further intensify Polish resentments, thereby making Poland even more
susceptible to external attraction from the West.

- In the long term, the United States faces the problem that Mexico's internal economic and political
failures might galvanize latent anti-American sentiments and merge them with the wider crisis in
Central America.

C. Stakes and Policies

- The United States, careful not to contest the Soviet
Union's hold over Eastern Europe, has concentrated its efforts on a strategy of indirect intrusion
to dilute over the long haul the effectiveness of
Soviet control.
- The Soviet Union, strategically bolder but tactically cautious, realizes that in a superpower conflict in Central America or the Caribbean it would
be at a massive geographical, logistical, and economic disadvantage to the United States.
- Should the internal problems of Central America
merge with a larger domestic explosion in Mexico
that inflames the U.S.–Mexican relationship, the
Soviet Union is almost certain to exploit it, thereby
opening up a fourth central strategic front.

IV. THE ONE-DIMENSIONAL RIVAL:
A THREAT ASSESSMENT

- An underassessment of Soviet power could be fatal, but an exaggeration of Soviet capabilities can
produce wasteful reactions that weaken America's
capacity to endure a protracted competition.

A. Soviet Military Capabilities

- A condition of ambiguous strategic equivalence exists today, with neither side at this stage entitled to

a high degree of confidence regarding the outcome of a nuclear exchange.

- It is possible that the continuation of the massive Soviet buildup in both offensive and defensive strategic systems might dramatically alter the balance to the disadvantage of the United States by the mid-1990s. All U.S. land-based strategic systems, communications, and command centers would become even more vulnerable to Soviet attack with the effectiveness of a U.S. second-strike significantly degraded by Soviet strategic defenses.
- Such vulnerability could induce geostrategic paralysis on the American side, thereby undermining the stability of the American-Soviet relationship.
- In Europe, since the threat of escalation to nuclear weapons is still the key deterrent to a massive Soviet military breakthrough, a deterioration of the strategic balance would result in a higher probability of a conventional war or successful military intimidation.
- In southwest Asia, both permanent geographical and transitional political factors could favor the Soviet Union. A U.S. response to Soviet aggression would face enormous logistical difficulties, and the probability of inadequate or tenuous political support from adjoining countries.

B. Socioeconomic Liabilities

- Soviet military power is actually the sole basis for the Soviet Union's status as a global power, for in all other respects it is not even a truly competitive rival of the United States.
- In the mid-1980s, while the United States was plunging headlong into the technetronic age, the

Soviet Union was still struggling to make its relatively conventional industrial economy more efficient and modern.

- Soviet economic and social stagnation is critical because in the long run, unless military means prove historically decisive, social creativity is likely to determine the outcome of the American-Soviet competition.

C. A World Power of a New Type

- Although Moscow may have outstripped the United States in the buildup of military power, neither the Soviet Union nor the Eastern bloc even comes close to matching the United States or the industrialized democracies in terms of socioeconomic capability or technological innovation.
- Because of the unique one-dimensional character of the Soviet global challenge, Moscow is manifestly unequipped to provide constructive and sustained leadership should it succeed by military leverage in unseating the United States as the number-one world power.

D. Domination and Disruption

- Its one-dimensional power has led Moscow to follow an erratic pattern of accommodation and competition with the United States because Kremlin leaders seek a transitional condominium with Washington but are fearful of becoming locked into the role of junior partner.
- It also leads the Soviet Union to continue to promote regional conflicts, to inhibit wider intranational cooperation, and to pursue a strategy of dis-

ruption, including active support for international terrorism.

- Historically, a Soviet triumph on the Eurasian continent would be less likely to create enduring Soviet hegemony than to promote increasing global chaos.

KEY POLICY RECOMMENDATIONS

V. U.S. STRATEGIC IMPERATIVES

- Once its military power is checked, the Soviet Union ceases to be a historically threatening rival.
- To neutralize Soviet military power, the United States must maintain a military capability sufficient
  - to negate Soviet efforts to intimidate strategic U.S. friends and allies,
  - to block direct and indirect Soviet expansionism,
  - to deprive Kremlin leaders of the certainty of quick conventional victory on Eurasia's three strategic fronts and to increase their uncertainty about a possible U.S. nuclear escalation,
  - to counter the Soviet Union's war-fighting capability at all levels of nuclear escalation,
  - to maintain a secure nuclear retaliatory force capable of inflicting massive societal devastation on the Soviet Union even after a Soviet first strike directed at U.S. strategic forces.
- The United States must maintain an integrated military capability for surface, sea, and space combat as the central point of departure for the waging of an enduring and consuming political contest for earth control.

A. Strategic Impotence: The Threat of Arms Control

- Arms control should be viewed as part of — not a substitute for — American national defense policy, especially since the Soviets have used arms control as a political tool to promote U.S. strategic impotence.

- Unless a truly historical transformation of the American-Soviet relationship takes place, the most promising route for arms control is to seek narrowly focused, highly specific, and perhaps interim arrangements.

- Agreements must be subject to genuine verification, including, in the case of mobile missile launchers, some form of on-site inspection. The United States must make a major public issue of Soviet strategic secrecy and insist that its veil be lifted for the sake of mutual security.

- Agreements must concentrate on the central issue: the first-strike systems that represent the most acute security problem for each side.

- The emphasis in future comprehensive arms control agreements must shift from quantitative reductions to qualitative prohibitions. The number of systems capable of undertaking a precise first-strike attack must be driven below the number required to make such an attack militarily effective. Such limits must be accompanied by binding and verifiable prohibitions on the introduction of new first-strike systems.

- Washington must address the basic obstacle to reaching a genuine arms control agreement: the U.S. lack of strategic arms programs with which to bargain.

B. Mutual Strategic Security

- Mutual strategic security — a mix of forces that makes a first strike militarily futile and societally suicidal — should be both the American and the Soviet objective.

- To best deter a nuclear war at any level, the United States must adjust its strategic doctrine and its deployments away from mutual assured destruction and toward greater flexibility in war-fighting options.

- U.S. strategic offensive forces should be deployed in numbers deliberately contrived not to pose a threat of a disarming first strike to Soviet strategic forces.

- The United States should move toward deploying a limited strategic defense, composed of a space-based screen to destroy missiles in the boost phase and a land-based terminal defense to intercept incoming warheads. This would inject a degree of randomness into any Soviet planning of a first-strike nuclear attack.

- In order to pursue mutual strategic security bilaterally, the United States should propose a renegotiation of the outdated ABM treaty of 1972 to permit some limited deployment of space-based defenses.

- If that effort fails, the United States should give notice of its intent to reevaluate its adherence to the treaty, and possibly abrogate it and proceed with the deployment of a two-tier, limited, counter-first-strike strategic defense.

C. Global Conventional Flexibility

- Washington must address a perilous strategic paradox: U.S. conventional forces are weakest where the United States is most vulnerable, along the

southwestern strategic front, and strongest where
its allies have the greatest capacity for doing more
on their own behalf, along the far western strategic
front.

- The United States should undertake a gradual —
  and certainly only partial — reduction in the level
  of American forces in Europe.
- A joint American-European anti-tactical-missile
  project and the application of SDI technologies to
  conventional warfare could more than offset the
  proposed reductions in U.S. forces in Europe.
- Budgetary savings from these reductions should be
  allocated to a significant expansion of U.S. airlift
  capability.
- Manpower withdrawn from Europe should be absorbed into an enlarged Rapid Deployment Force
  through the creation of additional light divisions for
  use on the third front or in Central America.
- Preserving sea control should be the U.S. Navy's
  central preoccupation, and its mission of carrying
  attacks directly into Soviet home ports should be
  de-emphasized.

D. The Centrality of Technological Superiority

- Although systemic factors in the American economy favor technological innovation, it is important
  that the United States channel its efforts into a
  powerful stimulus, like the Strategic Defense Initiative, that mobilizes and directs scientific and
  technological resources toward strategic applications.
- At the very least, the United States must hold a
  technological edge sufficient to make the value of
  Moscow's numerical advantage in weaponry ambiguous.

E. An Integrated Strategic Framework

- With an integrated strategy, combining mutual strategic security with conventional global flexibility, the United States should be able to maintain extended deterrence, to deny the Soviets a quick conventional victory in any Eurasian theater, and to ensure a conventional Soviet military defeat in the event of a non-Eurasian clash.

VI. U.S. GEOPOLITICAL PRIORITIES

- The United States must deliberately promote over a protracted period several key geopolitical objectives designed to transform the American-Soviet global contest into a somewhat less antagonistic relationship.

A. A More Self-Reliant Europe

- The United States should encourage the development of a politically and militarily integrated Western Europe, less dependent on the United States but still tied to it by a strategic alliance.
- Toward this end, the United States should encourage greater Franco-German defense cooperation, press for a greater European contribution to the common defense, and redeploy gradually some troops from Western Europe to meet other geopolitical priorities and to prompt European leaders to address the issue of their own defense.
- In the long term, the United States should welcome closer West European ties with Eastern Europe, which could eventually lead both America and Russia to disengage from their present confrontation in the heart of Europe.

B. The Pacific Triangle

- The United States should promote an informal geopolitical triangle in the Far East through wider economic and political cooperation among the United States, Japan, and China.
- Rather than simply increasing its defense spending, Japan should be encouraged also to make an indirect but still important contribution to common security by increasing its strategic economic aid to those developing countries in which the Western democracies have a vital stake. This effort should involve about 4 percent of the Japanese GNP.
- With Japan's emerging strategic role, the United States should seek to transform the annual Western economic summit into a meeting that would also take up strategic issues.
- Japan and the United States should actively promote China's economic modernization, especially in the critical regions of Manchuria and Xinjiang; and in this context the United States and Japan should seek quietly to expand the scope of informal security consultations with China.
- The United States should maintain its current deployments in South Korea to deter a North Korean attack.
- In the Philippines, Japan and the United States should seek ways to reduce the economic causes of the unrest, but Washington should be ready to intervene more actively to promote long-term political and economic recovery.

C. The Soft Underbelly

- Washington should work to reinforce the resilience against Soviet advances by providing more aid to

Pakistan and by being willing to improve relations with Iran.

- The United States should keep the Afghan issue alive by sustaining the resistance, while simultaneously probing for Soviet willingness to restore genuine neutrality and internal self-determination.
- The possibility of geostrategically dangerous Soviet leapfrogging into the Middle East should be minimized by a more intensive U.S. diplomacy designed to push forward the Arab-Israeli peace process.
- The United States should help stimulate through radio broadcasts and other means a more distinctive political consciousness among Soviet Muslims as a deterrent to further Soviet absorption of Islamic peoples.

D. Imperial Retraction

- Ultimately, change in both the scope and character of Soviet power will be needed to assure a more stable American-Soviet relationship, and the United States should promote such change in Eastern Europe and within the Soviet Union itself.
- The United States should encourage the EEC to provide Eastern Europe with economic options that even the Communist regimes would find attractive, for enhancement of all-European economic cooperation would inevitably lead indirectly to closer political ties.
- The United States should promote the development of an independent-minded and increasingly assertive East European public opinion, not only through radio broadcasts, but also with new communications techniques, such as videocassettes, miniaturized printers, and word processors.

- As economic cooperation widens and Communist ideology wanes, the United States should put forth proposals to deal with the security issue in central Europe, in the hope of eventually stimulating East European pressures for the progressive withdrawal of Soviet forces or even of applying at a more distant stage the model of Austrian neutralization to other regions of Europe.
- The United States should encourage evolutionary change within the Soviet Union itself by promoting greater assertiveness on the part of non-Russian nations through radio broadcasts and other means.
- The United States should triple its funding of programs to provide the peoples of Eastern Europe and the Soviet Union with greater access to news and information.

VII. PREVAILING HISTORICALLY

- To be effective, American policy toward the Soviet Union must be pursued steadily, over several decades, and be immune to the utopian dream and the apocalyptic nightmare.
- The United States must respond effectively to key regional crises not of Soviet making but susceptible to Soviet exploitation:
  - Greater American diplomatic activity in the Middle East, particularly to solve the Palestinian problem, is needed as an essential extension of the geopolitical undertaking to stabilize the third central strategic front.
  - The United States should intensify its efforts to accelerate a racial accommodation in South Africa.
  - Washington should advance regional economic development in Central America and work to

create a more solid base for political democratization in Central America.

- The United States must exert every effort — including the use of force if necessary — to obtain the external neutralization and internal self-determination of Nicaragua and must be prepared to apply force at an early sign of Soviet or Cuban military involvement in the suppression of opposition to the current regime in Managua.

- The United States should enhance foreign policy consultations between the executive and legislative branches, perhaps through regular monthly sessions of an enlarged National Security Council, and increase the emphasis on strategy within the executive branch itself by creating within the NSC a top-level, civil-military geostrategic planning staff to formulate and periodically revise the broad outlines of a long-term policy.

- Since victory in the traditional sense has been made anachronistic by the onset of the nuclear age and since a comprehensive accommodation is unrealistic, America should pursue the goal of prevailing historically over Moscow by actively promoting the decentralization of the Soviet orbit internally and the pacification of Soviet behavior externally, for these are the unavoidable and interrelated long-term requirements of enduring peace.

- The United States therefore should pursue strategic and regional agreements designed to reduce the scope for arbitrary Soviet actions. It is critically important that each initiative be carefully designed to promote the key American objective of checking the outward thrust of Soviet power and of gradually altering the manner in which the Soviet Union conducts the rivalry.

- Since external defeats have historically been the greatest stimuli for political change within the Russian system, the geostrategic goal of defeating the Soviet quest for domination over Eurasia is directly linked to the prospects for significant changes in the nature of the Soviet system itself.

Where Major U.S. Defense Forces Stand

Air Force / Alaska
- 2 tactical fighter squadrons
- 1 tactical air-support squadron
- 1 tactical airlift squadron
- 1 strategic reconnaissance wing

Land Unit / Alaska
- 1 army infantry brigade

Land Combat Unit / Hawaii
- 1 marine brigade
- 1 army infantry division

Marines / Pacific
- 2 attack helicopter squadrons
- 14 lift helicopter squadrons
- 7 attack squadrons
- 7 fighter-attack squadrons
- 1 photoreconnaissance squadron

Land Unit / Pacific
- 1 marine division

Air Units / Pacific Fleet
- 19 attack squadrons
- 9 tactical electronic warfare squadrons
- 7 early-warning squadrons

14 fighter squadrons
13 patrol squadrons
2 fleet air-reconnaissance squadrons
2 fleet logistics-support squadrons
6 anti-submarine warfare squadrons
6 anti-submarine warfare helicopter squadrons

Air Force / Continental United States
9 strategic missile wings
16 strategic bomber wings
6 fighter-interceptor squadrons
37 tactical fighter squadrons
3 tactical reconnaissance squadrons
2 tactical air-support squadrons
7 military airlift wings
10 tactical airlift squadrons
4 air refueling wings
2 air refueling groups
2 strategic reconnaissance wings

Army / Continental United States
1 airborne division
1 air assault division
2 armored divisions
4 mechanized divisions
2 infantry divisions
1 armored brigade
1 air cavalry brigade
1 infantry brigade
1 armored cavalry regiment

Army / Panama
1 army infantry brigade

Marine Air Units / Atlantic
1 attack helicopter squadron
10 lift helicopter squadrons

   6   attack squadrons
   1   electronic countermeasures squadron
   5   fighter/attack squadrons

Air Units / Atlantic Fleet
   17 attack squadrons
   6   early-warning squadrons
   11 fighter squadrons
   10 patrol squadrons
   1   fleet air-reconnaissance squadron
   1   fleet logistics-support squadron
   4   anti-submarine warfare squadrons
   5   anti-submarine warfare helicopter squadrons

Naval Units / Atlantic Areas
   6   aircraft carriers
   97 surface combatants
   29 amphibious types
   57 attack submarines
   31 ballistic-missile submarines

Land Unit / Atlantic
   1   marine division

Naval Air Units / Europe
   5   attack squadrons
   2   early-warning squadrons
   4   fighter squadrons
   3   patrol squadrons
   1   fleet air-reconnaissance squadron
   1   fleet logistics-support squadron
   2   anti-submarine warfare squadrons
   2   tactical electronic warfare squadrons
   2   anti-submarine warfare helicopter squadrons

Air Force / Europe
   28 tactical fighter squadrons
   2   tactical reconnaissance squadrons

3 tactical air-support squadrons
2 tactical airlift squadrons

Air Force / Iceland
1 fighter-interceptor squadron

U.S. Army Land Units / Europe
2 armored divisions
2 mechanized divisions
2 armored cavalry regiments
1 infantry brigade (Berlin)
1 armed brigade
2 mechanized brigades

Land Unit / Mediterranean
Marine Amphibious Unit with Sixth Fleet

Naval Units / Indian Ocean, Persian Gulf
1 aircraft carrier
10 surface combatants

Eighth Army / Korea
1 infantry division

Land Unit / Western Pacific
Marine Amphibious Unit with Seventh Fleet

Land Unit / Okinawa
1 marine division

Air Force / Pacific
10 tactical fighter squadrons
2 tactical air-support squadrons
1 tactical reconnaissance squadron
2 tactical airlift squadrons
1 strategic bomber wing
1 air refueling wing

Naval Units / Pacific Areas
    6 aircraft carriers
  85 surface combatants
  32 amphibious types
  41 attack submarines
    4 ballistic-missile submarines

Acknowledgments

THIS book is a by-product both of my experience as Assistant to the President for National Security Affairs during 1977–1981 and of my teaching on the subject of U.S. national security policy after my return as professor to Columbia University in 1981. Thus, my first debt is to my former NSC staffers and to my Columbia University students, with whom and for whom I sought to develop an integrated strategic outlook. Subsequently, in writing this volume I benefited greatly from my association with the Center for Strategic and International Studies at Georgetown University, which provided me with a setting in which there were manifold opportunities to engage in a serious dialogue on geostrategic matters.

More specifically, I also wish to acknowledge the help of several individuals who made substantial contributions to this book. Dr. Carol Hansen helped me in organizing the course at Columbia on U.S. national security policy that in turn was a stepping-stone to this volume, and she was a vital research aide in this enterprise as a whole. Subsequently, Mr. Marin Strmecki was relentless in polishing my prose, in offering substantive criticisms and refinements, in developing some of the charts and maps, and in drafting the executive summary. Ms. Trudy Werner supervised the preparation of the entire manuscript and more generally managed my professional affairs in an orderly and decisive manner, enabling me to meet my writing deadlines without jeopardizing other obligations. To her, to Marin, and to Carol go my special thanks, for their help was truly central.

The finished product was reviewed and criticized by two close friends whose judgments I especially value, Professor Samuel Huntington and General William Odom. They are not to be held responsible for the shortcomings of the final version, but their criticisms and recommendations improved greatly what the reader has seen. Parts of the finished draft were also read by Colonel Harry Summers, Jr., and I am grateful for his helpful comments.

A very special role in fortifying the argument and in refining my prose was made by my editor, Mr. Harold Evans, and I am grateful also to his colleague Mr. Upton Brady, executive editor of the Atlantic Monthly Press, who supervised the preparation of the maps and the overall production. I am pleased to acknowledge my obligation to them.

Finally, the book would not have appeared without the imprimatur of my severest critic but also most devoted encourager, my wife, Muška.

Zbigniew Brzezinski
January 1986

Index

ABM systems, Soviet, 108–109
ABM treaty, 109, 167, 261
Acheson, Dean, 45, 58
Afghanistan, 39, 154, 241, 247, 265; communism in, 242; geopolitical position of, 64; as neutral buffer state, 49, 50; and Pakistan as linchpin state, 52–53, 63–65, 220, 225; Soviet invasion and occupation of, 22, 50, 51, 72, 93, 119, 174–175, 211, 218, 221–222; and Soviet Union, 16, 27, 63–65, 221, 225, 227, 242
Africa, 27, 79, 95; and Soviet Union, 112–113; *see also* southern Africa
ALCMs, U.S., 105
Algeria, 128, 137, 225
American-Soviet conflict, 43, 236; and arms control, 148–159; attrition as Soviet strategy in, 240; Central America as factor in, 241; China as factor in, 211; economic, 195; European focus of, 182; geopolitical factors of, 11, 12–15, 153, 194–196, 231, 251, 263; geostrategic focus of, 242; as global conflict, 8, 26–30, 202–203, 246, 252, 263; as historical conflict, 8–15, 29, 246–247, 251; as ideological conflict, 195, 202–203, 246; as imperial contest, 16–26, 252; Iran as factor in, 43; military factors in, 100; as nuclear contest, 100; oceanic domination as factor in, 146–147; and Pacific triangle, 220; as political-ideological contest, 28; prevailing historically in, 239, 244–245, 250, 267; resolution

of, 10–11; scenarios for, 141–144, 247–250; as social competition, 9, 130; socioeconomic factors in, 100; Soviet policy and, 248, 267; strategic factors in, 11; strategic fronts in (general discussion), 41–52, 102, 117, 144, 145, 240, 253 (*see also* Europe; Far East; Rio Grande; southwest Asia); summit meetings for, 248; U.S. policy and, 246, 250; and Vietnam War, 45; war as possible result of, 15, 250, 251; and Western Europe, 197
Andropov, Yuri, 195
Anglo-Russian Convention, 63
Angola, 16, 27, 153, 242
antiballistic missiles. *See* ABM
antitactical missile defense (ATM), 180
Arabian Peninsula, 175
Arabian Sea, 64
Arab-Israeli conflict, 113, 186, 227, 228, 265
Arab states, 227–230
arms control, 111, 260; accommodation in, 167; agreements and arrangements for, 158, 159, 168, 192, 245, 247, 260; and defense policy, 155; and domestic politics, 153; and geopolitics, 153–154; prospects for, 155–159; Soviet attitude toward, 167; and Soviet military, 154–155; Soviet participation in U.S. activities for, 149–150; strategic impotence as danger in, 148–159; U.S. attitude toward, 168; and U.S.–Soviet relations, 153–154, 156, 165; and weapon systems, 154–156

arms control negotiations: ABM treaty, 109, 167, 261; MBFR, 207, 234; SALT I, 153, 154; SALT II, 153–154
arms race, 149, 237
Asia. *See* Eurasia; Southeast Asia; southwest Asia
Assad, Hafiz al-, 230
assault breaker/skeet technology, 186
Association of Southeast Asian Nations (ASEAN), 48, 212
Atlantic alliance. *See* NATO
Atlantic Community, 44, 47
ATM (antitactical missile defense), 180
Austria, 234
Austrian Peace Treaty, 208, 225, 266
Autonomous Republic of Azerbaijan, 43

Baader-Meinhoff Gang, 140
balance of power. *See* global balance; strategic stability
Balkan region, 233
Baltic region/states, 18, 34, 128, 231, 234, 236
Bangladesh, 73
Basque separatists, 140
Bay of Pigs invasion, 79, 95
Berlin blockade, 43, 171
Berlin crises, 67, 206
Beyond Containment, 20
Black, Cyril, 123
Black Sea region, 18
Bolivia, 79
Bolshevik Revolution, 129
Bolshevism, 34
Borneo/Malaysia, 47
Brezhnev, Leonid, 154
Brezhnev Doctrine, 81, 82
Britain, 9–10, 128; air force of, 182; and Anglo-American alliance, 24; defense budget of, 212; and France, 32; nuclear forces of, 206; as oceanic power, 41, 78; and Persian Gulf, 49; and Poland, 89; postwar position of, 42; prewar position of, 11; and Soviet Union, 43; and United States, 24, 78–79; as world power, 131; in World War I, 28; in World War II, 35
Bulgaria, 34, 36, 68, 81, 139, 233
Byelorussia, 18, 128

C-5 transports, 181
C-17 transports, 181
California Institute of Technology, 189
Cambodia (Kampuchea), 27, 242; Vietnamese occupation of, 211, 218
Camp David agreements, 229
Canada, 24
Caribbean region, 22, 78, 95, 98, 256
Carnegie-Mellon University, 189
Carter, Jimmy, 50, 93, 113, 160, 174, 228, 248
Carter Doctrine, 50, 143, 222
Castro, Fidel, 139, 241–242
Catholic Church, 87–88
Caucasian republics, 128
CENTCOM, 171
Central America: economy/GNP of, 84, 240; geopolitical importance of, 214; Soviet deployments in, 174; and Soviet Union, 76, 92, 95, 96–98, 143, 182, 256; and United States, 22, 78, 90, 92, 96, 97–98, 256, 266–267; U.S. deployments in, 171, 175; as zone of vulnerability for United States, 76–77, 79–80, 255
central Europe: nuclear zone in, 199; security of, 208, 234, 266; and Soviet Union, 198
China, 31, 47, 71; and Afghanistan, 225; economic modernization program in, 70, 216, 217, 218, 264; and Ethiopia, 136; expansion policy of, 46; geopolitical position of, 217; and Japan, 70, 135, 216–219, 254, 264; military capability of, 216; and North Korea, 59; nuclear capability of, 46; and Pacific triangle, 52, 58, 59, 61, 70, 135, 216–219, 254, 264; and Pakistan, 64, 217, 221, 223; and Philippines, 52, 61; and South Korea, 58; Soviet deployments in, 174; and Soviet invasion of Afghanistan, 211; and Soviet Union, 24, 26, 32, 34, 45–47, 69–72, 141–142, 211, 215, 220; technology transfers to, 218; trade of, with Japan, 216–217; trade of, with United States, 216–217; and United States, 25, 47, 58, 65, 69, 70, 93, 210–212, 215–219, 223, 254, 264; in World War II, 40–41

Chow, Brian, 158
Churchill, Winston, 9–10, 24
CIA, 79
circular error probability, 107
cold war, 9, 10, 22, 26, 45, 112, 119; *see also* American-Soviet conflict; war
Comintern Congress, 34
communication, command, and control (C³I) systems, 160, 165, 188, 192, 257
communications, 237; mass, 8, 28, 233–234; technology of, 197, 265–266
communism/Communist party, 176; and anti-Communist activities, 242; Chinese, 45, 46; East European, 82–83, 234; East German, 199; foreign, 126; French, 68; Soviet, 16, 21, 122, 123, 125, 129–130, 142, 238; and Soviet-backed regimes, 242; Vietnamese, 47
Constantinople, 33
conventional military balance: and arms race, 190; in Europe, 170–172, 174; in Far East, 170, 172, 174; geopolitical, 191; in southwest Asia, 170, 175; U.S. technological superiority in, 187–188, 190
Council of Mutual Economic Assistance, 19
counterinsurgency, 242
cruise missiles, 105, 163, 186–187, 188
Cuba, 16, 255; as Communist state, 79, 95; and East Germany, 96; and Mexico, 89; and Nicaragua, 97, 241, 267; as Soviet proxy, 95, 112; and Soviet Union, 26, 27, 50, 79–80, 95–97; terrorist activities of, 139–140; and United States, 22, 77, 79, 80; and Vietnam, 96
Cuban missile crisis, 95
Cutler, Robert, 176
Czechoslovakia, 34, 198, 233; and Soviet Union, 55, 81–82, 84, 93, 94; and terrorist activities, 68, 139; and United States, 93
Czechoslovak spring, 81

Dardanelles, 36, 39, 41
Deng Xiaoping, 70, 218

détente, 10, 29, 142, 154, 246
Djilas, Milovan, 39, 231, 238
Dominican Republic, 77

early warning satellites, 158
Eastern Europe: and Britain, 10; Communist regimes in, 81–83, 93, 255; economies/GNP of, 83, 131; geopolitical situation in, 94–95; isolation of, 236; and Radio Free Europe broadcasts, 233; self-assertiveness of, 231–233; Soviet control of, 16, 44, 52–53; Soviet integration with, 19; and Soviet Union, 26, 77, 80, 90, 92–94, 141–142, 144, 197, 198, 203, 231–234, 236, 254, 256; standard of living in, 84; and United States, 10, 92–94, 197, 231–232, 234, 265, 266; and Western Europe, 65, 83, 135, 143, 208, 263; as zone of vulnerability for Soviet Union, 76–77, 80–84
East Germany, 34, 56; and Cuba, 96; and East-West cooperation, 83; economy of, 83, 199; and Soviet Union, 56–57, 81, 197–198; terrorist training camps in, 139; and United States, 93; and West Germany, 198–202
EEC (European Economic Community), 56, 131, 136, 208, 233, 265
Egypt, 24, 113, 140, 230; and Japan, 214; and United States, 222–223
Eisenhower, Dwight D., 100–101, 176–177
El Salvador, 80, 140
England. *See* Britain
escalation. *See* nuclear escalation
Ethiopia, 16, 27, 153; and China, 136; and Soviet Union, 50, 136; and United States, 136
Eurasia, 65, 66; Far Eastern front of, 45–49, 51, 60, 253 (*see also* Far East); and Europe, 215; European front of, 42–45, 51, 253 (*see also* Europe); geopolitical centrality of, 30, 42; and Japan, 215; southwest Asian front of, 49–52, 65 (*see also* southwest Asia); and Soviet Union, 9, 30–41, 65–66, 74–75, 121, 146, 196, 221, 231, 250, 253, 259, 268; strategic fronts in (general discussion), 117, 145,

Eurasia (*continued*)
168, 170, 183; as theater for war, 114; and United States, 53, 66–67, 99, 114, 137, 144, 146, 175, 192–193, 196–197, 215, 220–222, 253; *see also* southwest Asia
Europe (first strategic front), 215, 253; atom-free zones in, 248; containment of, 27; defense effort of, 196–210; geopolitical situation in, 42–45, 51; international system in, 11; military buildup in, 176–177; partition of, 10, 197–198; political-military balance in, 56; security of, 67, 180, 204; self-reliance of, 247, 263; Soviet advantage in, 117; Soviet ambitions toward, 9–10, 43; Soviet redeployments from, 206–207; and Soviet Union, 203–204; as theater for conventional war, 151, 171, 172, 179, 204; U.S. defense commitment to, 171–172, 175, 176–177, 179, 180, 204, 223; U.S. deployments and military presence in, 142, 170–172, 174–177, 181–182, 191, 196; U.S. redeployments from, 205–207; *see also* central Europe; Eastern Europe; Western Europe; *individual countries*
European Economic Community (EEC), 56, 131, 136, 208, 233, 265
Europe-based international system, 11

Falklands campaign, 182
Far East (second strategic front), 45–49, 51, 60, 117, 135, 253; geopolitical situation in, 71–72; Japan's security role in, 210; Soviet deployments in, 174; and Soviet Union, 32, 34, 40, 44–48, 58, 72, 211; and United States, 22–23, 25, 44–48, 66, 196, 220; U.S. deployments in, 181; U.S. security obligations in, 210, 212
Federal Republic of Germany. *See* West Germany
Finland, 34, 36, 39, 89
first-strike systems and policies (general discussion), 156, 159, 260; counter-first-strike strategy, 167; *see also* Soviet strategic power, first-strike

capability; U.S. strategic power, first-strike capability; U.S. strategic power, second-strike capability
Foreign Affairs, 170, 232
France, 12, 128, 249; and Britain, 32; communism in, 43; defense budget of, 212; and Germany, 205, 263; as land power, 41; and NATO, 177; nuclear forces of, 206; prewar position of, 11; role of, in nuclear war, 177, 179; and Soviet Union, 67–68, 204; as world power, 131

Gandhi, Indira, 93
geopolitical determinism, 7
geopolitical divisions of the world, 5–7
geopolitical linchpin states (general discussion), 52–65, 254; *see also* Afghanistan; Iran; Pakistan; Philippines; Poland; South Korea; West Germany
geopolitics: and foreign policy, 3; and linchpin states, 52–65, 210; and maritime trade, 113; and military balance, 155; and zones of vulnerability, 76–98
German Democratic Republic. *See* East Germany
Germany, 11, 56, 65, 94, 185, 208; and France, 205, 263; Nazi, 12, 34–36, 41; nuclear forces of, 206; partition of, 59, 197–198; and Poland, 55; reunification program of, 58, 198; and Soviet Union, 33, 34–39, 55, 68; as world power, 131; in World War I, 27; *see also* East Germany; West Germany
Glenn, John, 207
global balance/status quo, 11, 135, 137, 139, 142, 205, 246; and arms control, 155; deteriorating, 203; geopolitical adjustments to, 181, 183; *see also* conventional military balance
Gorbachev, Mikhail, 83, 126, 195, 232
Great Britain. *See* Britain
Great Russian empire, 4, 16, 31, 126–128, 164, 192, 226, 231, 249, 252; geopolitical goals of, 195; imperial consciousness of, 20–21, 220; political tradition of, 236

Greece, 42, 43
Grenada, 77, 96
Griffith, William, 232
Gromyko, Andrei, 3–7, 35
GRU, 188–189
Guam, 173
Guatemala, 77

Haiti, 78
Harvard University, 189
Hauner, Milan, 37
Helsinki agreements, 206
historical discontinuity, 85–91, 255
Hitler, Adolf, 34, 35, 36–37, 39
Hitler-Stalin pact, 34–39
Holland, 12
Hopkins, Harry, 40
Hungary, 34, 55, 81–82, 83, 84, 233; and Soviet Union, 93; and United States, 93, 94
Hussein I, 230

ICBMs (intercontinental ballistic missiles), 186; launchers for, 157; Soviet, 95, 108, 164; U.S., 106, 154
India, 25, 31, 64, 137; and Afghanistan, 225; and Pakistan, 221–222; and Soviet Union, 225
Indian Ocean, 64, 170
Indochina, 27, 45–46; see also Southeast Asia
Indonesia, 27, 47
intercontinental missiles. See ICBMs
International Monetary Fund, 235
Iran, 22, 31, 42–43, 144, 226; economy of, 224; geopolitical position of, 64, 73; as linchpin state, 52–53, 63–65, 223; population of, 73; and Soviet Union, 34, 36, 41, 49, 53, 63–65, 72–73, 118–119, 182, 221, 224, 226; and Syria, 221; and United States, 23, 43, 49, 50, 63–64, 221, 223–224; war of, with Iraq, 221
Iran, Shah of, 23, 63, 73, 219, 221
IRA Provisionals, 140
Iraq, 36, 42, 73, 221, 222
Ireland, 25
Islamabad, Pakistan, 72
Islamic countries, 226–227, 265
Israel, 24, 112, 186; and United States, 228–230; see also Arab-Israeli conflict
Israeli-Syrian conflict, 186
Italy, 25, 35, 39, 42, 208; economy of, 124; terrorist activities in, 68, 139–140

Japan, 11, 35, 47, 122, 249; antimilitarism in, 213–214; and China, 70, 135, 216–219, 254, 264; defense budget of, 173–174, 212–214, 264; economy/GNP of, 48, 131, 134, 173–174, 212–215, 264; and Eurasia, 215; foreign trade of, 214; and Korea, 52; and Pacific triangle, 52, 58, 70, 135, 214, 216–219, 254, 264; and Pakistan, 223; and Philippines, 219; security of, 67, 210; security commitments of, 214–215; and South Korea, 58; and Soviet Union, 31, 33, 40, 44, 61, 72, 134; technology of, 202; trade of, with China, 216–217; and United States, 24, 25, 45, 58, 60–70, 71, 73, 173, 212, 215, 254, 264; U.S. deployments in, 173; U.S. security commitment to, 210; in World War II, 10–11, 212; as world power, 220, 264
Jordan, 230

Kampuchea. See Cambodia
Katyn, Poland, 86–87
Kazakhstan, 18
Kennan, George, 111–112
Kennedy, John F., 79
Kenya, 174
KGB, 139; Directorate of, 188
Khomeini regime, 72, 223
Khrushchev, Nikita, 122, 124, 138, 242
Kissinger, Henry, 80, 207
Korea: and China, 212; communism in, 253; reunification program for, 59; and Soviet Union, 44, 59; and United States, 25, 44; see also North Korea; South Korea
Korean War, 22, 24, 45–46, 69, 172–173, 210
Kurdish People's Republic, 43
Kurile Islands, 40, 41, 44, 69

Laos, 27
laser-based defense, 109
Latin America, 237; *see also* Central
    America; South America; *individual
    countries*
League of Nations, 11
Lenin, V. I., 125, 130
Libya, 126, 140, 227
limited strategic defense, 164–166
linchpin states. *See* geopolitical linchpin
    states
Lippmann, Walter, 9
Lithuania, 17, 55, 85

MacArthur, Douglas, 44
Mackinder, Halford, 194
MAD. *See* mutual assured destruction
Malacca, Strait of, 47, 211
Manchuria, 32, 44, 217, 264
Mao Zedong, 24
Marcos, Ferdinand, 23, 61
Marine Corps, U.S., 182
Marx, Karl, 82
Marxist-Leninist ideology, 77, 83, 136
Massachusetts Institute of Technology,
    189
MBFR (Mutual Balanced Force Reduc-
    tion) negotiations, 207, 234
Mexico, 22, 143; and Cuba, 89; econ-
    omy of, 88; emigration from, to
    United States, 88, 91; population of,
    90–91; and Soviet Union, 91–92;
    and United States, 77, 85–91, 97,
    98, 255–256
Michigan, University of, 189
microelectronics, 186
Middle East: and oil, 51; potential con-
    flict in, 112, 142–144, 240; and So-
    viet Union, 27, 36, 53, 113, 182,
    227–228, 237, 265; terrorist activi-
    ties in, 139; and United States, 24,
    170, 227–230, 240, 266; *see also*
    Persian Gulf; *individual countries*
Midgetman missile, 156, 158, 165
military balance. *See* conventional mili-
    tary balance
military draft, 14
Military Industrial Commission, 188
Ministry of Foreign Trade, 188
Minuteman III missile, 107

missiles. *See individual types*
Molotov, Vyacheslav, 35, 53
Mongolia, 40, 47, 71, 218
Monroe Doctrine, 78, 79
Monteneros, Argentina, 140
Moscow summit (1974), 155
Mozambique, 27
Mubarak, Hosni, 230
Muslims, 16, 17, 127; *see also* Soviet
    Union, Muslims in
mutual assured destruction (MAD), 152,
    159, 161, 162, 165, 167, 168, 193,
    261
Mutual Balanced Force Reduction
    (MBFR) negotiations, 207, 234
mutual strategic security, 159–168, 245,
    261, 263; and global conventional
    flexibility, 184, 192, 193, 261
MX missile, 107, 151, 152, 156, 158,
    163, 165

Nakasone, Yasuhiro, 217
Napoleonic Wars, 28
National Security Council (NSC), 101,
    160, 174; assessment by, of Soviet
    atomic capability, 101–102; geo-
    strategic planning by, 242–243, 267;
    and U.S. deployments, 176
National Security Directive Memoran-
    dum 242, 160
NATO (North Atlantic Treaty Organiza-
    tion), 172, 209, 210, 232; conven-
    tional military power of, 177, 180;
    and East European neutrality policy,
    234; European contributions to, 177,
    207; forces of, 117–118, 150–151;
    military expenditures for, 172–173;
    operational strategy of, 142, 177–
    178, 180, 186; and United States,
    170, 203; and U.S. troop levels, 207;
    and West Germany, 56, 68
Netherlands, 131
neutralism, 205–206, 234
New People's Army (Philippines), 61
New York Times, 165
Nicaragua, 140, 219, 255; communism in,
    242; and Cuba, 97, 140, 241; and
    Soviet Union, 16, 27, 79–80, 96–
    97, 241, 242, 267; and United States,
    77, 80, 96, 241

Nixon, Richard, 69, 228
Nixon-Brezhnev declaration of joint principles, 154
no first use policy, 150, 152
North America, 48; *see also* Canada; United States
North Korea: and China, 59; GNP of, 59; and South Korea, 58–59, 219, 224, 264; and Soviet Union, 16, 34, 59–60, 171
North Vietnam, 47
Norway, 39
nuclear deterrence, 15, 100, 102, 118, 152, 160, 162, 164, 251, 261; U.S., 179, 192
nuclear escalation: of arms race, 152; of conventional war, 118, 141, 145, 146, 151, 169, 172, 183, 191, 257; and United States, 259
nuclear freeze, 150–152, 202
Nunn, Sam, 207

Oder-Neisse line, 198
Odom, William, 161
Ogarkov, Nikolai, 187
oil, 51, 220
Okinawa, 173
Olney, Richard, 78
Oman, 174
Operation Barbarossa, 37
Orbis, 37
Organization for Economic Cooperation and Development, 136
Ottoman Empire, 17
outer space, 28, 122; arms race in, 153; combat in, 146, 259; control of, 147–148; deployment zones in, 158; systems in, 188; U.S. preponderance in, 185

Pacific Basin states, 48, 220
Pacific triangle, 215–230; and American-Soviet conflict, 220; and United States, 247; *see also* China; Far East; Japan; North Korea; Philippines; South Korea
pacifism, 148–149, 267
Pakistan, 31, 144; and Afghanistan as linchpin state, 52–53, 63–65, 220, 225; and China, 64, 217, 221, 223;

geopolitical position of, 64, 73; and India, 221–222; Islamic law in, 226; and Japan, 214, 223; population of, 73; and Soviet Union, 49, 63–65, 72, 118–119, 182, 221–222, 224; and United States, 24, 49, 50–51, 72, 221, 222, 265
Palestine, 42, 240, 266
Panama, 80
Panama Canal, 78, 214
Panama Canal Treaties, 77
Peres, Shimon, 230
Pershing II missile, 107
Persian Gulf, 32, 36–37, 39, 41, 64–65; and Britain, 49; and oil, 51, 220; and Soviet Union, 51, 53, 144, 175, 227; and United States, 143, 170, 175; U.S. deployments in, 181
phased-array radar, 109
Philippines, 22, 47, 61, 117; and China, 52, 61; and Japan, 214, 219; as linchpin state, 52–53, 58, 60–61, 210; and Soviet Union, 61, 71–72; and United States, 23, 45, 58, 60–61, 173, 264; U.S. security commitment to, 210–211
Pipes, Richard, 66, 207; quoted, 19–20
Poland, 17, 21, 25, 56–58, 86, 94, 198, 233; and Britain, 89; Catholicism in, 87–88; communism in, 89–90; and Eastern Europe, 235–236; economy of, 83, 88; and Germany, 55; as linchpin state, 52–55, 235–236; political unrest in, 91, 232; Solidarity movement in, 55, 81, 89, 93, 199, 236; and Soviet control of Eastern Europe, 52–53; and Soviet Union, 33, 34, 53–55, 81–82, 84, 85–91, 93, 94, 235, 255; and United States, 89, 91–92, 235–236; and Warsaw Pact, 55
Policy Planning Council, 243
Polisaro Front (South Sahara), 140
Polish-Lithuanian republic, 17
Pollack, Jonathan, 215
Ponomarev, Boris, 139
Popular Front (Arabian Peninsula), 140
Portugal, 131
Potsdam Conference, 39, 44
Pravda, 83

Presidential Directive 41, 160–161
Presidential Directive 53, 160
Presidential Directive 59, 160
prevailing historically, 239, 244–245,
　250, 267
Princeton University, 189
Prussia, 56
public opinion, 241–242; of American-
　Soviet conflict, 10, 195, 239; East
　European, 265

Qaddafi, Muammar, 126, 242
Quemoy-Matsu confrontation, 47

radar, phased array, 109
Radio Free Afghanistan, 226
Radio Free Europe, 90, 93–94, 233, 237
Radio Liberty, 237
Rapid Deployment Force, 113–114, 119,
　143, 171, 174, 224, 262; air-, sea-
　lift capability of, 175, 181–182, 262
Ravenal, Earl, 170
Reagan, Ronald, and Reagan administra-
　tion, 96, 108, 113, 158, 170–171,
　174; political frictions of, 216;
　southwest Asia policy of, 222; and
　Strategic Defense Initiative, 152–
　153, 162 (see also Strategic Defense
　Initiative)
reconnaissance satellites, 158
Red Army (Japan), 140
Red Army Faction (West Germany), 140
Red Brigades (Italy), 140
research and development of military
　systems: Soviet, 189; U.S., 187
Reserve Force (United States), 160
Rio Grande (fourth strategic front), 98,
　143, 241
Romania, 34, 81, 94, 233
Roosevelt, Franklin D., 9–10, 24, 26, 40
Russia. See Great Russian empire; Soviet
　Union
Russo-Japanese War, 32

Sakhalin Island, 32, 40
SALT I, 153, 154
SALT II, 153–154
satellite deployment, 158
Saudi Arabia, 49
Sazonov, Sergei, 53

Scandinavia, 234
Schlesinger, James, 160
Schmidt, Helmut, 199
Schroeder, Gertrude, 124
SDI. See Strategic Defense Initiative
seas, control of: Soviet, 114–115, 183–
　184; U.S., 12, 22, 28, 78, 114, 170,
　173, 183–184, 191, 192, 251, 259
SED (Communist party of East Ger-
　many), 199
selective subversion, 68
Seton-Watson, Hugh, 208
Shah of Iran, 23, 63, 73, 219, 221
Siberia, 18, 217, 254
Sinai disengagement accords, 229
Singer, Max, quoted, 20
SLBMs: Soviet, 114, 155, 156; U.S., 106,
　108, 155, 183, 185
Smith, Walter Bedell, 39
social creativity, 7, 258
socialism, 5–6, 239
socioeconomic power
　SOVIET, 6, 123, 129, 131–132, 232,
　　258; decay of, 143, 237; lack of
　　technological innovation in, 132–
　　133, 258; and standard of living, 84,
　　122
　U.S., 131–132, 136, 258; cultural dy-
　　namism of, 25–26
Soloviev, V. S., 70, 217
Somalia, 49, 174
Sommer, Theo, 199
Somoza regime, 70, 219
South America, 139
Southeast Asia, 24, 25, 61
southern Africa, 112–113, 142–144, 175,
　182, 237, 266; racial policies in, 240
Southern Yemen, 16, 27, 49, 140
South Korea, 117; defense budget of, 174,
　212; economy of, 48, 59, 219–220;
　and Japan, 214; as linchpin state, 52–
　53, 58–60, 210; and North Korea,
　58–59, 219, 224, 264; and Soviet
　Union, 31, 71–72; and United States,
　24, 45, 58, 170, 173; U.S. deploy-
　ments in, 219, 264; U.S. security
　commitment to, 210–211
South Vietnam and Soviet Union, 16, 26,
　27
southwest Asia (third strategic front):

geopolitical situation in, 49–52, 65, 220, 230, 253; Soviet advantage in, 117; as theater for war, 182–183; and United States, 119, 174, 175, 197, 224, 247; *see also* Eurasia

Soviet Union: agriculture in, 130; alcohol consumption in, 125; and allies, 26; as centralized state, 123, 128, 249–250; consumption in, 124; containment policy of, 11–12; defense expenditures of, 189; direct use of force policy of, 66; economic decentralization in, 126–128, 141–142; economy of, 13–14, 83, 122–124, 128, 133–134, 144; education system in, 14; encirclement of, 65; European, 18; expansionist policy of (*see* territorial expansion of, *below*); foreign policy of, 6, 83; foreign relations of (*see individual countries*); geographic position of, 31; geopolitical objectives of, 23, 34, 240, 246; geopolitical position of, 5–7, 45–46; global position of, 130–131; GNP of, 124, 129, 131, 206, 248; ideological defeat of, 81–84; ideology of, 14–15, 125; as imperial system, 16–21, 33, 208; infant mortality rate in, 124–125; intelligence agencies in, 188; internal change in, 231; as land power, 12, 28, 41, 251; life-styles in, 14; male longevity in, 124; military expenditures in, 128–129, 184, 189; multiethnicity of, 25, 126, 237; Muslims in, 222, 226–227, 231, 236, 265; non-Russian nations of, 127, 236–238, 249, 266; as onedimensional world power, 142, 255, 258 (*see also* as world power, *below*); peace offensive of, 203; philosophical values of, 13; political change in, 250, 268; political objectives of, 119; political organization of, 13, 237; political subconscious of, 12–13; population demography of, 16, 24, 127, 206; production in, 122, 124; promotion of regional conflicts by, 135, 136, 195, 240, 246, 258; religious philosophy in, 13; as revolutionary model, 125–126;

Russification policy of, 226; scientific capability of, 130; social deprivation in, 124, 249, 258; space program of, 185; standard of living in, 84, 122; technology in, 130, 132–134, 202; technology acquisitions of, from West, 188–189; territorial expansion of, 17–18, 19–21, 31–33, 41, 43, 55, 217, 236, 244, 259; and terrorism, 68, 138–139, 259; as Third Rome, 14, 21; as totalitarian state, 249; accommodation of, with United States, 240, 244–246, 258 (*see also* American-Soviet conflict); U.S. policy of, 240; as world power, 14, 125, 130–131, 248, 257; *see also* Great Russian empire

CONVENTIONAL MILITARY POWER OF, 99–101, 102, 117–121, 128, 134–137, 145, 146, 151, 162, 215–216, 240, 257–258; airlift capability, 112; air power, 69; first-strike capability, 161, 164, 168–169; force redeployments from Europe, 206–207; forces, 169, 178–179, 257; inventory sales, 136; naval, 27, 69, 114–115, 183–184; superiority, 119, 144, 186–187, 244–245; war-fighting capability, 187; weapons, 133, 189, 262

GEOSTRATEGY OF, 65–75, 146, 242, 254; in Central America, 97; condominium in, 66–67; decoupling in, 66–67; in Europe, 197; in third world, 27

SOCIOECONOMIC POWER OF, 6, 123, 129, 131–132, 232, 258; decay of, 143, 237; and standard of living, 84, 122; lack of technological innovation in, 132–133, 258

STRATEGIC DOCTRINE/POSTURE OF, 167–168; defensive, 166, 167; offensive, 161–162, 163–164, 166, 167

STRATEGIC POWER OF, 111, 165–166, 215–216; deployments, 107; first-strike capability, 106, 108, 109–111, 121, 141, 145–146, 159, 161, 166–168, 172, 191–193, 259, 261; forces, 102–106, 112, 158, 163; land-based systems, 108; nuclear inventory and

Soviet Union (*continued*)
    systems, 108, 109; sea-based sys-
    tems, 108, 112; second-strike capa-
    bility, 165; secrecy concerning, 157–
    158; superiority, 102–103, 154–155;
    technology acquisitions, 188–189;
    parity with United States, 74, 102,
    107, 113, 118; war-fighting capabil-
    ity, 145, 163–164, 259; weapons
    acquisitions, 189
space. *See* outer space
Spain, 12, 131
Spanish-American War, 78
Spasowski, Romuald, 21
SPD (West German Socialist party), 199
Spitsbergen Islands, 39, 41
Sputnik, 9, 185
SS-18 missiles, 105, 107, 156
SS-19 missiles, 107
SS-20 missiles, 74, 118
SS-24 ICBMs, 107, 108, 156
SS-25 ICBMs, 107–108, 156
Stalin, Joseph, 9–10, 24, 26, 33, 34, 35,
    40, 58, 125, 130; and Hitler and
    Germany, 34–39, 250; and purges
    in Eastern Europe, 81; at Yalta, 203
"star wars," 152; *see also* Strategic De-
    fense Initiative
State Department, 243
stealth bomber program, 185–186
Strategic Defense Initiative (SDI), 162,
    167, 262; and antitactical missile
    defense, 180; debate over, 152–153;
    and space control, 185
strategic fronts in American-Soviet con-
    flict (general discussion), 41–52,
    102, 117, 144, 145, 240; *see also*
    Europe; Far East; Rio Grande;
    southwest Asia
strategic stability, 153, 244, 247, 257
Study of History, A, 129
submarines, 183
surface-to-air missiles, 109
Survival Is Not Enough, 19–20, 66
Sutton, Anthony C., 132–133
Syria, 140, 186, 221, 225, 230

Taiwan, 45, 46
technetronic age, 122, 257–258

technological superiority in military sys-
    tems, 184–191
technology: in conventional combat, 177–
    178, 180; innovation in, 7, 153; in
    weapons, 154, 180, 184–191
Tehran Conference, 10
terrorism, 139–140; Soviet role in, 68,
    138–139, 259; training camps for,
    in Eastern Europe and Cuba, 139
Thailand, 24; and Japan, 214; and United
    States, 211, 212
third world, 48; and Soviet Union, 136–
    139
Tito, Marshal, 39
Tocqueville, Alexis de, 12
Toynbee, Arnold, 129
Trans-Siberian Railroad, 18, 164
Tricontinental Congress, 139
Trident D-5 missiles, 156, 158, 163, 165
Tripartite Pact, 35–36
Trotsky, Leon, 34, 139
Truman, Harry S, 43, 45, 253
Truman Doctrine, 43, 49
Tudeh party, 63
Tunisia, 140
Turkey, 36, 42, 43; terrorism in, 68; and
    United States, 49
Turkish Liberation Army, 140
Turkish Straits, 33

Ukraine, 16, 17, 231, 236; and Soviet
    Union, 53, 55, 127
United Kingdom. *See* Britain
United Nations, 230
United States: and relations with allies,
    25–26; arms control policy of, 150–
    152; atomic capability of, 101; con-
    tainment policy of, 100, 137; de-
    fense programs of, 154; differentia-
    tion policy of, 92–93, 94; economy
    of, 122–123, 262; European policy
    of, postwar, 41; and European se-
    curity, 67; foreign policy of, 23, 160,
    242–243, 252; foreign relations of
    (*see individual countries*); geopolit-
    ical objectives of, 23, 194–196, 197,
    243, 246, 263; GNP of, 7, 84, 129,
    131, 172; GNP/defense ratio of,
    212; ideology of, 14–15; as impe-

rial system, 23–24, 252; indirect intrusion policy of, 93, 256; integrated strategic framework of, 191–193, 263; internal arrangements of, 49; and alliance with Japan and China, 65; and Japanese-Soviet relations, 72; military expenditures of, 129, 172, 175; multiethnicity of, 25; as nuclear power, 27, 79; as oceanic power, 12, 28, 78, 251, 259; philosophical values in, 13; political culture in, 194; political organization in, 13; postwar position of, 11, 42; prewar position of, 11; radio broadcasts of, to Asia, 236; radio broadcasts of, to Eastern Europe, 237, 265–266; religious philosophy in, 13; and Sino-Soviet relations, 72; socioeconomic power of, 25–26, 131–132, 136, 258; and Soviet occupation of Afghanistan, 174–175, 224–226; Soviet policy on, 241, 242; accommodation of, with Soviet Union, 94, 240, 244–246, 258 (*see also* American-Soviet conflict); standard of living in, 84, 122; strategic imperatives of, 145–148, 259; technology in, 70, 122–123, 130, 135, 184, 202, 262; territorial expansion of, 22, 252; as territorial power, 27; third-world policy of, 23; weapons acquisition policy of, 160; world image of, 14; as world power, 131, 134–135, 258; in World War I, 28; in World War II, 35, 40–41
CONVENTIONAL MILITARY POWER OF, 145–146, 173, 191, 258; airlift capability, 113, 175, 181–182, 262; buildup of forces, 171–172; flexibility, 184; force deployments, 58, 146, 159, 162–167, 169–171, 180, 183–184, 187, 190, 207, 261–262; force redeployments, 205–207, 262, 263; imbalance of deployments, 169–171; naval, 12, 22, 28, 78, 114, 170, 173, 183–184, 191, 192, 251, 259; sealift capability, 113, 175; technological superiority, 184, 187–189, 190; and technology, 135; troop reduc-

tions, 181; war-fighting capability, 191; weapons acquisition policy, 160
GEOSTRATEGY OF, 141, 144, 154, 184, 242, 244, 246; in Central America, 98 (*see also* Central America, and United States); doctrine, 160, 249–250; in Europe, 197; geopolitical objectives, 23, 194–196, 197, 220, 243, 246, 263; in southwest Asia, 222; strategic consciousness, 194; and technological superiority, 184, 187–189, 190
STRATEGIC DOCTRINE/POSTURE OF, 159–162, 167–169, 224; defensive, 161–164, 166, 167; lack of integrated policy, 191–193; offensive, 161–164, 166, 167
STRATEGIC POWER OF, 111, 113, 151; as deterrent, 119; European deployments, 142; first-strike capability, 111, 161, 163, 165, 166; forces, 102–106; lack of programs for, 158; land-based, 114, 257, 261; limited offensive forces, 193; mobility, 181–182, 191; modernization program, 149, 154, 163, 168; programmatic mishandling, 158; second-strike capability, 107, 110–111, 121, 141, 145, 163, 191–192, 257, 259, 261; parity with Soviet Union, 74, 102, 107, 113, 118; space-based defense, 185, 261; superiority, 100, 113, 121, 162, 166, 243; war-fighting capability, 192; weaponry, 149, 154, 185
U.S. Navy, 183–184, 262; *see also* United States: conventional military power of, naval
U.S.–Soviet conflict. See American-Soviet conflict

Vangarda, Brazil, 140
Venezuela, 78, 79
verification of weapons systems, 155–156, 157, 166–167, 168, 260
Vietnam, 47; and Cuba, 96; and Soviet Union, 47, 60, 61, 174, 211; and Thailand, 211; and United States, 97
Vietnam War, 46, 172–173, 242
Vladivostok talks, 153

V-rockets, 185
vulnerability, zones of: Central America, 76–77, 79–80, 255; Eastern Europe, 76–77, 80–84

Wakhan Corridor, 223
Walker, William, 78
war: and American-Soviet conflict, 15, 250, 251; atomic, 101; chemical, 199; conventional, 121, 141, 143, 146, 168–170, 172, 179, 180–181, 257, 262; electronic, 188; in Eurasia, 114; in Europe, 151, 171, 172, 179, 204; global, 28, 252; nuclear, 102, 118, 141, 146, 160, 161; in space, 146; "winning" fallacy of, 243–244; *see also* nuclear escalation
War and Christianity, 70
Warsaw Pact, 19, 55, 199; forces under, 68, 117–118, 178, 190; and Soviet Union, 67, 83, 203, 236
weapons: and arms control, 154–157; and computer technology, 188; conventional, 28, 186; innovation in, 154–156, 159, 184–191; nuclear, 29, 66, 107, 110, 147, 162, 180, 186 (*see also* nuclear deterrence); space-traversing, 147; technology in, 154, 180, 184–191; verification of, 156, 157, 166–167, 168, 260
Weinberger, Caspar, 169
West Bank, 230
Western Europe, 22–23, 48, 219; defense budgets in, 212; and Eastern Europe, 65, 83, 135, 143, 208, 263; economies and GNP of, 134, 177, 206; and Europe's defense, 178; self-reliance of, 196–210, 263; and Soviet Union, 5, 65, 68–69, 95, 134, 144, 150, 196–210, 231, 254; technology in, 202; terrorist activity in, 139; unification program for, 67; and United States, 22–23, 25, 26–27, 43, 55, 65–68, 73, 119, 142, 144, 196–210, 220; U.S. defense commitment to, 171–172, 179–180; U.S. deployments in, 170
Western European Union, 205
Western Technology and Soviet Economic Development, 132–133
West Germany, 56; army of, 177; defense budget of, 212; and East Germany, 198–202; as linchpin state, 52–53, 56–57, 204; and NATO, 177; and Soviet Union, 144, 198; terrorist activities in, 139–140; U.S. deployments in, 172
Williamsburg summit, 213–214
Wohlstetter, Albert, 107, 158
World War I, 28, 32
World War II, 34; geopolitical consequences of, 26, 27–28

Xinjiang province, 217, 223, 264

Yalta Conference, 9–10, 40, 44, 203
Yugoslavia, 26, 94, 142